THE
EXPENDABLE
MARY SLESSOR

Her Majesty the Queen laying a wreath on Mary Slessor's grave during her visit to Nigeria in 1956.

THE
EXPENDABLE
MARY SLESSOR

JAMES BUCHAN

THE SAINT ANDREW PRESS
EDINBURGH

First published in 1980 by
THE SAINT ANDREW PRESS
121 George Street, Edinburgh EH2 4YN

Copyright © James Buchan 1980

ISBN 0 7152 0414 9 (Cased)
ISBN 0 7152 0438 6 (Limp)

Printed in Great Britain by
Robert MacLehose and Co. Ltd.
Printers to the University of Glasgow

To
My Wife

CONTENTS

ACKNOWLEDGMENTS

In 1915, W P Livingstone made a collection of Mary Slessor's 'voluminous correspondence' to provide him with the material for his book *Mary Slessor of Calabar*. Unfortunately this collection was destroyed in World War II. The first part of this book therefore is based largely on Livingstone's.

Thanks are due to the Church of Scotland for access to its Foreign Missions' Library, to Dundee Museum and Central Library for access to those of Mary's letters, diaries and Bibles which have survived, to all three for permission to use extracts and photographs, and to retired Calabar missionaries for passing on memories of Mary Slessor from colleagues who once worked with her.

ILLUSTRATIONS

Frontispiece: Her Majesty the Queen laying a wreath on Mary Slessor's grave during her visit to Nigeria in 1956.

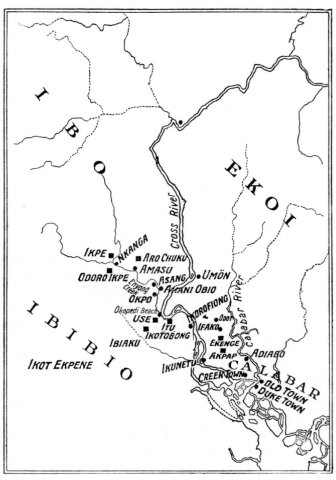

The Calabar area of 1915 showing Mary Slessor's work

PROLOGUE

Margery Perham, the historian, has written 'Mary Slessor . . . can justly be described as one of the greatest women of her generation.' Mary Kingsley, the author and explorer, wrote of 'roustabouts like Mary Slessor and me' and that in insight into the African mind, and knowledge of his law, customs, and religion, 'Miss Slessor stands alone'. The two Marys met in Africa in 1893 and became great friends.

Expendable – the word applied during and after the Second World War to assault troops who accepted that most of them would become casualties – fits Miss Slessor, the Scottish redhead. When as a young woman she went to work in Calabar in West Africa, she knew that even if she survived the fevers and the humid climate her health would be ruined. It fits her too when thirty years later as a sick and ageing woman she drove what she called her 'poor carcase' on into the forests to help break up a rule of terror in the way in which only she could. By then, she had trained herself to live and to think like an African. She spoke the local language fluently, and went barefoot, usually wearing old cotton dresses, which she was not averse to removing if in the rainy season they were slowing her down. For most of the twenty-eight years which she spent in the forests she lived in mud huts which, with the help of a group of orphans whose lives she had saved, she built herself.

Calabar is now a province in the new Nigeria with a modern port of the same name, but when Mary Slessor arrived in 1876 it was one of the most unattractive places on Earth. Its miles of swamps, where millions of insects swarmed, bred fevers for which, at that time, there was no preventative, and two centuries of the murderous slave trade had cheapened human life, split and mixed the tribes, destroyed their simple way of life, and perverted their religion. The people were living under a tyrannical and corrupt régime which, as Nigerian historians agree, ruled by terror. It could have given lessons in terror tactics to the Nazi Gestapo. Its chiefs looked on most of their tribal slaves and most of their women, whether slave or free, as of less importance than their cattle. They killed and tortured these people not only with impunity but as of right under their laws.

Before the British moved in to govern and to police the area Mary Slessor took on this régime in the forests single-handed. Pax Britannica eventually ruled in them. But Pax Mary Slessor preceded it in some of them. Until she died in 1915, she continued to move further and further into them, with only her orphans as company, often into places where no other white person could go without a military escort. Often she was near to death from violence, fevers, and malnutrition. That it took until 1915 for the expendable finally to become spent is astonishing.

Long before then she had become famous along the rivers of Calabar as one who wanted nothing for herself and could be trusted. The end of the nineteenth century was a bewildering time for the West Africans. They had been held back for centuries in a medieval world by their inaccessible forests and swamps, and then that world had been plunged into savagery by the slave trade. Now they were suddenly being thrust towards the modern world.

Margery Perham – who first travelled in Africa by horse and camel in the 1930s – wrote in 1959, 'The key to the African situation lies in the astonishing fact that . . . the great solid block of tropical middle Africa lay almost completely shut off from the rest of the world until some sixty or seventy years ago. It was then that modern Europe, with all the power of its new science and equipment, penetrated this lonely Africa with great power and speed. This trick played by geography and history has thrown a strain on poor human nature almost greater than it could bear. It had a literally shattering effect upon the societies most directly exposed to the new influence.'

The Africans badly needed the help of those rare and precious people, the builders of bridges between conflicting sections of the human race. Mary Slessor was one of these. The British described her as 'a tornado'. But the Africans called her, quite simply, '*Eka Kpukpro Owo*' – 'Mother of All The Peoples'.

1. RAIN, DARKNESS, AND DEATH

The rain ran from the breasts of the Efik women come to weep and to wail over their friend Mary Slessor who was determined, it seemed to them, to go to her death. It spattered over the naked bodies of the paddlers as they loaded her goods into the canoe. It had been raining for hours. It was certainly no day for paddling a heavily loaded canoe against the rising current of the Calabar River.

The crew grumbled and dawdled over the loading. The river god must be against them making the journey which, even if the canoe were not swamped on the way, would end in a meeting with their old enemies the Okoyong. Had not Mary's friends, both black and white, been trying for days to persuade her to give up her foolish idea of going to live in the forests with such a fighting tribe of drunken habits and hair-trigger tempers as the Okoyong? Did she not know that when they had no common enemy to fight they fought continuously among themselves; that even their women went into battle; that only people who had Okoyong blood could risk going near them; that Efiks who strayed near their border often disappeared without trace? How could their chief expect them to risk their lives by going with her – and on such a day too? Perhaps if they took long enough over the loading she might, after all, change her mind.

Eyo, chief of the Creek Town Efiks, was lending Mary his personal canoe. It had been dug out of a tree-trunk over forty feet long, had a crew of thirty-six, and a little cabin amidships, fitted, in honour of Mary, with a piece of red carpet and a new curtain. He had come to the landing-place himself to try, like everyone else, to persuade Mary to wait for a better day. But she, during a sleepless night, had screwed her courage to the sticking point and would not be persuaded. Eyo knew her well enough to realise that he was wasting his breath so he turned instead to persuading his crew that it was safe for them to make

1

the journey. They would be under the white woman's protection and she, as everybody knew, was especially protected by the gods. How else could she already have made a journey into the Okoyong forests and not only come back safe but with their consent to her going to live with them?

Mary herself would normally have been facing up to her problems in her usual wise-cracking way, chivvying the crew along and making them laugh. But the general gloom had damped even her spirits and she was wondering if she was being arrogant in ignoring the advice of her friends and whether she really was, as the white ones were saying, 'flying in the face of Providence': a view which was much the same as that of the paddlers.

It was 1888 and Mary had been working in Calabar for twelve years, with breaks back in Scotland on sick-leave to recover from the inevitable fevers. Even nine years earlier two deputies, who had come out from Edinburgh to inspect the work of the mission, had reported that she preferred to live with Africans rather than with Europeans, that she had walked the two of them off their feet, and that her success with the people was helped by 'the singular ease with which she speaks the language'. The Africans found her a different kind of missionary: one who went among them as one of themselves and who could sleep soundly on a clay bench even down by the river among the mosquitoes, in the mud huts which they lent to her.

Now at last the day had come for which she had been training herself. She would break the mission out of the straitjacket into which the blockade of the rivers against it by the Efiks, and the blockade of the forests by the Okoyong and other tribes, had locked it for over forty years. Never before in the history of the missions to West Africa had a woman been allowed to break new ground by going alone into the forests to live with an unknown tribe. Today she would do it, rain or no rain. The Okoyong were about to be taught a new, peaceful, way of life. In less than a year their war with the Efik would be over and the two tribes would be trading together. This would be achieved on her own by the small, fine-drawn, whipcord, woman sitting soaked to the skin among her boxes waiting for the crew to get on with the loading.

Because there was nowhere else for them to go, she had decided to take five orphans with her. These were three boys aged eleven, eight, and three, and two girls, one aged five, and one only a few months old.

Eventually the crew finished the loading and to renewed wailing by her black friends and head-shaking by her white friends Mary and the children climbed into the little cabin. By now it was clear that it would be dark before the paddlers had battled their way up the river to the landing place for Ekenge, the village where she was to live, and once they had landed Mary and the children would have to walk four miles up a forest path to the village. Because of the leopards and the head-hunters few people risked the forests at night without an armed escort, and Hugh Goldie, the senior missionary at Creek Town, could not bear the thought of his obstinate colleague facing these added dangers alone. At the last minute he called for a volunteer from among his white staff to go with her, and William Bishop, the mission printer, stepped into the canoe for the adventure of his life.

To help the paddlers to keep the rhythm of the stroke there was one drum forward and one aft. The steersman shouted his orders, the drums beat a preliminary tattoo, and they were off. Creek Town, true to its name, was on a creek which ran down from the Cross River into the Calabar. At first the swirling current took them racing along. But when they hit the cross current at the junction with the Calabar the canoe bucketed and lurched in the broken water. Mary, who would face up to 'devil-men' in hideous masks and armed and painted warriors, was frightened in canoes in rough weather. She had nearly drowned in one during a tornado. Now, as the crew fought to swing the canoe up-river, she grabbed Mr Bishop's arm and prayed aloud. Perhaps Mr Bishop prayed too.

Gradually the light faded, the mud brown river changed to black, and the forest drove darkness down at them over the banks. The drums tapped on over the hiss of the rain. The paddlers grunted 'Ho!' as they dug in their paddles. Mary wondered about her reception at Ekenge.

It was still raining when they reached the landing-place. The battle with the river had exhausted the paddlers and in any case none of them was going to risk a journey through an enemy forest on such a night. Mary asked Mr Bishop to wait with the crew while she took the children up to the village. She would ask its chief, Edem, with whom she had negotiated her stay, to send down some of his men to carry up her boxes. She waded on to the muddy beach carrying the baby astride her shoulders while Mr Bishop carried the other girl and the youngest boy. Mary

The Cross River at Itu

carried a bundle of dry clothes for the children and the older boys carried food and a cooking pot.

Like the other Calabar tribes, the Okoyong usually walked in single file, so the path was narrow. Bushes clawed out into it and the dripping trees met over it. When they reached its mouth it must have looked to the children like a tunnel into a huge black cave and they all began to cry. Mary comforted them and distributed some of her home-made toffee. Then with the baby still on her shoulders and the two other little ones clinging on to her skirt she led them through the mud and the puddles into the forest.

'Our singing', she wrote to a friend, 'would discourage any self-respecting leopard.' So now, to keep up both their spirits and her own, she tried to get the children to sing hymns with her. But they were in no mood to sing. So she sang the hymns herself and some of the nonsense songs which she had a habit of making up for them. At the speed of the little ones, which was no more than a potter, and with many halts for rests and toffee, they splashed on into the dark.

In the Okoyong country, village still raided village and the approaches to them were therefore guarded by sentries. But on this night no armed warriors stepped out of the bushes to intercept her as they had done on her earlier visit. The villages themselves were made up of scattered groups of huts; each group was built round a yard, like sheds round a farmyard, and thorn stockades surrounded the huts and the family lands to keep out enemies and leopards. As Mary approached the first of the stockades she expected to see the glow of the watch-fires. But there were none. Then from the direction of Ifako, a neighbouring village which she had also visited, she heard the sounds of screaming, yelling, drumming, and gunfire. It was most unlikely that a night battle was in progress, so it had to be some kind of celebration. That meant that the men would not only be keyed up to a high pitch of excitement but would also be drunk. The children were however too exhausted by now for her to turn back even if she wanted to.

When they reached Ekenge she found the tracks between the stockades deserted, except for a few goats, dogs, and chickens. It was like a ghost village. The children who had been looking forward to a fire and to hot food, began to cry again. Then two old women came creeping out of the shadows. They told her that the people had all gone to Ifako to celebrate the funeral of the wife of one of its chiefs. Mary knew now that, as was customary, slaves were being slaughtered there to provide an escort for the noblewoman into *obio ekpu* – the spirit world. She had arrived at Ekenge on a night, not only of rain, but also of killing.

2. ROOTS AND ORIGINS

The woman standing, drenched and tired, in the Ekenge mud with her orphans had undergone a long conditioning process which had prepared her for this moment. In the beginning the squalor, the poverty, and the hunger of a Scottish slum had taught her how to share the squalor, the poverty, and the hunger of the West Africa of her day.

Mary Mitchell Slessor was born in Aberdeen in December 1848. In Scotland the 1840s were 'The Hungry Forties'. At the beginning of the century the population of the country had risen sharply. Then crops failed. The harnessing of steam to drive factory machinery destroyed the old cottage industries. To escape from starvation the people began to migrate into the cities in search of work and of food: cities which were quite unprepared to receive them. Many found neither work, nor food, nor shelter. They slept on pavements and they died on them. And their unwanted orphans begged, and stole, and starved.

Mary was the second of a family of seven children. Her father, Robert, was a shoemaker. Her mother, also named Mary, was a weaver. When three of his children died, including his eldest son, the struggle to bring up his surviving children, Mary, John and Susan – Janie was born later – was too much for Robert and he became an alcoholic. By 1859 he had drunk himself out of his job. Her mother's wages of ten shillings for a fifty-eight hour working week were not enough to keep the family so they moved to Dundee. There Robert could try to make a fresh start, and since the city's main industry was weaving Mrs Slessor could easily find work.

The mill owners of Dundee were beginning to make fortunes out of the new power-driven looms, and the city was booming. As immigrants packed into it in search of work its population doubled and then trebled. The Abertay Historical Society reports that in the 1850s the city was an insanitary place with heaps of animal manure, human excreta, and rubbish piled in the lanes and backyards. 'Immigrants were crowded into Dundee . . . adequate social services and accommodation simply did not exist for them'. Families were so packed into buildings that it was impossible for them to live like human beings.

When, at the age of ten, Mary arrived in the city, over thirty-thousand people were living in one-room homes known as 'single-ends'. The family had been forced to sell most of their possessions to pay for the journey from Aberdeen and, with no friends and no money, the only accommodation they could get for the first few years was one of these single-ends.

Her parents did find work, but their combined wages were barely enough to keep the family in food and shelter. For the first few months while her parents were at work, Mary was able to run wild with the other grubby, barefoot, children. They swarmed and screeched among the filthy narrow lanes between the slum buildings which were as closely packed together as the families who lived in them. A contemporary writer called them 'sunless rookeries'. But when her father began to drink again and needed money for whisky he decided that Mary, now his eldest child, must go to work in the mills as a half-timer.

The half-timers were children between the ages of ten and thirteen who worked either one day in the mills and one day in school or from six to eleven in the morning in the mills and from midday to six in the evening in school. At fourteen, if they were lucky, they went on to work the full fifty-eight hour week. Most of the girls could find regular work in the mills but when a boy reached the age when he qualified for a man's wage he was usually sacked and replaced by another boy. Nimble fingers rather than strength were required at the looms, so since a woman's wage was little more than half of a man's, and a child's only a quarter, few men were employed at them. Since there was no other work which they could find, many men hung about miserably at home or in the lanes while their wives and children earned their keep. The sacked boys grew into bitter and anti-social men. Drunkenness leading to violent assault was the main crime in the city and illegitimacy was common as men and mill-lassies tried to escape from the degradation of their lives.

Mary was eleven when she became a mill-lassie. In later years she wrote, 'At that time I was wee and thin and not very strong.' For the next fifteen years hers was the world of the 'knocker-up' who hammered on doors at five in the morning every day except

Sunday. Month after month, year after year, when the bells and hooters sounded from the mills, the bare feet of the children slapped on stone stairs beside the clattering clogs of their mothers; and slow-moving columns of people shuffled down the lanes to an incessant accompaniment of coughing, blending together in the streets into processions of thousands of people.

Inside the long mill-sheds it was a world where the driving belts whirred from the steam-driven pulleys to the looms on which the weaving frames clattered. These made such a din that communication was by signal or by shouting in the ear.

In the tiny one-room home, with no supply of water or of lighting and with no toilet, it was a world of no privacy whatever; bed was a mattress stuffed with straw on the floor; dressing was done jammed in between walls and elbows – if you were fussy you did it under your night-gown looking in the process like an itching ghost. A bath was a zinc tub on the floor once in a while in which you knelt in tepid water while the men-folk were out of the way. There were no public bath-houses any more than there were public lavatories, beyond the communal bucket closets placed for convenience next to the manure-heap in the backyard.

Towards the end of their long day in school and in the mills the half-timers were often half asleep. But lack of attention in either place brought a strapping over the hand with a leather belt. This helped to produce a tough breed of child resulting in tough men and women.

It would have been difficult for God or man to have found a better place than the slums of Dundee to prepare Mary for the conditions under which she was to work in Africa. And while the slums were toughening the barefoot lassie, her mother, who was a gentle and deeply religious woman, was planting in her daughter's mind the seeds of the great ideal which was to captivate the lassie and drive her relentlessly on from the back streets of Dundee into the Calabar forests.

Back in the Aberdeen days a sermon by a missionary on leave from Calabar – in which he described the fearful conditions created by the slave trade under which the Africans were living, and what the mission was trying to do for them – so fascinated Mrs Slessor that from then on her great ambition was to see one of her sons a Calabar missionary. She began to borrow the *Missionary Record* magazine from her church library, and to read it to her children, and to encourage them to play at

Barefoot children in Dundee

teaching black children. So Mary grew up with 'Calabar' as a household name. Then, when another Calabar missionary, the Reverend William Anderson, came to give a series of lectures in Dundee, Mrs Slessor took Mary and her brother John to hear them, so that Mary listened for the first time to the man who would one day be among her greatest friends.

But Mrs Slessor never seems to have looked on Mary as a possible missionary. This was probably because, by the time she was fourteen, the redhead had developed into one of the toughest of an extremely tough breed of girl. Mary described herself as having been 'a wild lassie' in those days. Her nicknames at the time were 'Carrots' because of her flaming hair, and 'Fire' because of her flaming temper. She was, and always would be, a warrior, and this and her strong personality made her the leader of a group of young girls who were forever up to mischief. She was definitely not, it seemed, mission material.

In 1862 Mary became a full-timer, and in that year her mother bore the last of her sisters, Janie. Now there were six of the family living in one room. But even that was below the average number for the Dundee single-ends.

Robert Slessor was gradually losing his battle against his alcoholism and soon Mary's fighting qualities were tested nearly every week in her attempts to protect her mother from her drunken father. Saturday was payday and Saturday night became nightmare-night for the family. The marriage bed was in a recess curtained off from the room and the younger children were put into it until it was required by their parents when they were lifted down on to a floor mattress. On Saturday nights, with the little ones asleep in the bed behind the curtain, Mary and her mother waited for her father to come home. It was always a problem to decide when to cook his meal. If he came home early, and only a little tipsy, his good cheer turned quickly to anger if his meal was not ready for him. If – and this was more usual – he came staggering home late and the meal was dried up through being kept hot, he flew into a rage and threw it either at them or into the fire.

Mrs Slessor was a patient woman, resigned to poverty and unhappiness, but her red-haired daughter would never be resigned to anything. In the violent Saturday scenes she drew her father's anger on to herself. Sometimes she managed to dodge him round the plain wooden table and chairs and the boxes, which were their only furniture, until he collapsed into a chair. Sometimes he caught her, clouted her, threw her out of the door, and locked it. On winter nights everything was in darkness. People either used candle lanterns or groped their way as best they could. When she saw the huge flickering shadows and heard the shambling drunken footsteps the shivering Mary, waiting until her mother could let her in, hoped that the drunk would not come her way. If he did, then she had to dodge quickly past him. She got used to moving quickly in the dark and to humouring drunks: skills she was going to need in Calabar.

Inevitably the day came when her father's employer warned him that he must stop drinking or be sacked. Robert tried to keep off the whisky, but he failed, and he joined the ranks of the unemployed who hung around the taverns hoping to scrounge a drink from old friends. Now, towards the end of the week, the family had no money to buy the oatmeal and the bread which was their main food. Their mother had to look out something on which a pawnbroker would lend them a few pennies to tide them over until Saturday when, by returning the loan plus interest, they could 'redeem' the articles. These might be their Sunday clothes or, if these had been handed over already, her wedding ring.

To Mrs Slessor the trips to the pawnshop were the ultimate in shame. She made Mary wait until it was dark before she allowed the lassie to slip out, with the disgraceful parcel under her shawl, to dodge her way through the gangs of young men who had nothing better to do and nowhere better to go than to hang about the lanes. This too called for speed and for humouring, and, since kicking with bare feet was not much use, sometimes for the use of teeth and finger nails. To maul and try to kiss a lassie was one of the few sports the gangs could enjoy.

But Sundays were different. Then, the family – except for their father – went to service in the Wishart Memorial Church. Mother was in her carefully preserved hat and dress and the children in their home-made Sunday clothes – and even boots! Churches were the only large buildings into which Mary had ever been: an entirely different world, spacious, clean, and respectable. But although she enjoyed the singing, she was not much interested in the rest of the proceedings, until through a strange episode, she took the first steps along the road which would take her into the Calabar forests.

An old widow who lived nearby began to worry about the immortal souls of Mary and her friends. She took to inviting them in to sit on the floor in her nice warm room while she talked to them about the dangers of running wild. This suited the gang because each of them would have been unpopular hanging about her one-room home. One evening, perhaps because she was making no impression on Mary, she took the lassie's hand and held it near the fire. 'If you were to put your hand in there', she said, 'it would be awful sore. But if you don't repent your soul will burn in blazing fires for ever and ever.'

Mary could laugh about it in later years but, at the time, the event made such a deep impression on her that she began to have nightmares in which an old crone was about to push her hand into a fire. For days afterwards, when she looked into a fire, she remembered the nightmares and for the first time she began to think about life and death and about eternity and God. Could you really talk to this Jesus of Nazareth about whom she had been hearing all her life? She tried talking to him and decided that you could. Gradually she began to chat away to him in her mind at any time and in any place. Life at home was becoming more and more miserable and in religion she began to find an escape from unhappiness and squalor. She began to read the New Testament and to borrow books from the church library. But although her mother helped her with the reading, she found that she could not understand the books. Then the idea came to her that she should go to night school and educate herself. But would an ignorant mill-lassie be welcome? Anyway fifty-eight hours a week in the din of the weaving shed, plus the chores at home, were more than enough. But the need to open up this closed world of books and ideas grew stronger and at the beginning of the next term she enrolled for classes on two evenings a week.

Then her father died suddenly. In a way it was a relief because alcohol had destroyed him and in doing so had given Mary a bitter hatred of it which lasted for the rest of her life. But since she was – and always would be – an emotional, romantic, even a sentimental person, she grieved for the man he had once been and who had played with her as a child.

Now, with one mouth less to feed and with John apprenticed to a blacksmith and Susan working as a half-timer, the family was able to move into a bigger home. But it was still in the slums.

Then, in 1866, when she was seventeen, Mary received encouragement in her work to educate herself from reports in the *Missionary Record* about David Livingstone, the famous Scottish missionary and explorer, who was setting off on a new expedition to Lake Tanganyika. Like her, he had been a mill-worker before he educated himself and became a doctor. He had sailed for Africa in 1840, had survived hair-raising adventures including being mauled by a lion, had travelled hundreds of miles up several rivers, and had discovered the Victoria Falls on the Zambesi. He regarded himself as a pioneer missionary: one whose work it was to open up the country so that others might follow.

In later years, Mary would model her own pioneer work on Livingstone's. Now he became her hero. He had read books while he worked at his loom. So she would too. She applied for permission to do so from her employers and, perhaps because they too had been reading about Livingstone, was given it, provided it did not interfere with her work. Apparently it did not, because soon she was promoted to operating not one but two of the large looms. The wild lassie was becoming a competent young woman.

As her reading improved, her keen, logical, brain, which would one day so impress British officials, began to probe the teaching of the New Testament. In later years she showed a great ability to go direct to the heart of a matter. Now she began to grope her way towards the heart of the teaching of Jesus of Nazareth. In doing this she was helped by her conviction that she was in direct communication with him and that he was guiding her, a conviction which would never leave her. She was naive enough to pay the writers of the New Testament the compliment of thinking that they meant what they wrote and from this she developed another conviction: that the worship for which Jesus was looking was the worship of active love of God and Man, that Christianity demanded a life of service. This too was a conviction which never left her. It helped her to develop her own individual attitude to Christianity, which one day a Chief Justice of Nigeria would describe as being 'above religion', and which would cause her to write to a friend: 'No! No! . . . Creeds and books and ministers are all good enough but look you to Jesus.'

After her death it was customary in the Sunday schools of Scotland to pretend that at this time Mary Slessor was a pious, timid, young thing in whose mouth butter would scarcely melt.

But she herself never pretended that she had been anything but 'wild', and an elderly minister, who had met contemporaries of hers in Dundee, wrote shortly before his own death that he had heard things about her both good and bad which none of her early biographers ever seem to have discovered. Again, Dr John Hitchcock who worked with her in Calabar, wrote that, '. . . she was recognised as a forceful personality from the start.' It seems hardly likely therefore that Mary changed from a 'wild lassie' into a pious lassie and then back again into the tough, aggressive, wise-cracking warrior of Calabar fame.

What does seem likely is that her mother's fight for respectability in the middle of squalor, with an alcoholic as a husband and a wild lassie for a daughter, divided the Slessors from their neighbours and made them the tight-knit family which they continued to be; and that as Mary changed into a thoughtful, religious, young woman, she too became divided from her wild lassies. She certainly began to escape more and more into her talks with Christ, her Bible, and her books.

An entirely new world was opening up for her.

3. MARY EDUCATES HERSELF

Mary moved into her twenties. She had striking blue eyes under the equally striking red hair, but her face was too strong to be pretty, and although her vitality and sense of humour attracted men to her in later years, there is no record of any romance in her life in Dundee. Perhaps, in the enforced intimacy of the single-end, the closing years of her mother's marriage to a man who had become an alcoholic made sexual relations repellent to all the Slessor girls, for none of them married.

Mary no longer needed to go to night-school now, and she began to think about helping with the work of the parish. A new minister, James Logie, came to work in it, and, because she stood out in his congregation, he invited her to teach a class of the youngest children in his Sunday School: an invitation which she had, she wrote later, 'the impudence to accept'.

Logie gradually became what she described as 'the best earthly friend I have'. He and his wife began to help the uncouth mill-lassie to learn how to behave in polite society. The world of polished floors and furniture, of carpets and pictures, was strange to her; these things were not to be found in the slums any more than were bathrooms. And although a Scottish minister's home – the manse – was not an elegant place, Mary's visits to the Logies may well have been her first introduction to these luxuries. She learned quickly, but she was desperately shy and tongue-tied in the presence of 'better class people'. She knew that, just as in the army officers did not mix with sergeants, nor sergeants and privates, so, as a mill-lassie from the slums, she was only tolerated by 'better class people' provided she kept her place. Instead of coming forward therefore she drew back, and it took months of patient work by the Logies to bring her out of her shell.

She worked hard at 'bettering herself', began to speak without the rough Dundee slum accent, found that she had a good sing-

Posh young Mary

ing and speaking voice and that she could hold her class of children fascinated with stories from the Bible, making them laugh too. But she was very much a learner and an imitator, anxious to conform to the strict rules of middle-class Victorian society. She was only saved from becoming prim and proper and an imitation 'lady' by her earthy commonsense, her belief in Christ's own teaching, and her great sense of humour. The photograph for which she posed at this time shows the type of person she could have changed into. In it, with her stiff voluminous skirt, her tightly corseted waist, and her carefully arranged hair with not a ringlet out of place, she looks as unlike the real Mary Slessor as anyone possibly could. It was not until she had established herself as a missionary in Calabar, and had sized up what had to be done about its problems, that she broke completely free of Victorian convention and followed in her own way where she was convinced that her Lord was leading her. But even in her diffident days in Dundee there are flashes of the rebel which she would become.

Logie had ideas about parish work which were ahead of his time for, although church members visited homes and distributed money to the sick, the elderly, and the paupers, there was no organised social work or youth work in those days. In order to bring the church nearer to the people of the slums he opened a mission in the middle of them, and when he started what would nowadays be called a youth club, Mary volunteered to be one of his assistants. The club was novel enough to attract a small membership. Logie put on 'magic lantern' shows and held discussion groups and, when the weather was fine, Mary took the members for long rambles in the countryside where they had picnics and ran races. There was not much more which they could do. There was no space available for organised sport, and even playing cards were looked upon by the church elders as 'devil's instruments', so that Mary could not even teach the youngsters 'Snap'.

Soon, even her rambles incurred the displeasure of the elders. They asked Logie if he knew that his Sunday school teacher was wandering the countryside with groups of uncouth young people; that she had been seen to pull her skirts above her knees and run races with them; even worse, that she had been seen to climb trees? Logie thought that he better suggest to Mary that she should be more prudent. But his normally respectful assistant flared up and told him what she thought of elderly hypocrites.

The rambles, the racing, and the tree-climbing continued.

It was not only with the elders that the mission ran into trouble. In fine weather, because his mission rooms were so small, Logie held meetings out of doors. To the youngsters of 'the sunless rookeries' these soon became the most entertaining things which had ever happened. They threw horse manure at the speakers and charged into the audience in groups to break it up. They were encouraged to do this by some of the men who did not find the mission at all amusing. They wanted work and better wages and living conditions, not 'pie in the sky'. To them the Church was part of the Establishment which was exploiting them and Logie had not yet been able to put his ideas about social work into effect. Groups of men and youths began to attack the mission workers on their way to meetings. They punched and kicked the men and pelted and jeered at the women. Logie had to advise his workers to go to meetings in pairs.

Mary, typically, did not always bother to find a partner. Because of her sense of humour and her reputation as a fighter she was usually left alone. But one Sunday afternoon when she was on her way to one of her meetings for young people a gang of youths surrounded her. The leader had a big lead weight on a cord which he swung round his head towards Mary. She did some quick thinking and made a deal with him. If she stood up to the swinging weight without flinching then they would all come to her meeting and, furthermore, behave themselves. He accepted. Mary took off her Sunday hat, and the gang stood round her in a circle while the leader began to swing the weight again. As he let out more and more cord it swung two feet from her nose, then barely a foot. Mary stared at him. Suddenly he pulled back the weight and let it fall. 'She's game boys!' he said. We'll just have to sing

Mary had picked some good rousing hymns, in the talk which she gave to them she made them laugh, and, to their surprise, some of the gang enjoyed themselves. Afterwards Mary explained to them that the mission was not just about singing hymns. Would they help with her rambles, picnics and races? They thought about it. Would they have to go to meetings no matter who was speaking? – No. – Right! They would help her.

This was a beginning. Soon Mary had youngsters helping her with what would now be called social work. The boys ran errands for the sick and the elderly and the girls helped Mary to scrub floors and to do the washing for mothers who could not cope.

Years later, after Mary died, a member of the Wishart congregation wrote, 'She sat down among the poor as one of themselves . . . She stooped very low. She became an angel of mercy in miserable homes.' The words were well meant. But Mary herself would not have been impressed. She was not 'stooping low'. These were her people. She was only doing what Jesus of Nazareth was teaching her to do.

Later, when she and her sister Susan were preparing to scrub out one of the mission rooms, a church elder protested that they should get a charwoman to do it. 'It's no job for ladies', he said. Mary's temper flared again. 'We're nae ladies!' she snapped. This would have been a new idea for the man. In the class-conscious Victorian world, in which even a washer-woman who took in work looked down on one who had to go out to do it, every woman wanted to be considered a 'lady'.

The experience which Mary gained in the losing battle which Logie's mission fought with the slums in Dundee was invaluable to her. Here, she learned that because she was one of themselves and lived among them, the people would speak openly to her about their problems, whereas they would keep quiet about them in front of 'better-class' church visitors. Here she found that she was better able to help with problems because she had shared them and still shared some of them; she was not a well-meaning visitor, who, even when the problems were explained still did not understand what it was like to face them. She did not blame the members of her church who would not have dreamt of going into 'the dreadful slums', or those who did work in them out of a sense of duty but held themselves aloof from the people. These members had a position to keep up in a hard world where class barriers were sacred. But between her and the people of the slums there were no barriers. Here, she learned that the conditions under which they are forced to live, and from which they cannot escape, shape peoples lives, that they have to adapt or go mad; that in order to lead an oppressed people to a new way of life it is necessary to improve their standard of living. This experience was part of the conditioning process which helped to produce '*Eka Kpukpro Owo*'.

Logie was becoming more and more impressed with his assistant. He persuaded her first to join a church discussion group and then to write a paper for it. The paper took her several weeks of night work and much crumpled paper. When she gave it to him she said it was no good but he could tell her what was wrong with it later. Logie however found it surprisingly good and tried to persuade her to read it to the group. But this she flatly refused to do. They would, she said, only joke afterwards about her rough accent.

For a joke one of the group did indeed lend her the weighty *Sartor Resartus* by the philosopher Carlyle. She returned the book to him the following Sunday saying that she had found it 'just grand' and had sat up all one night reading it. He thought that she in turn was joking until she began to discuss it with him. Then he found that it was he who was out of his depth.

Logie lent her *The Rise and Progress of Religion in The Soul*. The following Sunday he found that she was sighing a lot. 'It's yon book', she explained, 'and this silent meditation. I canna manage it at a'. My mind jist gings a' roads. I aye have to be talkin' or up and doin'.' Logie assured her that the talkin' and up and doin' were what mattered most.

Now her brother John was found to have tuberculosis: one of the scourges of the slums along with cholera, smallpox, typhoid and dysentery. He was advised to sail to a warmer climate and he managed to get an emigrant's passage to New Zealand. It was too late however and he died shortly after he arrived there. Mrs Slessor, Mary, Susan and Janie were now alone in the world and became an even tighter group. The girls all worked together in the mills and became almost inseparable, and, since they were now all working, they were able, at last, to get a house away from the slums.

Then in 1874, when Mary was twenty-five came news of David Livingstone's death. He had died the year before in the interior of Africa hundreds of miles from any other white man, and his two African servants had struggled for weeks to carry his body back to the coast. It was a romantic story and the Scottish newspapers were full of it.

He had written: 'I direct your attention to Africa. I know that in a few years I shall be cut off in that country which is now open . . . Do not let it be shut again. Do you carry out the work I have begun. I leave it with you.'

Mary read the reports about her hero's death and a ridiculous idea began to come into her mind and to keep returning there as often as she threw it out: she was to follow Livingstone to Africa. The family had known for years about Mrs Slessor's ambition to see one of her sons a Calabar missionary. They were dead. It was she, Mary, who had all along been steered gradually towards Calabar and who was now being directed to go there.

But it really was a ridiculous idea. Women missionaries − 'female agents' as they were called in Scotland − were educated people drawn usually from the families of the professional classes like ministers, doctors, and teachers. Who would want a mill-lassie as a missionary? She would only be snubbed if she applied. Besides, she knew from the *Missionary Record* that Calabar was a most unhealthy place. Who wanted to go and live there anyway? For over a year she tried to forget the idea. But she was not allowed to forget. Often, when she talked to her Lord the word 'Calabar' flashed up on the screen of her mind.

Meanwhile she continued to help Logie with his mission. She was, by now, one of the most successful of his teachers, and he tried to persuade her to talk not just to children but to adults too. But the thought of standing up in front of a gathering of men and women was too much for her and she refused. Then one evening, without realising it, she held the attention of a group of workers in a discussion on the text, 'The common people heard him gladly'. Logie kept quiet and let her do the talking. Afterwards he told her that she had been given a gift and that she must use it. She thought about it, and no doubt prayed about it. The following week she told him that she wouldn't mind talking to her 'ain folk'. But she was not going to go up on any platform. She would just sit in the middle of the folk like she did with her bairns.

She was surprised when gradually she was invited to speak in other parishes. But she never went up on to any platform. And still the word 'Calabar' nagged at her.

In 1863, Hope Waddell had written a book about the first twelve years of the Scottish Mission to Calabar of which he was the founder. From his book and from the *Missionary Record* Mary was able to get a picture of what life was like out there. He had worked for sixteen years among the West African slaves in Jamaica, and of Calabar he had written 'To the European constitution the climate is most exhausting and debilitating. It sucks out the vital energy . . . Five years there bring one down like ten or fifteen in Jamaica.' Then there were the fevers, especially the mysterious malaria which everybody got but nobody knew why. The *Record* had reported recently that two more of the female agents had died. New recruits had died within months of arriving in Calabar; others had gone on working there for thirty years. But Captain J B Walker of the Royal Geographical Society, who had made a survey of the area, had written in the *Record*, 'It is a mistake to suppose that any *ordinary* man can discharge the duties of a missionary in Old Calabar.' What made her think that she could discharge them?

Then there was the blockade of the rivers and the forests against the mission, which had locked it in the coastal towns for nearly thirty years while, beyond them, hundreds of thousands of Africans still lived in the world of war and violence which the slave trade had created. Was it worth risking her health just to work in the towns where already the mission had greatly improved living conditions for the women and the slaves?

She was about to make one of the most agonising decisions which she would ever make; others would be more perilous, but they would be made by an experienced woman in the face of known risks; this would be a step into the unknown by an inexperienced mill-lassie who had probably never even spent a night away from home.

Another Calabar missionary came to lecture in Dundee. The mission was, and would continue to be, very short of funds and it had discovered that speakers who took with them carved masks, headdresses, drums, and other things from Calabar which people could see and touch, raised most money. So after lectures Mary actually handled things from the place about which she had been hearing all her life. Now the ridiculous idea became a certainty. She was to apply to go to Calabar. If she were turned down that would be that. But she must apply.

In recent years the missionaries to West Africa have been written off as people who went, simply because they wanted to follow Jesus of Nazareth into martyrdom, and so find a 'heavenly crown', to impose an alien culture on happy primitive peoples for whom they had no feeling whatever and whose way of life they despised. But unless they had some burning ideal of service to God, or man, or both, or were in search of fame and fortune, no one in their right senses would have gone to a hellish place like Calabar. It could have been the ideal of world revolution which sent the missionaries there. It so happened that it was the Christian ideal of a kingdom of peace and brotherhood upon Earth. And it is not surprising that the first letters from new recruits — including the few early letters from Mary Slessor which have survived — should be full of references to the degradation of African life, for it was indeed degraded. But what the critics do not seem to recognise is that it took more than an ideal of self-sacrifice to keep people working under appalling conditions, and sick with fever most of the time, for ten, twenty, thirty or even forty years. They arrived with no liking for the country or the people. They did not know them. But either they fell in love with Africa and developed a liking and respect for its people or, if they had not already died, they quit. This is clear from mission records and from the books, diaries and letters of experienced missionaries. At this time, to go to Calabar was to Mary Slessor a frightening duty which was thrust upon her. But one day Calabar would be her chosen home — 'If you don't send me back', she would tell the Foreign Missions' Board, 'I'll swim back!' — and among its people would be her 'true and intelligent friends'. Today, that she should write this is not remarkable. But it has to be remembered that in her day most Europeans looked on Africans as being only slightly more intelligent than chimpanzees.

Now, as usual, Mary went to James Logie for advice. She knew that other people might laugh at a mill-lassie's silly idea but that he would not. He told her that if only they could get over the education problem he thought that she would make a good missionary. He promised that, if she were accepted, he would look after her family and advised her to write to the Foreign Missions' Board asking what qualifications were required for a female agent in Calabar.

The Board replied that she should make every endeavour to improve her education, since it would have to be of a standard high enough for her to teach English and the Scriptures to women and children. If she were accepted, then in Calabar she would have to learn to speak and to write the native language, Efik, since she would have to teach that too.

Mary now told her family that she was thinking of volunteering for Calabar. Her mother was delighted. But her sisters were upset. Calabar was a terrible place. Couldn't she volunteer for Jamaica or China or India where their church, the United Presbyterian, ran missions also?

Mary hung back for a few more months and then in May 1875 she finally found the courage to apply to the Board. To it she sent recommendations from Logie and from other ministers whom she knew.

All her life she was a quicksilver, excitable, and emotional woman, and it was with shaking hands that she opened the letter which would tell her whether she had been accepted or not.

Provided that, in Dundee, she continued to improve her education, Mary Mitchell Slessor was accepted. In March 1876 she would go to Edinburgh at the Board's expense for a four month course of instruction. After that she would sail for Calabar.

But the brink of action is often worse than the action itself and on the night before she left home to go, not overseas, but only to Edinburgh for her course, the enormity of her decision overwhelmed her. The woman who would one day be described as 'a tornado' crept down to the door of the lobby of the tenement building where she lived and cried her eyes out.

When James Logie came to say goodbye and to wish her luck, he found her there. As he left her she said, 'Pray for *me*!' with such emphasis on 'me' that it was more of a wail than a word.

In years after she said that her course in Edinburgh had not been 'sufficiently practical'. Certainly instruction in carpentry and cement work would have been of more use to her than was theology. However, at the end of July and of the course Mary went home on leave. She was now a female agent with a salary of sixty pounds a year. She had received a uniform allowance of twenty-five pounds and in her new cases were the white blouses, the dark skirts and the sunhelmet which she would wear in Calabar.

She was committed now and much too excited to be afraid. She signed farewell letters to friends 'Yours in Royal Service, Mary M Slessor.'

On August 5th 1876 she said goodbye to her family and friends and set out by train for Liverpool and the SS *Ethiopia*. Two friends went with her as far as the ship. They reported that when they reached it scores of casks of rum were being loaded for bartering in Africa. Mary regarded them and said, 'All that rum! And only one missionary!'

Ethiopia sailed next day and Mary spent most of the voyage either in her cabin or on deck. The ship would be calling in at ports along the Guinea Coast before it reached Calabar. The hard-bitten, hard drinking, old-timers returning to 'The Coast' were probably amused at the soberly dressed, shy, young woman. They were probably sorry for her too, even though many of them had little sympathy for missionaries who wasted their time on 'niggers'.

In a storm in the Bay of Biscay a young deck officer found Mary sheltering on deck. He asked her if she thought that they were going to sink. 'Na! Na!' said Mary, 'God wouldnae send me all this way jist to drown in your silly old ship!'

Ethiopia sailed past the Canary Islands and began to close 'The Coast'. One evening the offshore breeze brought out of the darkness to the ship and to Mary the first puff of the perfume of The Dark Continent, a spicy, warm, hothouse smell which set the senses tingling for the many lovers of what was then a beautiful Jezebel of a country: fascinating but often fatal. To Mary it would always be exciting for it would always mean that she was nearing the only world to which she really belonged.

After they passed Cape Verde they sailed along first the Ivory Coast and then the Gold Coast. Soon the flat coastline was familiar to Mary, with its trees, monotonous and mysterious, which marched on for hundreds of miles. They were like a green ocean which hid in its folds the forest townships in which hundreds of thousands of people lived but of which there was no sign.

Ethiopia was heading for the main Calabar anchorage called, in those days, Old Calabar to distinguish it from New Calabar a few miles to the north of it. The anchorage was about fifty miles up the Cross River at a place called Duke Town. As the ship entered the mouth of the river, which at this point is twenty miles wide, Mary saw the hills of the island of Fernando Po astern and the mountains of the Cameroons to starboard.

They passed Tom Shotts Point where she saw the skeleton of a British sailing ship. Some of its crew had been eaten by cannibals. She saw too for the first time how the mangrove trees pushed their roots out into the water and trapped mud and debris making a belt of swamps ten miles wide along the coast. These swamps, along with the maze of rivers and creeks, created, under the blazing sun, the humidity which left people breathless and drenched with sweat even at night.

They passed the islands in midstream where she knew that young men and women had been sacrificed to the river gods by being impaled on stakes and left on the mud-banks. They passed the 'barracoons': stockades where tens of thousands of slaves had been penned before they were shipped across the Atlantic; where thousands had died of misery and hunger; where thousands of others, because they were too ill to travel, had been turned down by the ships' surgeons and, being worthless, butchered.

At Seven Fathom Point the *Ethiopia* turned out of the Cross River and into the Calabar. Five miles further on they sailed round a bend and, at last, the lassie from the slums saw the anchorage of Old Calabar.

Although it was September 11th 1876 and the rainy season, brilliant sunshine greeted Mary Slessor and she, flowery for once, was misled into describing the climate, in her first letter home, as 'delightsome'.

The land sloped upwards from the river which was coming down in spate, yellowish-brown after the rains. On the higher ground the painted houses of the rich African traders sat above the red clay walls and yellow thatch of the clustered mud huts of the town. In the anchorage itself, old sailing ships – the 'hulks' on which the white traders lived – dismasted, painted, and with their decks thatched over, looked like Noah's Arks as they swung at their cables. Canoes were threading in and out of the shipping, some with the palm oil which had replaced slaves as the main export, some with stores. Mary heard the rhythmic chanting of the paddlers and the tap of the drums as, black muscles gleaming, the men swung to the stroke. The colours of the houses, the hulls, the head-scarves and loincloths of the Africans, and of the ships' ensigns, backed by the green of the trees and under a blue sky which went up forever and ever, made for the excited lassie from the mucky, smoky, streets of grey Dundee, an unforgettable picture.

As the ship anchored Mary looked first for the white buildings on Mission Hill: the house, school, church, and dispensary, surrounded by a garden. Then she looked for the mission boat which she had been told would be crewed by oarsmen wearing red caps and dark loincloths.

The arrival of the steamer was always a great occasion, with newcomers to be greeted, old friends to be welcomed back, and letters and goods from home. The captain held what amounted to a reception as canoes for Africans and boats for Europeans surged up to his ship.

William Anderson and his wife were on leave in Scotland, and it was Alexander Ross who came out in the boat to welcome Mary. The mission had complained to the Board, after some early deaths, that recent recruits had been too delicate for the climate. When he saw the slight woman with the glowing ringlets peeping from under the white hat, Ross may well have thought that she also was too frail to last the pace.

When her turn came the new female agent went down the companion-ladder while black hands held the boat steady and white teeth beamed a welcome out of smiling black faces. The woman who was to be '*Eka Kpukpro Owo*' saw for the first time a black hand reaching out to her, grasped it, hitched up her long skirt and, on this the greatest day of her young life, Miss Slessor jumped into the boat. 'The upholding, the freedom from all anxiety, the sense of his presence which I have experienced since I left home, have been all that I could have asked or expected . . . We had a very pleasant voyage . . . But I did feel a little lonely.'

The key to the forests, for which the missionaries had been praying, had arrived.

4. INTRODUCTION TO OLD CALABAR

The 'Calabar Welcome' from the mission staff to new recruits was well-known. A later arrival wrote that it beat even the old traditional Highland welcome. The children from the school formed a guard of honour on the mission jetty and, since nearly all its stations were within a few miles of Duke Town, the mission staff gathered there in the evening to meet the newcomer.

As the boat pulled in towards the jetty Mary smelt for the first time the sweet, cloying reek of the palm oil and got her first whiff of the stink of a Calabar town.

Mrs Sutherland, who was in charge of the school at this time, was on the jetty with the children. She had joined the mission as Miss Miller in 1849, and a few years later had married one of its teachers. He had died of fever five months later but she had gone on working in Calabar for twenty-seven years. This was the woman who, when the victorious side in a battle had begun to burn the town of the defeated with men, women, and children still prisoners inside it, had searched through the huts and released many of them; whom white traders had found among the smoke trying to break the padlock on the chains of one prisoner with a bit of an old gun; who, after they had gone and she was alone again and the victors had opened fire, had walked out with the bullets whistling past her and stopped the shooting. She had made journeys into the forests to places where no white person had been before in spite of warnings that she would be killed and had more than once defied the officials of the ruling body, Egbo, and stopped them flogging a slave to death by intercepting the lash with her umbrella. She was one of the few white women honoured by the Africans with the title of *Ma Akamba* – Great Mother.

So, when the boat was tied up and Mary walked over to the line of young Africans beaming their welcome, the first of the women missionaries to greet her was a small grey-haired woman who summed up in her person everything which the new recruit wanted to be and who would help to shape her into *Eka Kpukpro Owo*. Then, escorted by the excited children, a nervous but equally excited Miss Slessor went up the path to Mission Hill with Mrs Sutherland: past and future chapters of mission history walking side by side.

The hill was only about two hundred feet high but before she reached the top of it, Mary, properly uniformed in all the underwear of a Victorian lady topped off with voluminous skirt, blouse, hat, and gloves, and shored up with knee-high boots, was drenched in sweat. She soon found that in a climate where the temperature was constantly above 90°F in the hot season and never fell below 70°F at the coolest even at night, sweat-soaked clothes were going to be the order of all her days.

The garden at the top of the hill was one of the best places from which to see the landmarks. This was where, before they allocated the land to the missionaries, the Efiks had thrown the corpses of slaves not worth the trouble of burying, and where now, from the cemetery beside it, the headstones of dead missionaries looked out over Old Calabar.

Looking down from the garden, the steamer, the hulks, and the canoes coming and going made the anchorage a bowl of colour in a great sea of green, in which, shimmering in the heat, wave after wave of trees rolled away to the horizon. Most of the land had been reclaimed from the rivers over the centuries by the gradual spread of the mangrove trees. It was flat and rarely higher than twenty feet above sea level. To her right, partly hidden by the shoulder of the hill, was Duke Town. Beyond it, two miles further up the Calabar and hidden in the trees was Old Town. Directly opposite her, across the river and four miles of creeks, mangrove swamps, and trees was Creek Town. The mission had a station there which was also built on a hill so that on a clear day the missionaries could send messages to and fro by semaphore.

The Calabar flows diagonally towards the Cross River so that there is a wedge shaped area of land between them. Creek Town was towards the point of the wedge with its farm villages behind it. Above them was the unknown territory of the Okoyong. They were the enemies, not only of the Efiks, but of every other neighbouring tribe except the Aro for whom they had fought at one time as mercenaries.

The Cross River was the main trade route. There were no

roads. Horses, donkeys, and mules had been imported from time to time but the tsetse fly had killed them. So everything was carried either along the narrow bush paths on the head or in canoes along the maze of small creeks and small rivers which flowed into the main ones. The Cross is tidal in its lower stretches and in Mary's day it was navigable, even in the dry season, by steam launches and large canoes for the first one hundred and fifty of its five hundred miles.

On the west bank of the Cross, as far as the important market town of Itu about fifty miles up, there were a few Efik settlements by the riverside but most of the territory belonged to the Aro-dominated Ibibio. The Aro territory proper was inland beyond Itu up an old slave route called the Enyong Creek. Their territory like that of their friends the Okoyong was a blank space on the map. Both tribes chased out white intruders and a British officer called Carr who had tried to reach the Aro from the Niger side had been murdered. All that the mission knew about the Aro at this time was that they possessed the oracle of the great god Chuku which was respected and feared by all the other tribes and that they were wealthy enough to hire the best of the warrior tribes to fight for them.

After she had pointed out the landmarks to Mary, Mrs Sutherland showed her round the mission buildings including the school and dispensary where she would be working. For the first few weeks new recruits were always given duties on Mission Hill itself and discouraged from doing much walking because the continual sweating was thought to weaken them and make them more susceptible to malaria. The cause of this fever was still a mystery. Most people thought that the germs were probably carried from the swamps by the night mists, and the missionaries – who were the only whites allowed to live ashore – always built two-storey buildings and slept on the upper one.

The mission had, with Mary, a staff of thirteen. Some were Scottish and some Jamaican. There were four ordained missionaries, four men teachers, and five women teachers. Mary met most of them that evening including the veteran Hugh Goldie. He, poring over the work by the light of candles or paraffin lamps after the hard day of a missionary, had produced the first English/Efik dictionary and the first Efik grammar. The work had taken fifteen years to complete and had ruined his sight. Now he was nearly blind. But in spite of this he was working on his book *Calabar and Its Mission* which would be published in 1890. He taught Efik – which was the trading language of all the Cross River tribes – to the new recruits and, thanks to the years of research which his book had involved, he would give Mary the foundation of her wide knowledge of Calabar law, customs, and religion which would so impress Mary Kingsley and the British.

Mary met another friend that evening, the famous Mammy Fuller. She had been a slave in Jamaica, then a children's nurse, then one of the first Jamaican women to join the mission. Down through the years she had been the friend and comforter of many of the young Scots and was remembered by them, including Mary, as 'Dear Old Mammy Fuller'.

The reason why the mission had always included Jamaicans on its staff was that it had originated on their island where the Scottish Missionary Society had been working among the slaves since 1824. Most of the slaves came from West Africa and when the British freed them the Jamaican Presbytery devised a plan to take some of them back to their homeland to teach Christianity to their fellow countrymen. Its plan was 'not to evangelise the native tribes but to set up an African agency to do so'; to set up, not a European branch of its church in West Africa, but an African one.

In 1841 it put up its plan to the Society. It pointed out that the British, who had prospered so much from the slave trade, had a duty to make some form of reparation for all the cruelty which it had encouraged. Hugh Goldie was a member of the Presbytery at the time, and he wrote that the trade had exposed the Africans to, 'all the miseries of the most iniquitous system that ever defiled or desolated the earth'. But the Society replied that it was impossible for Europeans to live in the West African climate and turned the plan down. Recent British expeditions to the Niger area had failed disastrously because of the high casualties from fever and missionaries already working in the area had suffered heavy casualties too – fifty of them had died.

When two of the presbytery went home to Scotland on leave in 1842 however, they talked the Society into changing its mind. Then they made contact with a Captain Turner who traded in palm oil with West Africa from Liverpool. He suggested that the Efik chiefs of Old Calabar, whom he knew well, might be only too pleased to have a mission. They were firmly pro-British and wanted to learn 'white-man's fashion' in order to compete on better terms with the European traders. They themselves had a genius for trade and it was one of the most important activities in their lives.

When a British commander had negotiated a treaty with them by which, in return for compensation, they had agreed finally to stop exporting slaves, King Eyamba of Duke Town had written to him, 'Now we settle for not to sell slaves I must tell you something I want your Queen to do for we. Now we can't sell slaves again we must have too much man for country, and want something for make work and trade . . . Plenty sugar cane live here, and if some man come teach we way for do it we get plenty sugar too and then some man must come for teach book proper and make all men saby God like white men and then we go on for same fashion . . . What I want for dollar side is fine coat and sword . . . and the rest in copper rods (Calabar currency) . . . Also I want bomb and shell'.

At the same time King Eyo Honesty of Creek Town had written on the same lines. He ended, ' . . . Mr Blyth tell me England glad for to send man to teach book and make we all understand God all same white man do'.

The missionaries asked Captain Turner to apply to the chiefs on their behalf for permission to come to Calabar and to buy land. They then returned to Jamaica and reported to the presbytery.

Early in 1843 they heard from Captain Turner that the chiefs had favoured their application but that they had not yet made a firm decision on it.

Communications by sailing ship from Old Calabar to Liverpool and then on to Jamaica were slow and six months went by before the presbytery heard from Captain Turner again. He explained that the chiefs had asked him to write a letter of invitation to send a mission but that because of native laws it would not be possible for them to buy land allocated to it. He wrote however that, 'The land will be at your service to make such establishments on as you see proper. It will be guaranteed to its occupants forever; a law will be passed for its protection; and the colonists Africans from Jamaica will dwell in peace and safety none daring to make them afraid. There seems no doubt of your obtaining land, when once here and established, sufficient for plantations for a number of families. The King and chiefs say they are desirous of your coming amongst them, and are full of the scheme, hoping to have their children taught in English learning.'

To his letter the chiefs added, 'We the undersigned, Kings and chiefs of Old Calabar, having consulted together, agree to those things before written, and request you to come amongst us . . . King Eyamba the Fifth, Henshaw Duke, Mr Young, Duke Ephraim, Egbo Jack, Adam Duke, Bashey Offerey, Antera Duke.'

The comic pidgin-English of the chiefs' letters and their anglicised names summed up their position part-way between a medieval African and a modern one. Most beginners, before they learn to do something their own way, have to follow the advice and the example of experts and in doing so become pale imitations of them. Except for infant prodigies there is no other way to learn. Professor Onwuka Dike, himself a Nigerian, has written that at this time the Efiks had 'an avid desire for Europeanisation'. They were happy to abandon tribal customs if to do so brought them more power and wealth. Inevitably they were becoming imitations of the Europeans whom they so much admired. Inevitably too the white traders found them laughable caricatures of themselves and despised them. It was possible that some of the whites might have recognised and respected a great Efik warrior in the tall figure of Eyo Nsa when he was wearing his tribal robes. But under the new name which he chose, Willie Honesty, in the top hat and the tatty old British uniform which he had taken to wearing as his ceremonial dress, and against the background of squalor and misery which the slave trade had created, it was almost impossible for them to do so.

The Jamaican Presbytery of course accepted the invitation from the chiefs and Hope Waddell with Mr and Mrs Edgerley, who were Scots, and Andrew Chisholm and Edward Miller who were Jamaicans, finally arrived in Calabar in 1846. They were one of the most experienced missionary groups to arrive in Africa. The Jamaicans were of African descent and the whites had worked among Africans for years and were accustomed to treating them not as 'savages' or 'heathen souls to be saved' but as people. This gave them an advantage over newcomers from Britain who saw their first African community under the worst possible conditions and, not surprisingly, took years to see any-thing good under the ugly face of cruelty and filth which con-fronted them. Even so Hope Waddell's group were shocked at what they found. They had known the slave trade at the import-ing end – he had described it as 'murderous' – now they were to see what it had done to the people at the exporting end.

The Efiks had moved into Old Calabar from the Ibibio territory probably in the middle of the seventeenth century. Since trade with the Europeans had not yet caused the tribes to migrate to the coast and grab the best anchorages they had been able to get permission from the Qua tribe, which owned the land, to settle first at Etunko (Creek Town) and then, after a quarrel had split the tribe, at Obutong (Old Town).

At this time the tribe was made up of five families descended from a common ancestor. In the Ibibio society, from which they came, the smallest unit was a man and his family. Several related families made up an *ufok* or compound: sons built their huts and yards near those of their father. A group of *ufoks* made up an *ekpuk* or extended family community. Several *ekpuk* made up a village and each village was self-governing under its family head (*Obong*) and its council of family elders. The tribe made their living as fishermen, trading their catches with the tribes of the interior for vegetables, fruit, and the palm oil which they used for cooking.

The tribes all traded one with the other. They tended to specialise. Some were farmers, some fishermen, some made canoes, some pottery, and some wove raffia cloth, while a tribe of travelling blacksmiths did metal work. The population of the coastal areas was small and tribes like the Efik owned few, if any, domestic slaves. It was this simple way of life which the slave trade destroyed.

At the beginning of the eighteenth century, as the colonies in the New World developed, so did their demand for slave labour. The West African tribes soon realised that to trade in human beings was the way to power and wealth and those which did not have an anchorage already, migrated to the coast and occupied one. Soon too, by bartering slaves for guns, they had the fire-power to keep other tribes back and to set themselves up as middlemen between the tribes of the interior and the Europeans. All along the Guinea Coast the tribes fought to keep their anchorages and the monopoly of the trade in their area.

In the successful tribes like the Efik the small *ekpuk* units developed into powerful Houses each with its head, its sub-chiefs, its freemen, and its domestic slaves. As the trade developed and they needed more warriors and more labour the coastal tribes began to keep back more and more of the captives for their own use. A small House, slave and free, could number up to a thousand. But a large one, like those of the Calabar towns,

Egbo officials

owned thousands of slaves and hundreds of the trading and war canoes on which their wealth and power depended.

Professor Dike writes that the House rule was, 'the direct result of the trade with the Europeans . . . The mixture of peoples often meant that African law and custom vanished and a new law and order was evolved . . . In its full development the House became at once a co-operative trading unit and a local government institution.'

But once a tribe had established itself in an anchorage and set up its monopoly, its Houses began to fight for supremacy among themselves. In Calabar, Creek Town tried to cut Old Town off from trading. So some of the Old Town Houses moved nearer to the sea and established Duke Town. Soon all three towns were fighting one another until, in 1767, British traders tired of the contest interfering with their trade and helped eliminate Old Town from it. They invited the Old Town chiefs aboard one of their ships for a palaver (meeting), chained them up, and then opened fire on the war canoes of their bodyguard. The Duke Town warriors then joined in and helped slaughter those of Old Town. Afterwards the traders handed over the chiefs to their enemies who beheaded one on the spot and sold the rest into slavery.

This incident was typical of the violence which the slave trade had created not only along the Coast but in the interior as well where tribe now raided tribe for prisoners for export. The brutality of the trade gradually brutalised the tribes which were profiting from it. Between 1720 and 1830 about a million slaves were shipped out of Calabar while thousands more died in the anchorage or were butchered there. The chiefs grew accustomed to looking on human beings simply as merchandise. But because they shared the same human life, the cheapening of the lives of the sold cheapened the lives of the sellers, and the cruelty and fear which the Efiks had helped to spread up the rivers spread through their whole society. By the beginning of the nineteenth century the Calabar life which confronted the European traders, and later the missionaries, was a squalid travesty of what it had once been. In 1833 MacGregor Laird, a famous explorer, described Calabar as 'The most uncivilised part of Africa ever I was in . . . I was much struck by the demoralisation and barbarism of the inhabitants in comparison with the natives of the interior. The human skulls seen in every direction and that are actually kicking about the streets attest the depravity of feeling among the people.'

Since, unlike some of the other coastal tribes, the Efiks had no hereditary ruler, they tried in the Egbo Order to create an overall ruling body which would draw up a new legal system and enforce it. Dike writes, 'For all practical purposes the Egbo Order was the supreme political power in Old Calabar; it exercised not only executive and legislative functions but was the highest court of appeal in the land. Its president became the first citizen of the community.'

Outside the affairs of their own Houses men like Eyamba and Eyo only had power according to their standing in the Egbo Council and their influence over it. The titles of 'King' and 'Duke' were only assumed to impress the white traders. Within Efik society they were meaningless.

Egbo ruled by a system of crippling fines on Houses which refused to obey its rulings and by burning their villages and massacring their inhabitants. Individuals who broke its laws were flogged, tortured or executed. Freemen, who had the right to substitute one of their slaves for themselves for punishment, were rarely tortured or executed, but the great mass of the slaves were terrorised into subjection.

Dike gives a list of punishments which Egbo officials meted out, ' . . . crucifixion round a large cask; extraction of teeth; suspension by the thumbs; . . . fastening the victim to a post driven into the beach at low water and leaving him there to be drowned by the rising tide . . .; impaling on stakes; driving a steel ramrod through the body until it appeared through the top of the skull'.

But, although the Egbo Order held down the slaves, it failed to stop the quarrels between the Houses. Now they fought over which was to have the president. Fighting between the Houses and between them and the white traders was still breaking out spasmodically when the mission arrived. It would continue to break out until, at last, over forty years later the British would accept the invitation of the chiefs and move in to govern Old Calabar. Until then the British, provided they could continue to trade without interference, would see no reason to go to the expense of colonising the area, for the wealth of the African interior was not yet discovered. In 1847 a French naval squadron would sail up the Cross and offer a French Protectorate to the chiefs and they, afraid for their compensation and their trade monopoly, would refuse it and petition London for a British one. This however would be denied them for the time being. But, while she would not move in and govern, Britain would continue to interfere in the affairs of all the coastal states and use her naval power to overrule their chiefs. In this way she would weaken what authority they had, aggravate an already violent situation, and create a state of near anarchy all along the Guinea Coast.

Her interference had begun in 1810 when she sent a naval squadron to blockade the Coast, intercept slave ships, and free their captives. Her sudden switch from being the chief supporter of the slave trade to being its chief opponent threatened to ruin the economy of the coastal states because it was to trade in slaves that they had been established. They saw no reason why a sudden change of mind by a foreign power should be allowed to ruin them and tried to continue to export slaves. This led to friction with the squadron, which by 1830 was even seizing slave ships inside African ports.

It was the palm oil trade which came to the rescue. This oil, made from the crushed fruit of a palm tree which grew in great numbers in West Africa, was found to be the best for lubricating the new metal machinery of the Industrial Revolution and for making soap. From being negligible in 1810 the trade rocketed by 1840 to being worth half a million pounds sterling a year. Soon the white traders could make the modern equivalent of sixty thousand pounds a year out of it. This was why tough men known as 'The Palm Oil Ruffians' risked their lives on the Coast which had already earned the name of 'The White Man's Grave'. Because the profits were so high new traders tried to cut in on the established ones. This led to more fighting and to what was literally cut-throat competition. The violence along the Coast became too widespread and the British had too few warships to make more than an occasional visit to the worst trouble spots to protect traders. So in 1845 the mission arrived into a situation which was politically, socially, and economically chaotic. They were the only white people allowed to live ashore and they would find themselves living in the middle of violence for the next forty years. The more they found out about the way in which Egbo enforced its laws the more they disapproved of it. But they had to admit that it was only because they were under Egbo protection that they were able to operate in Calabar.

They found that Duke Town had a population of close on seven thousand but Creek Town had only about one thousand five hundred because most of Eyo's people lived on his farms. In all, Hope Waddell estimated that at least sixty thousand people lived on the farms in the 'bush', the Calabar name for all land outside the towns whether forest or scrub.

In Duke Town he wrote, 'There was hardly anything like a street and the passages between the houses were narrow, crooked, rugged and dirty'.

Eyamba's House was the most powerful at this time and he intended to keep the benefits of 'God' and 'Book' for Duke Town alone. He allocated land to the missionaries on a hill outside the town and invited them to dinner in his 'palace' which was a pre-fabricated building from Britain made of iron. The meal was held at an enormous polished mahogany table and beforehand Eyamba showed his guests through his storehouses which were crammed with European goods of all kinds.

Eyo, who was Eyamba's rival in everything and who was building up the fortunes of Creek Town to the equal of those of Duke Town, was determined to win 'God' and 'Book' for his town too. He also invited the missionaries to dinner. His house was not as elaborate as Eyamba's but Hope Waddell counted 'eight or nine court-yards surrounded by low thatched buildings, and opening into one another. These were for his wives, principal and secondary, his domestics, trade goods etc . . . Inside his public, or court-yard . . . the walls were tastefully painted in gay and bold native patterns, by native pigments – his women being the artists . . . the houses and yards of all the natives of any rank were similarly constructed and adorned'. Eyo too had storehouses in which clocks, tables, sideboards, sofas, mirrors, china and other goods were piled. Hope Waddell found him more agreeable and intelligent than Eyamba and the dinner 'better served and of higher character. The table was well laid out and everything in excellent order.'

The white traders lent Hope Waddell some Krumen to clear his land and to help erect the frame-houses which he had brought with him from Britain. Krumen were workers from Liberia further up the Coast who spoke pidgin-English and were considered more reliable than Efik workers since they had no local ties. When they started clearing the trees and scrub which covered the hill they soon came on the skeletons and the rotting corpses of the slaves which had been dumped there. As fast as they cleared one section slaves arrived with more corpses slung on poles and dumped them on it. The work was held up for weeks until Egbo passed a decree ordering that a new dump be found.

When at last the houses were erected the missionaries were plagued by the leopards which had lived well off dead humans and now began to attack live ones after dark and to carry off livestock including Hope Waddell's pet dog. It was not a good beginning.

The missionaries soon clashed head on with the Efik chiefs over their appalling treatment of their lesser slaves. In Calabar it was no disgrace to be a slave. Some were prisoners captured from other tribes, some were Efiks who had sold themselves and their families into slavery to pay a debt or to avoid starvation. Slaves born in the service of a House were particularly favoured and could be given land for their own use, own hundreds of slaves themselves, and become as rich as freemen. But the great mass of the slaves were of no importance to the chiefs. They had a high birthrate as well as a high death-rate and since they could no longer be exported the chiefs had too many of them and they had become an embarrassment. Floggings and executions of slaves were a daily occurrence and when a chief or one of his relatives died dozens, sometimes hundreds, of slaves were killed or buried alive with him to escort him into *obio ekpu*, the spirit world. The Efiks believed that everyone without a retinue would be treated as a slave in the spirit world. While in earlier years probably only a few wives and slaves were killed at funeral celebrations, the surplus of people and imported alcohol had turned what had been religious ceremonies into orgies of killing.

An Efik trader, Antera Duke, writing between 1785 and 1788 described what happened on a single day after a chief had died: 'About 4am I got up; there was great rain, so I walked to the palaver house and I found all the gentlemen there. So we got ready to chop heads off and at five o'clock in the morning we began to cut slaves heads off, fifty heads in that one day. I carried twenty-nine cases of bottled brandy and fifteen calabashes [big hollow gourds] of chop [food] for everybody'.

Men like Eyo and Eyamba really did want to see an end to the worst of their bloody customs and a more settled and better way of life for their people. When the plan of bringing freed slaves back to West Africa from Jamaica had been explained to him Eyo had written, 'Let them come. I will be glad to see them and give them land. I will look on them as white men because they have learned white men fashion. Let them come and teach my people. Nobody will trouble them.' But the 'Kings' were powerless to act without the consent of the Council of the Egbo Order.

When Hope Waddell discovered that slaves had been brought in from the farms to be slaughtered at a funeral he reminded Eyamba that he had promised 'to knock off this bad fashion'. Eyamba replied 'It be knock off a little bit, but not quite. Them old fashion can't knock off in one day, must take time and me can't make law for all country.' Eyo said much the same when more slaves were killed at a funeral.

The chiefs began to find that the missionaries, with their revolutionary teaching that all men were equal in the sight of God and should be treated with respect and love and that in the spirit world slaves might have preference over chiefs, were attacking the very foundations of their rule. That 'God' and 'Book' should bring such strange ideas into their world came as a shock to them. 'The Palm Oil Ruffians' who boozed, had African girls, and fought and flogged and killed, and the slave traders who preceded them, had until now been the only white people whom they had known well. The behaviour of these men had not led them to expect that Christianity involved such extraordinary ideas. In their world, given the opportunity, everybody exploited everyone else, and they only knew one way to rule and that was by the fear of flogging, torture and execution. Their religion taught them that terrible things would happen to them if they offended the powerful gods, demons, and spirits of the dead which surrounded them. In it they looked for protection from human enemies and from spirits. The Christian God must be a very weak God if he allowed his laws to be broken in the way in which white men broke them. It might be more profitable to keep to their own religion and their own Gods. Christianity was very disappointing, inconvenient and confusing. It was going to be a hindrance rather than a help.

A kind of love-hate relationship developed between the chiefs and their mission. Some were for throwing it out. Others, like Eyo, decided that since Gods gave power and white men were powerful they must find a way of coming to terms with the white man's God. They argued that it would be better to humour the missionaries and wait and see how things developed. But at an outdoor meeting, convened by Egbo to decide the mission's fate, it began to look as if the verdict would be for expulsion. Then a freak storm of rain and wind swept into the anchorage and broke up the meeting. The chiefs decided that this was a warning from the white man's God and that perhaps Eyo was right. They would wait and see how things worked out.

Much to Eyamba's disgust Hope Waddell opened schools in both Duke Town and Creek Town. The mission settled down to a situation in which it was merely tolerated by the chiefs who were hoping that 'Book' would come up to expectations and not be a disappointment like 'God'.

In 1847 Hope Waddell went back to Jamaica to fetch reinforcements. These included Hugh Goldie and his wife and Edward Miller's fiancée. But when she arrived she found that Miller had died of fever a few weeks before. William Jameson, who had arrived from Jamaica to run the mission while Hope Waddell was away, also died shortly afterwards.

Eyamba too had died and Jameson and Edgerley had been powerless to prevent the slaughter at his funeral. Several freemen, thirty wives and concubines, and over fifty slaves had been buried with him in a great pit along with his regalia and weapons and all the food he and his retinue would need on their journey into *obio ekpu*. Afterwards his warriors had gone berserk and hunted through the bush for slaves who had run away to escape the celebrations. For several days the traders in their ships and hulks and the missionaries on their hill heard the screams of the victims. The ships' crews got so sick of the sight of headless corpses floating out and in with the tide that they took to firing into them to sink them.

But life in Calabar was not all grim. Hope Waddell wrote: 'The dry season is play time in Calabar . . . both farm labour and oil trading are suspended . . . The evenings are spent by the young people in plays and games in the open'. His own 'magic lantern' shows were attended by 'uproarious audiences', and the missionaries in turn attended several of the miming plays in which the Africans specialised.

Hope Waddell was particularly interested in the cleansing ceremony of *Ndok* which was held every two years: 'The night preceding the ceremony a message from the King desired me not to be alarmed next morning if I heard noises in the town "because every man and woman will begin at three o'clock to knock door". Notwithstanding this warning the tempest of noises, which woke me at the hour named, gave me such a dreadful start, that I leaped from my bed confounded and rushed to the window to learn the cause . . . It crossed my mind next moment that the town was stormed by an enemy. Everywhere were the rattle and flash of musketry; from time to time the cannon on the beach thundered; thousands of voices were shrieking and howling; the King's great bell was all the while tolling; and every yard resounded with the horrid din of great sticks belabouring doors like the clash of weapons in battle . . . All this din was designed to frighten the 'devil' out of town and was enough to frighten everyone but the devil. The cows, which usually slept quietly in the market place nearly went mad, galloping up and down the streets.'

After the celebration, in which everybody joined, both slave and free, the town was swept clean of all the piles of filth and rubbish which had accumulated over the two years. These, and carved effigies of little men, birds, and animals were thrown into the river. Then the town was free not only of rubbish but of all the devils and ghosts both big and small which had crept into it.

More reinforcements arrived in 1849 including William Anderson and his wife, and Miss Miller and the man she was to marry, Mr Sutherland. With its new staff the mission was now able to open a school in Old Town.

In that year too the British appointed a Consul to the Bights (Bays) of Benin and Biafra which made up the Guinea Coast. He was John Beecroft, a trader who knew the area well and was liked and respected by the chiefs. Since Britain had no base on the Coast he was stationed on the island of Fernando Po. The Calabar chiefs particularly welcomed his appointment because they were still worried about being taken over by the French. Soon they and the rulers of the other coastal states, partly because they were happy to have an arbiter in their own domestic squabbles, and partly because they respected the power of the British warships, were recognising Beecroft as in effect the governor of the Guinea Coast. He supported those who did not interfere with what he considered the trading rights of the British and deposed those who interfered with them, although he had no legal right to do so. The missionaries knew him well because it was he who had met them on their arrival in Calabar and had introduced them to its chiefs.

The Scots began to explore the Cross and Calabar rivers. But Beecroft warned them not to go beyond the trading stations on them. 'If you do', he said, 'your lives will not be worth a moment's purchase'. In 1843 he himself had tried to explore up the Calabar but had been forced back by the Okoyong.

More recruits joined the mission in 1854 to replace those who had been invalided home. So Goldie, with the permission of the chiefs, was able to open a station on the east bank of the Cross at an Efik settlement called Ikonetu about twenty miles above Creek Town.

By now a regular steamship service, subsidised by the British, was operating along the Coast. An area which had a few years earlier been almost as remote as the moon was now open to more traders because they no longer needed to own their own ships. The African chiefs too could trade direct with Liverpool using the steamers. But the established traders, to whom they were in debt because they had not been able to provide enough oil to meet the advances of money and of goods which they had received, refused to let the chiefs trade with anyone else. This led to more fighting and more visits from the British warships to protect the interests of the established traders.

The Efiks were now even more touchy about their control of the rivers and in 1857 they let the mission know that it would not be allowed to go beyond the Efik settlement of Ikorofiong fifteen miles above Ikonetu. No whites would be allowed to settle with the tribes further on. The rivers were closed to them.

In other ways 1857 was a bad year for the mission. Hope Waddell's health gave way and he and his family had to go home while Mr Edgerley, Mr Sutherland, Mr Hamilton, Mrs Timson and Mrs Thomson all died of fever within a few weeks of each other.

Because of the high casualties recruits would be scarce from now on. At any one time during the next thirty years there would never be more than fifteen Scots on the mission staff. Twenty-nine of them would die during this period and about the same number would be invalided home. From time to time African teachers would be stationed up river among the other tribes, but the never-ending tribal wars would always drive them out. In all that time there would never be more than a hundred names on the roll of church members. Sporadic visits by warships would never stop the continuing fighting between the Houses and between the traders so that the mission would cling to Calabar by its fingernails in the middle of the confusion and violence. For all these years and for ten more it would, in effect, be in its straitjacket while the Goldies, the Andersons, Mrs Sutherland and Mammy Fuller, watched recruits come and go and only a handful last for any length of time.

James Luke, who arrived shortly after Mary Slessor, wrote: 'For years as each new worker arrived, he was absorbed at the base, played out, and sent home or fell; and the passing days were marked by new graves in old ground.'

Appeals to Scotland for new recruits brought only a few. The United Presbyterian Church which now controlled the mission's affairs, had lost its enthusiasm for it; the casualty figures were too great and the results achieved too small.

Nobody would have blamed the pioneers if they had decided to give up. The plans drawn up in Jamaica must have seemed starry-eyed to them. It was clear that because of the violence the idea of using Africans to teach Christianity to the tribes did not work, and, even if the rivers were opened up to whites, how could they reach out, with their pitifully small staff, to all the hundreds of thousands of people along the rivers? But Scots are obstinate people and they were still as convinced as some of them had been in Jamaica in the first place that their God would find them a solution to their problems. When it arrived however nobody of course recognised it. That a small redhead called Slessor would one day be described as 'dragging a great church behind her' into Africa would have seemed too unlikely a solution even for a God who was known to have extraordinary ways of doing things.

5. DUKE TOWN AND THE FORESTS

Although by the time Mary joined it the mission had converted few people to Christianity – and indeed it would continue to have little success on that score for the next fifty years – it had, with the help of pressure from Beecroft and the Royal Navy, persuaded the chiefs to put an end to human sacrifices and ritual killings in and around the Calabar towns. They had also stopped torturing their slaves although floggings both of slaves and of wives continued.

Mrs Sutherland was detailed to look after the new recruit, guide her, and supervise her work. The main duties of the female agents were to teach in the schools, help in the dispensary, and visit the women in the yards of their families. Slave women could move about freely but, ironically enough, free women could only leave the family yards with the permission of their fathers or husbands.

When Mrs Sutherland took her down to Duke Town, Mary found that it had not changed much since Hope Waddell's day. The family huts were still built round interconnecting yards and were still decorated in the way in which he had described. The backs of the huts were presented to the lanes and there was usually only one entrance to both huts and yards. This was guarded by watchmen to keep out human intruders and by charms to keep out evil spirits. In a corner of the main yard there was always a shrine dedicated to the family ancestors with offerings of fruit and vegetables in front of it and the remains of the latest sacrifice – usually a chicken – hanging beside them. Naked children, goats, dogs, and chickens wandered through the yards so that they were usually dirty, stinking, and buzzing with flies. But the huts themselves were comparatively clean inside. Rubbish was thrown in pits in the lanes which, after the rainy season, were filled with stinking water in which mosquitoes bred. The stink in the overcrowded town was so bad that new female agents, sweating in their unsuitable clothing and breathless in the humid atmosphere, were known to keel over in a faint. To Mary however, apart from the heat, the conditions were not unlike those of the Dundee of her childhood. What she commented on most in her first letters home were the sores which covered the bodies of many of the children and of the slaves. In the tropics any scratch or insect bite can quickly go septic unless properly treated and eventually Mary, living her primitive life, would have her own share of sores. Now she was taken aback by the sheer quantity of them. She also commented on the half-starved appearance of some of the slaves. Their principal food was the yam – cooked like a potato – and the festivals of the yam harvest, with their human sacrifices, were usually held up-river in September. So perhaps the new crop had not yet begun to reach the markets. It was difficult to preserve food in the Calabar climate so that between crops there was often hunger among the slaves and in years when the crops failed many of the children and old people died of starvation.

Although Mary was not seeing Duke Town at its worst, living conditions there for most of the population were as bad as any which could be found in a West African town in the 1870s. She quickly developed a strong dislike for the place. In a few years she would be able to see some good under all the squalor, cruelty, and fear. But for the time being she could see nothing good about the place whatever.

Luckily, after a few weeks she was given three Krumen to interpret for her, guide her, and look after her, and sent on a tour of the out-stations which the mission had set up in the bush. Then her delight in the wonder of Africa quickly balanced her dislike for Duke Town.

She had of course to be warned beforehand of what wildlife to watch out for. On the mud banks along by the rivers were the crocodiles, mud coloured themselves and difficult to see, and given to darting out and grabbing people. There were the many kinds of poisonous snakes and the pythons which hung from trees and crushed their victims to death. The leopards were unlikely to attack people in daylight but she was warned to return before sunset. Hope Waddell had described how nobody went out into the bush at night without company, lights and weapons, and how a leopard had even carried off a boy who had fallen asleep in the kitchen of the Old Town station with the door open.

The driver ants merited a special warning. They were black, half an inch long, equipped with vicious jaws and teeth, and travelled in columns thousands strong. They quickly stripped the bodies of any sick or dead human being or animal which they found. Once they got under the clothing their quick bites were maddening. Anyone who 'got the drivers' was said to resemble a pocket circus. There were really only two remedies: to strip, or to run for the nearest water and plunge in.

It was such a different jungle from the one of bricks and mortar which she knew that Mary first went into it as one entering a lion's den. But she quickly forgot the fangs big and small which surrounded her in the excitement of seeing, for the first time, her faraway places. On these journeys Mary fell in love with them. She never fell out of love with them. Whenever she left them they called her back.

Along by the creeks and in the scrub were the brilliantly coloured butterflies and the equally brilliant birds; the electric blue of the kingfishers flashing over the still green waters; the herons fishing along by the banks of tall, sword-bladed, reeds; the grey parrots with red tails, the white cranes, the green doves, and the red bee-eaters hovering over the blossoms of the creepers which cascaded down from some of the trees; white frangipane with its strong perfume, scarlet hibiscus, and blue, white, or yellow convolvulus. But the monkeys were her favourites. Their antics had her in peals of laughter.

For the longer journeys she started out, as was usual and sensible, at dawn. Then, before the sun's first glittering spears pierced the trees and dazzled her, she watched the night mists on the river curl and lift and the red blaze of the advancing African day rim the forest trees with flame.

On some of her journeys she had to wade through creeks almost up to her breasts. At these crossing places the water often ran crystal clear over sand and the Africans bathed at some of them. Soaked with sweat, she would have envied the men, women and children splashing in the cool water. But even if she could have found a quiet place and got rid of the Krumen, it would have been unthinkable at that time for a lady missionary to bathe out of doors. It would not always be however, for Daniel Slessor, one of her adopted orphans, wrote years later: 'In spite of advancing age Ma cared little for warm baths. Often when we returned from service somewhere, wherever there was a stream, she would prefer to have a long dip in the sparkling water.' What she wore, if anything, for her bathes he did not say, but it cannot have been much. It certainly was not on the day when a colonial official saw her canoe anchored in a creek and, as he approached, heard frantic splashing on the far side of it and an agonised cry of, 'Oh losh, Jeannie, gie me a pin!'

When they moved away from the rivers and into the forests she found herself among smooth grey trees which towered up a hundred feet and more like the columns of a cathedral which had no walls to limit it. By cutting off the sunlight they had cleared the floor of vegetation, and they marched on in ghostly twilight supporting a vaulted roof of branches under which the thick stems of creepers curved like arches. From this roof, most marvellous to her of all, the petals of their blossoms drifted down like snow.

Mary was used to the Krumen by now and would sometimes grab the arm of the nearest and point to whatever excited her. But in the villages she was still wary of the Efiks, with their intense expressions, their brows screwed down against the sun, and their quick movements and noisy chatter. In the more distant places a white woman was still a novelty and Mary was followed by a procession wherever she went. The women and children crowded round her and fingered her clothes and sometimes her skin until she slapped their hands away. Once or twice she had to be rescued by the chiefs.

The villages were usually sited in thick bush which concealed and protected them. The approach was along narrow winding paths which led off the main market trails. These too were narrow and sometimes cut deep into the ground by the bare feet which had pounded them for centuries. The markets to which these led were held in large clearings often near a river or creek for transport purposes and beside which a town or village had sprung up.

The women did the trading in the markets just as they did the work of digging, planting, and harvesting in the fields. They spread their produce on the ground and squatted beside it to haggle with their customers. Sometimes they bartered their goods. Sometimes they were paid in the thin copper rods, shaped like a hoop, and worth less than a penny, which were still the Calabar currency.

Every village, whether a market or not, had its clearing where the people gathered for mimes, dancing, war games, floggings, and executions. On the edge of it was the palaver house where the chiefs and elders met to discuss and decide on village affairs. At the palaver house was the big drum of the village branch of Egbo. This was made out of a hollowed log and was only sounded on special occasions: to call the people back from the fields in an emergency, or to hear an Egbo decree, or to warn them to stay indoors when an Egbo procession was about to be held. Only members of the Order could watch a procession. Any outsiders caught out of doors – and these included all women – were flogged by the masked runners which went ahead of it.

The fields, Mary discovered, were often several miles from the villages. When one patch of land had been cropped for a few years the people moved on and burned the vegetation off another. Tribe still raided tribe and young warriors proved their manhood by collecting skulls. So the women were always guarded by armed sentries on their way to and from the fields and while working in them, and lookouts were posted in trees nearby.

When her tours were completed Mary had to settle down to trying to come to terms with Duke Town and also with life at Mission House. This she found stiff and starchy, with an excessive amount of etiquette and protocol.

Even in Hope Waddell's day the upper-class Efiks had been on their dignity and very touchy about receiving the proper salutation according to their rank. He had written that to fail to give the proper salutation gave great offence. The white traders and sea captains were also anxious to keep up their positions in the eyes of one another and of the Efiks. Indeed 'The Palm Oil Ruffians' had now taken to calling themselves 'The Gentlemen of the River'. The missionaries therefore had in their turn to be on their dignity and to keep up their position as befitted representatives of their church. Mary found the Sunday afternoon tea parties, which the mission gave for the white traders and captains, particularly trying. She had not yet learned the art of small talk, and since the guests were not particularly interested either in God, the Bible, or the Efiks, she was often very much a fish out of water and tongue-tied as ever. She wrote to a Dundee friend, 'I am now living among an entirely different class of people.'

Mrs Sutherland and Mammy Fuller did their best to help her to adjust to this new starchy way of life and she did her best to accept it. But to wear too many clothes and a silly great sunhelmet and try to make polite conversation was not what she had come to Calabar to do. She was still very conscious of being 'lower class' and her rough upbringing, which was to be such an advantage to her in later years, was at this time a handicap.

She was teaching in the school now and part of her duties were to take the children for walks in the bush. Here, safely away from adult eyes, she discarded helmet, blouse and skirt, and ran races with the children in her petticoat. Tired of being boxed in by trees, she took to climbing them. Soon, outside school hours, the children could tell which tree she was up by the gear piled at the foot of it. Soon too she could write that she had been up every tree worth climbing near Mission House.

In December the Harmattan came, a hot, dusty, wind which blew down from the Sahara desert for days at a time. Hope Waddell wrote, 'It loads the atmosphere, dulls the eyes, parches the skin, withers vegetation, and obscures everything.' The white traders called this season the 'smokes' and everybody hated it. It made the unhappy Mary thoroughly miserable.

In January 1877 William Anderson and his wife Louisa returned to Duke Town from their leave in Scotland. He was a big bearded man, in his sixties now, but still with a strong temper. He had always been known as the warrior of the mission. At one time or another he had battled with chiefs, traders and British consuls alike on behalf of the Africans. Neither he nor his wife suffered fools gladly and they were used to getting their own way. Louisa was said to rule Mission House 'with a rod of iron'. A clash between her and the new recruit was probably inevitable, although in later years Mary found that Louisa was a compassionate woman and they came to understand and to like one another.

Their first clash was over the wakening bell which it was part of Mary's duties to ring. She had no alarm clock and sometimes slept late. When this happened she was severly reprimanded by Louisa, who was a stickler for punctuality. Mary became so determined not to receive any more reprimands that sometimes when the brilliant African moonlight flooded her room she would waken suddenly and stagger out and ring away only to find that it was nowhere near dawn. This did not please Louisa either!

Their other main difference of opinion was over the matter of running races and climbing trees and in consequence being late for the evening meal. Mrs Anderson announced that if Miss Slessor must be late for the meal then in future she would get none. But what with one thing and another Mary often was late, and William Anderson would smuggle a snack up to her room. Soon they became not only conspirators but friends. It was not until years later that Mary discovered that the snacks were prepared by Louisa herself.

Duke Town was now even less to Mary's liking, so when to complete her tour of the out-stations Samuel Edgerley and his wife took her up to those at Ikonetu and Ikorofiong, it was a pleasant escape for her from Louisa and 'proper' behaviour. Edgerley was one of the ordained missionaries. He was the son of the pioneer and had lived in Calabar with his family until he went to Scotland to train as a medical missionary. He had arrived back in 1857 in time to see his father die of fever.

Krumen paddled them up to Ikonetu with the tide. The station, because of shortage of staff, was not manned. Mary wrote home that there was 'such a nice house which has been standing empty for so long. The walk to the station was pushing at undergrowth and climbing and jumping and wading. I enjoyed it!'

Here she stood beside the graves of the missionaries who had died while running the station, including those of Euphemia Johnstone and Mr and Mrs Timson. Miss Johnstone had been one of the first white women to go up to the station. When, in 1857, she jumped ashore the people who had come to see the white men all ran away. Anything unusual was likely to have a devil in it. White men devils were bad enough, but a new kind with long hair was more than they could take. She died there in 1873, of bronchitis and malaria. Edgerley found her lying dying, but fully dressed, on her bed. 'I'm going home', she told him. 'It is a good time to go because new friends are coming and one of them can take my place.' Until he discovered just how ill she was he thought she meant that she was going on leave.

'At the graves at Ikonetu, I was much moved', Mary wrote. 'All the past and the present and the future seemed to crowd into my sight and between recollection of the dead and anticipation I hardly knew whether I felt more solemnized than stimulated and comforted.'

They visited a village nearby: 'I have forgotten how to spell its name. The women and children crowded round me. Their gesticulations would have frightened me had not Mr Edgerley told me that they wished to be friendly . . . It was painful to have to say goodbye and not have a missionary to leave among them.'

C

Edgerley was now the explorer of the mission and Mary listened fascinated to his descriptions of his journeys. He had gone up the Cross River to make contact with the Akunakuna tribe above Itu, right up the Calabar and then across country to some of the villages in the interior. Most of the tribes had welcomed him and told him that they too wanted 'God' and 'Book'. The most notable exception had been the Okoyong who had ambushed him and his Krumen on their way back down the Calabar, taken them off to a village, and chained them up. It looked as if they were about to be killed but after a palaver the Okoyong demanded a ransom of rum for their release. After a few more days of bargaining Edgerley talked them into forego-ing the ransom against a promise that he would not pass through their territory again. It was lucky that his paddlers were Krumen. If they had been Efiks they would not have lived long enough to need chains. One of the principal pastimes of the Okoyong was still the raiding of Efik farms for livestock, women, and heads.

After the excitement of the trip up river Mary had once more to try to settle down at Duke Town which by now she thoroughly detested. The more she found out about the way in which the Efiks treated their women, children and slaves, the more it disgusted and angered her. As in the Roman world of the early Christians, a freeman had the right to do what he liked with his family and slaves, even to kill them. They had no rights whatever as citizens except through him. Because in the eyes of the Efik males the fatter a woman the more beautiful she was, a free girl was cooped at puberty in a fattening house where she was fed on special foods and allowed no exercise. When the time for her wedding feast arrived she was hardly able to waddle to it. Then, when her husband died, unless she was one of the wives selected to accompany him into *Obio ekpu* the process was put into reverse and she was cooped in a widows' mourning shed where she was starved and not allowed to wash so that she was soon covered with sores and vermin. This 'mourning' in the widows' sheds could last for years. In between the fattening and the starving a freewoman was cooped in her husband's yard except when she was out on the farms supervising the work of the women slaves.

'Marriage' in the Christian sense did not exist. Even the free wives, like the concubines and slave women, had to support themselves and their children by their work on the farms. A wife could always be rejected by her husband at any time and for any reason.

For a slave woman, unless she was chosen as a wife by a free man, there was never a wedding agreement of any kind. She could be taken as a concubine by her owner, given to his friends, or failing this be taken by any man, slave or free, who fancied her.

Eventually Mary would be the first to make it possible for women to live independent of men in Calabar, but for the time being her anger at their treatment had to be bottled up inside her along with her anger at the way unwanted babies were thrown into the bush to die, and twins always killed and their mother driven out of the tribe. The Efiks – along with the other Cross River tribes – believed that one twin was the child of a devil which had secretly mated the mother, and since it was impossible to tell which was the devil's baby both must die. Mary developed an almost fanatical love for African children and in her thirty-eight years in Calabar saved the lives of hundreds of them. At any one time she rarely had less than a dozen rescued babies in her huts.

But although Mary was sorry for the free wives she disliked the round of visits to their yards which she had to make with Mrs Sutherland. The visits of the white women broke up the monotony of their days and made them feel important, but some of the wives in the wealthy families could be very condescending to the missionaries and they were no more interested in Mary's Bible readings than they were in callisthenics. Mary much preferred to work among the slaves. Because she had once been a half-starved, despised, little half-timer herself she knew something of what it was like to be a slave, and she felt more at home among them than among the upper-class Efiks. The slaves did not even speak the pidgin-English of the free men so she soon began to pick up Efik phrases. Efik was something which she would have to master if she was to do the work which God had chosen for her. So she worked at it with that intense concentration which had helped her to educate herself. She pointed to things, imitated the Efik names for them, and laughed with the people at her mistakes. She found that her eagerness to learn their language began to create a bond between them. Soon they were saying that she had been 'blessed with an Efik mouth', and both they and Hugh Goldie and the other missionaries were amazed at the speed with which she was beginning to learn the language.

But, although she was learning to communicate with the people, she was still of course far from being able to see anything good in their way of life. This is clear from the eight page letter which she wrote to 'dear Maggie' on April 17th 1887. She must have run out of paper because she turned page eight on its side and wrote at right angles over what she had already written. She begins with 'I am tired as an old horse and the pen is just flying over the paper.' So what with the scrawl and the sideways writing, page eight is exceedingly difficult to read. 'The surrounding heathenism has such a depressing effect and the slow progress which is almost a necessary consequence of their utter debasement makes one's heart sick. Oh for power! Oh for a heart full of love to Jesus and to these perishing ones for His sake for, oh, one cannot love them for their own, at least not some of them. We may read and hear but to *see* the state of society here is sickening, however, as you say, one gets used to anything. I never thought my sense of delicacy would be so blunted. The scenes we cannot speak or write of – so that when one comes to see them there is something to learn.'

How amused Mary would have been if, twenty years later, she could have read this prim letter. Comparatively speaking she had hardly seen anything yet.

Maggie had apparently been wondering whether God was calling her to the foreign missions or whether it was just a silly idea of her own and she had written to Mary for advice.

Mary replies: 'If He has work for you here – I mean in Africa – He will fit you for it in His own time and bring it to your hand. Just serve Him where you are. Let it be your great love to serve Him well and faithfully. Don't trouble about the sphere. If He is to call you for this work don't wonder if He gives you severe discipline and keeps you long waiting. I have passed through deeper waters and darker valleys than you are aware of. But down there I learned to trust Him. I feel so humbled by your opinion of me . . . because I feel it so different from the true. But I love Him and I trust Him'.

In answer to Maggie's worries about some sections of the Creed she tells her to 'take it all to Jesus . . . There is no distance here . . . Where I am there shall my servant be!'

And then comes the statement of the Slessor theology by which she will live for the rest of her life: 'No! . . . No! . . . Maggie! Creeds and ministers and books are all good enough but look you to Jesus!'

Later she wrote home: 'One needs a special grace to enable one to sit still . . . It is so difficult to wait . . . Nothing of great interest seems to come my way'.

She does not say what she was waiting for but it seems it was the opportunity to get out of Duke Town to one of the bush stations, around which Egbo was still terrorising the people, poison bean trials were still being held, and twins were still being killed. That so many thousands of Africans were still beyond the help of the mission already seems to have been worrying her.

Malaria inevitably, however, did come her way, and she took it very badly. She was delirious for long periods and was unconscious for a spell too. It began to look as if she was going to be one of the recruits who did not survive their first bout for in those days, when only quinine was available to combat it, malaria was often lethal. By her own admission she was a great 'babbler' when she had fever and in this, one of her worst bouts ever, she babbled exceedingly. Her colleagues took it in turns to sit up with her night after night. But her chief nurse was Louisa.

After she had recovered, Mary wrote home, 'After a bout of African fever one looks as if one had escaped from a lunatic asylum.' Sir Richard Burton, the explorer and Consul to the Bights, wrote that women who had recently recovered from malaria '. . . looked like galvanised corpses, even those who had left England a few months before radiant with pleasure, bright with youth and beauty'. So it was some weeks before Mary began racing and tree climbing again. The fever recurred at intervals and Mary found that to feel ill for days on end was an inescapable part of Calabar life. She knew now that, if she lived long enough, she would be as sallow and as gaunt as Mrs Goldie, Mrs Anderson and Mrs Sutherland.

On her visit to Creek Town she had been introduced to King Eyo VII who had been educated in the mission school, spoke English fluently, and was a Christian. He was also one of the chiefs who wanted the British to move in and put an end to the struggle for supremacy between the Calabar houses and the threat of a takeover by the French or the Germans whose warships still visited the anchorage.

An enormous Egbo fine on Eyo II, who had been in power when Hope Waddell arrived, had reduced Creek Town from being the equal of Duke Town to being second-rate, but Eyo VII was building up its fortunes again. Because of his mission education he had the advantage of being able to talk to British consuls

King Eyo's state canoe

in their own language and had considerable influence with them.

A strong friendship now began to build up between Eyo and Mary Slessor. Her colleagues recorded it but never tried to explain it. He was impatient to see an end to the 'old customs'. and the fighting between the tribes which to him were a waste of resources and a brake on trading. He, like Mary, wanted to see the rivers and the forests opened up. It seems likely that the shrewd businesslike brain which she was seen to have in later years was already showing itself and that this was why the equally shrewd Efik began to consult her about his affairs. What is certain is that he did consult her and later supported her in every way he could in her attempts to open up the country.

He also supported the mission in its attempts to get the bloodiest of the 'old customs' finally banned by law in a treaty with the British. In 1878 they both gained their wish when Consul Hopkins arrived and obtained the agreement of the Egbo Council to put an end to human sacrifices, ritual killings, poison bean trials, the killing of twins, the outlawing of their mothers, the ill-treatment of widows, and the stripping and 'indecent assaults' on women by Egbo officers. The treaty was a great victory for the mission which it had taken thirty years to win.

Towards the end of that year, Thomas Campbell, who joined the mission two years before Mary, made another survey up the Calabar River and, through a trader, made contact with the Okoyong. He reported that the group which he met were heavily armed and told him that they had to keep their guns and swords at hand at all times. 'We trust no man', they said, 'and know not when we shall be attacked. All men are our enemies.' Their attitude to missionaries had not changed. But Campbell was pleased because at least they had not chained him up. He arranged for an African teacher to join the tribe. The man had Okoyong blood. But even so in a few weeks he had to run for his life.

So the Okoyong remained very much an unknown quantity. What little Goldie knew about them he had gathered from Eyo VII who had fought against them in 1867, when, although greatly outnumbered, they had beaten off the Calabar attacks. 'The Okoyong', Goldie wrote, 'rejoice in a wild freedom and this feeling, with their distrust of each other, separates them so that each family has its own settlement in the bush, living a life of thorough independence . . . Their mutual distrust and their dread of the power of spells is so great that they arm themselves when they go out and when sitting down to partake of food . . . This cloud of dread overhangs the whole of their life and takes all the enjoyment out of it, leading them to occasional escape from it in wild drunken revelry . . . All the customs of blood which have been abandoned in Calabar still prevail amongst them.'

The war had begun because three Okoyong had been killed at the market in Ikonetu and in revenge the tribe had overrun several farming districts belonging to Ikonetu, 'plundered and burned the houses and slaughtered the people.' As a result Duke Town had decided to put an end to the Okoyong raids once and for all. But the Okoyong territory was densely forested and intersected with streams, and their warriors were expert in bush warfare. Duke Town could make no progress and withdrew. Next Creek Town attacked. But again the Okoyong held their ground. Eyo described the savagery with which they fought and how their women followed the men into battle and roped and dragged away their wounded to prevent the enemy from taking their heads. In the end, because they depended on Calabar for gunpowder, salt, rum, and gin, the Okoyong made an offer of peace which Eyo accepted. But although a truce was declared the Okoyong still considered themselves at war with Calabar because Eyo would not ratify the peace in a proper manner by burying a slave alive.

Just why Mary Slessor got the idea that God wanted her to go and open up the forests by tackling this fighting tribe of mercenaries is not recorded. Perhaps it was because they reminded her of her own Highland clans of two centuries before: always fighting among themselves when they had no common enemy to fight and, not content with that, fighting as mercenaries for other countries too. Perhaps it was because they were described as being of 'superior physique and intelligence' to the Efiks. Or perhaps it was just because their name kept flashing up on the screen of her mind.

When she suggested that she might join the tribe no one seems to have taken the idea seriously. Women sometimes went to live in new territory with their husbands, but never alone. The risks for men could be great enough but, because the tribes looked on them as second-class citizens, the risks for women were unspeakable. Anyway Mary herself, with her malaria still recurring, was soon so run-down and depressed that it began to look as if even Duke Town life was too much for her health. In a report to the *Missionary Record*, Alexander Ross wrote that

Miss Slessor was 'continuing to teach in the Duke Town school when not indisposed', and there seemed to be a hint of criticism there.

At this time all her dreams may have seemed to be crumbling to dust. If she could not stand up to Duke Town she could certainly not realise her ambition to go and help the forest tribes.

Early in 1879 she wrote home, 'I want my home and my mother.' Although her four year tour of duty would not be completed until September 1880, the mission sent her home in June 1879. Less than three years in Calabar and she seemed to have crumpled under the strain.

6. LEARNING TO BE AN AFRICAN

Mary must have been very run-down indeed because the Foreign Missions' Board kept her in Scotland for sixteen months. At this time leave from Calabar was for one year every four years but later this had to be increased to every five years because of the shortage of staff. From the Guinea Coast the Royal Navy and the Colonial Service allowed leave every three years.

The veterans may not have expected to see Miss Slessor back at all. She had been ill for weeks and clearly miserable at Duke Town. They may have thought that she was just one of the people who had set out to work for the glory of God only to find that in Calabar there was plenty of drudgery, little excitement, and no glory at all, and whose names soon vanished without comment from the lists of mission staff printed in the *Record*.

But in Dundee, as Mary's health returned, so did her determination to get out into the Calabar forests. She talked to James Logie about her dislike for Duke Town and he advised her to write to the Board and ask to be sent somewhere else. She did this, but dutifully added that of course she would do whatever the Board thought best. She also talked to Logie and to other friends about her ambition to tackle the Okoyong but said that Mr Anderson was entirely against it.

As soon as she was well enough she had to go on the lecture tours which all the missionaries had to make during their leave to try to raise money and recruits for Calabar. She disliked this work intensely, was always sick with nerves before she went up on to the platform, and was consequently only moderately successful.

But she enjoyed giving informal talks to young people and here she was much more successful. In a class at a school in Falkirk were Janet Wright and Martha Peacock. Mary's visit was important both for them and for her. Because of her talk they too would volunteer for Calabar and each of them would help her at a crucial time in her life.

Meanwhile early in 1880 Hugh Goldie and his wife had also come home on leave. When Mary met them they told her that they would shortly be returning to Calabar, so without asking the Board's permission, she promptly arranged to travel back with them. She wrote to the Board from Calabar saying that she had made the decision on her own responsibility because time had been short.

At Duke Town she was pleased to hear that she was to be in charge of the Old Town station. Here she would be on her own and able to try out the ideas about mission work which she had formed on her first tour of duty. This was a sensible move by the mission. At Old Town her colleagues would be able to keep an eye on her, and both they and she would find out how suited she was to out-station life.

The station house had not been lived in for over a year and it was badly in need of repair. It was built on the usual mission design: an upper storey supported on poles, with a room for the missionary and one for the girls, and underneath it a schoolroom and a room for the boys.

The mission sent Mary a team of Krumen to repair it and she was in such a hurry to get the work done that she helped with it herself. She took to wearing a simple cotton dress and canvas shoes and since sweat-soaked ringlets got in the way she cut them off.

She opened out-stations at the farm villages of Qua, Akim, and Ikot Ansa, and was within a year preacher, teacher, district nurse, and social worker to several thousand people scattered over about twenty square miles of bush.

Her work in the dispensary at Duke Town had taught her first aid and there too she had learned what simple medicines to give for simple ailments.

Now she began to live on local produce and to cut out imported foods entirely, except for one important item – tea. (In years to come she would be able to do without food and shelter, but not without tea. It would always be her weakness.) It must have been a good growing season for she had plenty of foods to choose from: chickens, fish, yams, plantains (a kind of banana), rice, corn, sugar-cane, and of course palm oil, which according to Hugh Goldie was much relished by Europeans when they got over the uncomfortable sensation of eating oil.

By eating local food she saved not only money but also time, because soon she could safely leave all the cooking to her African girls, who boiled everything, and free herself for other work. Time of course was something of which she could never have enough; for although her stations were only a mile or two apart, walking between them was very time consuming as well as toughening her body.

She had started schools at Qua and Akim, and on Sundays she held services at all four of her stations; at the villages, under a tree in good weather and in the palaver house in bad; and at Old Town in her little church.

Every few years deputies from the Foreign Mission Board came out to inspect the work of the mission and it was the two who came out in 1881 whom she walked off their feet. They reported that on the Sabbath she set out at sunrise for Qua, held a service there, went on to Akim half a mile further on and held another, and returned at midday to Old Town for Sunday school. In the afternoon she went off to Ikot Ansa and held a service there, then returned to Old Town for evening service.

'Worn out by the work of the day', they wrote, 'we returned to Old Town wondering how she can go through the like every Sabbath . . . Miss Slessor is a devoted, diligent, and energetic agent . . . Her labours are manifold and arduous but she sustains them cheerfully.'

One of the deputies preached at one of her services in a palaver house with Mary interpreting. The floor was of clay packed round the skulls of tribal enemies and somebody must have caught a toe in one. In his report the deputy mentioned that he was considerably surprised to see a skull roll out between his feet. But whether the incident suited his text or not he did not say.

For Mary herself evening service in her little church at Old Town was outstanding. She wrote that she was always moved by 'the homeliness, the attention, the emotion, almost always visible on the dusky faces, just revealed by the flickering light of primitive lamps.'

Services in Calabar were a little different from those in Scotland in more ways than one. A typical collection at this time in Creek Town was: '1 worsted cap, 2 papers of needles, 1 packet of fish hooks, 1 reel of black thread, 7 pewter snuff boxes, 51 brass rods.'

Another duty which took up a great deal of her time was that of children's nurse. She was already showing the almost fanatical love of African babies which would cause her to make lone journeys through the bush, sometimes at night, to rescue them. And now when she heard of a twin birth she always hurried off and came back with the babies unless they had been killed before she arrived. Soon she had a room full of orphans to nurse and feed. They took up so much of her time that she suggested to the mission that it should establish a central orphanage run by a white or a Jamaican missionary and staffed by African girls. 'If such a crowd of twins should come to her as I have to manage she would require to devote all her time to them.'

This was a sensible suggestion but as with many others which she made no action was taken.

Towards the end of 1881 there were more deaths in the mission. First, William Anderson was ill for several weeks and, although he recovered, the strain of nursing him on top of all her other work and her own fevers was too much for Louisa and she died. Then Mrs Sutherland, whose health had been gradually ebbing away, collapsed in Alex Ross's house. She had to stay there for three weeks while Dr McKenzie, who was himself too ill to walk, was carried up to the house by Krumen twice a week to prescribe for her. She recovered, insisted against everybody's advice in going back to work, and died a few months later. She had asked to be buried at Creek Town in the same grave as the man to whom she had been married for five months twenty-seven years earlier. The *Record* reported that the launch which took her coffin up from Duke Town was escorted by scores of African canoes and 'by all the Europeans on the river.'

Mary was upset by the deaths of the two *Ma Akamba* and wept at their funerals among all the wailing of hundreds of African women.

By the time the 'smokes' ended in 1882 Mary must have been satisfied that her African girls could look after her orphans for a few days at a time without supervision because now, at last, she was able to get right out into the bush to the remote farm villages and up the Cross by canoe to Efik settlements on its banks. To the people among whom she had worked in the Dundee slums she had been one of themselves. Now she began to try to break down some of the barriers which separated the white missionaries from the great mass of the Efik people.

Shortly after her death W P Livingstone, who was editor of

The Missionary Record at the time, wrote a book about Mary in which he described how in the Old Town area, 'The people found her different from other missionaries, she would enter their townships as one of themselves, show them in a moment that she was mistress of their thought and ways, and get right into their confidence. Always carrying medicine, she attended the sick, and so many diseased and maimed crowded to her that she would miss the tide twice over . . . In her opinion no preaching surpassed these patient, intimate, interviews on the banks of the river and by the wayside, when she listened to tales of suffering and sorrow and gave sympathy and practical help.'

He was in a position to know better than most people that the mission women had never lived in ivory towers but had been willing to tackle emergencies. But to him, in Mary Slessor, the mission clearly had a new type of female agent: one who was prepared to live not only as an African but as a poor African.

The deputies who had tried to keep up with her that Sabbath also noticed the difference. They recommended that she be allowed to go on living among her Africans, 'because she prefers this manner of life to being associated with another white person on a station.' That they took the trouble to include this recommendation in a long report shows that her way of life was unusual and also under criticism by others.

But Mary was not yet 'mistress' of the thought and ways of the people. She was only beginning to grapple with all the intricacies of their religion and customs which shaped their attitude to life. She was only beginning too her own 'Africanisation'. Over the years she would develop it steadily and deliberately until she was no longer a sympathetic observer of African life, like somebody gazing into a goldfish bowl, but *Eka Kpukpro Owo*. The process started now, when she was thirty-four, and it would end only with her death thirty-three years later.

She knew from Hugh Goldie that it was impossible to begin to understand the way in which the minds of the Africans worked without first studying the factors which affected their outlook. That she made up her mind to learn to understand them was in itself an important decision which few white people made. She knew already that they were a deeply religious people (although at this time she wrote of the local 'superstitious beliefs' and only in later years promoted them to the status of 'religion'), and she was beginning to see that to the Africans the spirit world was as real as the material world; that unlike most Europeans they could not switch their religion on and off to suit themselves. They were surrounded by mystery and wonder and by forces which could be benevolent and beautiful if you obeyed the laws of the gods and of the tribe, and would most certainly be malevolent and ugly if you disobeyed them.

First to be placated were the gods. There were gods of earth and sky, of sun and moon, of wind and rain, of fire and water, and many others. But *Abassi* was the chief of all the gods; from him had sprung everything which existed. And it was his mother *Eka Abassi* who gave fruitfulness to women.

Next were the spirits of the dead, especially of your own ancestors. They, like the gods, had to be kept on your side and worshipped at the family shrine. If they were pleased with you then, like the gods, they would protect you from devils and from human enemies, but when offended not only would they not protect you but they might punish you themselves.

Then – as for the Ancient Greeks – there were the spirits which lived in stones, rocks, rivers, and in all living things. These could reach out to you and affect your life. Most of them were small fairy-like beings, but anything extra-large, or extra-beautiful, or extra-powerful, held not a fairy but a god who needed to be worshipped. So there were sacred groves, sacred trees, sacred eagles, sacred crocodiles, sacred pythons, and other creatures and things which were special in some way.

Everybody had three souls. There was the soul which lived in your shadow and went with you into the spirit world when you died. There was your bush soul which stayed with you when you were awake but could go wandering while you slept and perhaps get up to mischief if your ancestors did not watch over it. Then there was your twin soul or affinity which lived always in some animal, bird, or fish. If you belonged to a family which had pythons as affinities then you were careful all your life never to kill or injure a python in case you killed or injured yourself or a relative. And if as you went through the bush a python attacked you or behaved in an odd way, then it was best to hurry home and offer sacrifice at the family shrine for either your ancestors were angry with you or else they were trying to pass a message to you, perhaps of some danger.

But while everybody had an affinity some people could by magic take over the body of living creatures in order to do harm to people. One man would be feared and hated because it was

Efik shrine

well known that he could take over the body of a huge crocodile and prey on the village from it. No member of the village could kill it because it was sacred. But if a stranger could be persuaded to kill it while the man was occupying it then the man would be found dead too and that was clear proof that he had taken over the crocodile. Everybody knew that these things happened because there were so many examples of wicked men dying when the creature they were occupying was killed.

Finally, as if all the rest was not enough to think about, there was *ifot*, which is best translated into English as witchcraft. Any person could use *ifot* against any other person and even children could use it against their parents. A disaster was never due to natural causes or to an accident, it was always caused by someone using *ifot* against the sufferer. The *mbiaidiong*, or witchdoctor, must be sent for to name suspects. He could discover them because he was trained in magic and the use of spells. The suspects must then prove their innocence by undergoing the poison bean trial. The *mbiaidiong* ground dried *esere* beans, which grew locally, into powder, mixed the powder with water and gave it to the suspects to drink. Vomiting meant innocence and life. Failure to vomit meant guilt and execution in one. Unless the *mbiaidiong* had been bribed to substitute a harmless powder or to mix an extra strong dose of the *esere* to induce vomiting the suspects usually died. A series of poison trials caused by accusation and counter-accusation could decimate a village, and the death of a free man or free woman was an extra fearful event because, even before the killing of the retinue began, those suspected of causing his death were forced to take the poison bean.

At Old Town Mary began to see that Africans often seemed lacking in commonsense, slow, and stupid to a European because what was to him a straightforward issue was not straightforward to them at all. Gods, devils, ancestors, affinities, or *ifot*, could be involved and needed to be thought about. Their spirit world brought both beauty and fear into their lives; it was part fairytale part nightmare. There were so many forces surrounding them, quite apart from human enemies, that they tended to live in the present and not look to the future which was full of disasters looking for a victim. Like antelope living in lion country they enjoyed life while they could and hoped that trouble would pounce on somebody else. Mary found that, when cool, calm, and sober, the Africans were a kindly, hospitable people with a happy-go-lucky attitude to life. She found too that, while life was grim in the overcrowded towns, life in the farming settlements was pleasant enough for those who did as they were told. The men hunted and fished and guarded the people day and night against enemy raiders; the women did the farm work; and morning and evening everybody bathed in the creeks.

It was at Old Town where Mary got to like most of the Africans whom she met, and where she found great satisfaction in working for them. There was so much to be done: for the sick; for orphans thrown out to die; for wives and slaves flogged for trivial offences; for the women who had been under the thumbs of the men for centuries – the list was endless. Now she knew that she had made the right decision. Calabar was where she had to be.

She began to spend days and nights in the villages, sleeping on a clay bench in a hut as the local people did. Down in the river settlements she was plagued by the swarms of mosquitoes and sand-flies which drove many Europeans to distraction, but she had no net for her bed any more than she had a bed. Already she was showing a capacity for enduring African life as an African.

It was at this time, when she missed the tide and simply had to get back to Old Town, that she first began to make night journeys along the narrow paths through the bush, which was something that few people would do except raiding parties, head-hunters, and monkey-hunters.

At night the bush was a frightening place. Not only was there always the possibility of a shot or an arrow or a spear from the dense undergrowth but, while in the heat of the day the wildlife dozed, as the sun went down it wakened, and with a chorus of screaming, hooting, whistling, chirping and snarling, began the business of hunting and killing and eating in earnest. Now too the vampire bats, which had bodies as big as rats, added their swoops and their high-pitched screams to the activities of the daytime menagerie.

The Efiks who carried her medicine chest and her 'chop-box' would never have gone near the place at night without her, and she admitted that she herself was often frightened although this was stupid because God protected his servants. 'Fear not for I am with Thee', was a text which she actually believed in, as a surprised Thomas Hart would note in years to come. She herself said that she had never really appreciated the Bible story of Daniel in the lions' den until she made one of these journeys and that when she heard the snarls of the hunting leopards she prayed a special prayer: 'Oh Lord of Daniel shut their mouths', and got her little group to sing.

On one of her journeys she had met Okon, the chief of a village called Ibaka on the Cross estuary thirty miles below Duke Town, and later he made several journeys up to Old Town to try to persuade her to visit his people. But it was not until the middle of 1882, when she decided her girls were sufficiently trained to allow her to leave them for two weeks, that she made the journey. She told Eyo that Okon would be sending his own canoe for her. The King however insisted that she must have his own royal canoe. The wide estuary was often whipped by sudden storms and she must have a properly trained crew.

The people of Old Town too were worried for her safety. So great was the distrust of House for House that for her to make such a long journey and go and live among strangers was to risk death. Before she left, her yard was often crowded with people all begging her not to be so foolish.

Eyo had promised that his canoe would call for her at nine in the morning of the day fixed for her departure. But by midday there was still no sign of it. Luckily Mary had not expected to leave before lunch anyway. She cooked and ate this, somewhat hampered by well-wishers, and when in the late afternoon the canoe arrived, she set out for the river accompanied by a large crowd. Her procession to the jetty took nearly an hour because the free women who could not leave their yards crowded to the gates and called her over to be embraced and to warn her to be careful. Her departure had developed into a real African happening. Everybody was now enjoying it immensely except perhaps Mary herself who may have been tired of being crushed by large women.

She discovered that the canoe had been newly painted in bright colours for her, which probably accounted for the delay. She was taking four of her older children with her and when she had placed these among the paddlers, and a couch had been arranged for her in the cabin out of sacks of rice, which she was taking as a present to Okon, she expected to set off. But last minute advice had to be given by the Old Town men to this Creek Town crew. And what with one thing and another it was getting dark, and torches made out of bunches of dried reeds tied to thick resinous sticks had been lit before they finally pushed off.

The drums beat, the paddles swung into the stroke. The lanes of water, glittering red from the torches on the bank, lengthened, and the glow faded from the naked shoulders of the paddlers. Mary curled herself up among the rice sacks.

It was customary for crews on the Calabar rivers to sing to help pass away the time and to keep the rhythm of the stroke. The steersman made up impromptu verses and sang them three or four times before he made up another, while the crew joined in with a chorus of 'Ho!' . . . (dip paddle) . . . 'Ho!' . . . (dip paddle) . . . 'Ho!'

Now, of course, the verses had to be about Mary:

Our beautiful Ma is with us . . .

Ho! . . . Ho! . . . Ho!

The swing of the canoe, the steady rhythm of the drums, and the deep voices of the paddlers, soon lulled their beautiful Ma to sleep. And the next thing she heard was the clatter as the paddles were shipped for the canoe to glide into the Ibaka landing beach under all the flaring red, yellow, and gold of the African sunrise.

Mary was ready to jump out and wade ashore as the canoe grounded. But this was not good. She must land like a chief. Two senior members of the crew made a chair for her with their arms and carried her not merely ashore but right through the village to Okon's yards. Since they were doing things in the proper manner the rest of the crew formed an escort and fussed about clearing a path through the chickens, goats, and dogs, cuffing small boys out of the way as they would have done for Eyo. But since few people at Ibaka had seen a white man let alone a white woman nobody wanted to get near her anyway. Indeed at this stage some people were already on the run. But the crew were showing these 'small' down-river people how a white Ma must be treated.

Okon gave up his own hut to Mary and the children. This, since he was not rich and could not afford doors and windows, was open to his main yard with all its comings and goings both human and animal. Soon the comings outnumbered the goings as more and more people plucked up the courage to come and look at this new kind of person which they had been hearing so much about. White skin, red hair and blue eyes? Even the wise men of the village had never seen anything like this before. Would she bring good things or bad things down on them?

Mary did not want to offend. She knew how fascinated the

people were by anything strange which came into their lives. So she only rigged up blankets in the doorway at night for undressing and washing purposes.

At meal times Okon's senior wives squatted in the doorway and did a running commentary for the people packing into the yard. Yes, it was true. The white Ma ate just like everybody else, and the same food too. Edgerley reported that on one occasion the head of an outlying village had bent down in front of him as he took each mouthful to try to see where the food went. But this never seems to have happened to Mary. When she went out into the yard some of the women came up shyly to touch her skin. Others, giggling, were dragged up to do it by their friends. For the next few days she was followed by a procession of villagers and – as the news of her visit spread – of people from the surrounding bush farms too. Everybody was enjoying this amazing event.

Mary herself found the days tolerable. But the nights were hell. Calabar etiquette demanded that she should sleep with the senior wives and that they should lie down as close to her as possible. They had all been well and truly fattened, the only ventilation was the open doorway, and everybody was perspiring freely. Mary could hardly breathe. She lay on her back in the darkness wedged in between the large women, while lizards performing trapeze acts under the thatch sent showers of dust down into her eyes, and the occasional rat made a hop skip and jump across the sleeping women. She wondered how on earth she was going to survive twelve nights of this and was glad when the chorus of cockerels announced the dawn.

For the whole of her stay Mary had to give several hours each day to dispensing medicine, lancing boils, bandaging wounds and burns, and cleaning and disinfecting hundreds of sores. She also held morning and evening service, spent hours trying to explain the fundamentals of Christianity to uncomprehending audiences, and was so tired after a day or two that at night the lizards, rats, cockroaches, grunts, snores, and sweat no longer kept her awake.

Half way through her stay a tornado came in over the estuary and hit the village. It uprooted trees and swept away canoes, roofs and fences. The roof of Okon's hut went whirling away with the rest amid the thunder and lightning. Next everyone was drenched by the torrential rain which followed the thunder. As usual when frightened, Mary began to sing a hymn and got the children to join in. So, to the surprise of the African women, 'Oh let us sing!' quavered through the storm.

When it was all over Mary got dry clothes for herself and for the children out of her boxes, stripped and rubbed them and herself down, and dosed them all with quinine. Then, to stop her shivering, she wrapped herself in blankets and spare clothes while Okon's men rigged up a temporary roof. She went into a fever following the drenching but after a couple of days on a clay sleeping-bench in the hut she recovered.

A few days before she was due to return to Old Town, she noticed that the morning chatter and laughter of the wives had changed to whispering. When she asked what was the matter they told her that two of the girl wives of one of the chiefs had done a bad thing. They had crawled out of his yard in the night and gone to the hut of a young man. They had been caught and now the village council was holding a palaver about them.

As soon as the palaver finished Mary asked Okon what had been decided. He told her that each girl was to receive a hundred lashes. It was in effect a sentence of death. Neither girl was likely to survive for long after her back had been cut to ribbons by the terrible rawhide lash used for these floggings. Mary immediately asked Okon to reconvene the palaver and let her speak to the chiefs on the girls' behalf.

Okon was worried. His people would think God's law not good if they could not punish people who did bad things. He agreed however to postpone the floggings and to let Mary speak to the council.

Mary first told the girls that they had shamed their chief and brought punishment on themselves. This pleased the chiefs. Then she turned on them. It was a disgrace to coop up young girls as wives to elderly men who already had all the wives they needed. Girls had a right to expect more fun from life than to live it out penned in a yard with other women.

This down-to-earth approach was typical Slessor. But in Victorian Britain sex was very much a dirty word and it is doubtful if the church elders in Scotland would have approved of such a direct reference to the immodest desires of young women.

The chiefs did not approve of it either. Who did this white woman think she was to question their judgement, and to interfere with their customs? They were angry and began to shout at her. But why had they asked her to come, Mary asked? First they said they wanted 'God', now they said they did not want him. After an hour of angry discussion they decided to reduce the sentences to ten lashes each. This was the least punishment to which they would agree.

Mary thanked them for listening to her and for their mercy, went back to her hut and prepared bandages, and got out her bottle of laudanum, a pain-killing drug. Soon afterwards she heard for the first time the sounds of a flogging. She would hear them again many times.

While the second girl was still screaming the women brought the first to her naked, quivering in agony, and her back, buttocks, and legs covered with blood which was pouring from the deep bites of the lash.

For the rest of Mary's stay at Ibaka they lay on their stomachs on the floor of her hut, dosed with laudanum and bandaged against the flies. But what happened to them afterwards? There is no record of this. Was 'the palaver forgotten' in typical African fashion, or were they turned out of the village? Or were the chiefs so afraid of upsetting Mary's 'white man's God' that they left them alone? In later years, when the people were certain that Ma had special powers, her *ifot* alone would have protected them. Perhaps it did now.

For her return journey Okon provided his own canoe, which was smaller than Eyo's and had no cabin. He commanded it himself. They set out with the tide in the afternoon, seen off by most of the population. Soon afterwards a storm swept in from the sea and whipped up short, steep waves in the estuary. Okon had seen it coming and had ordered the steersman to head for the shelter of a small island. But before they could reach it, with the wind tearing at them, the waves breaking into the canoe, and the spray flying, the crew panicked and lost their rhythm and the drums stopped. Mary who had been crouching, terrified, beside one of Okon's senior wives, now lost her temper as she would often do in emergencies, and shouted at the drummer nearest her to start the beat again and the crew to begin paddling. Perhaps they were more frightened of the *ifot* of Mary than they were of the river god who had a moment before, it seemed, decided to destroy them. The drummer began to beat again and the paddlers turned the canoe towards the island. They struggled across to it, and for over an hour clung to the branches of a mangrove tree which overhung the water while the rain lashed them and the water swilled round their knees as the canoe writhed up and down.

After the storm had passed and it was safe to get under way again, Mary was shivering so much that her teeth were chattering. Okon and his wife cuddled up to her to try to warm her, and for once she was grateful for the bodyheat of large women!

They arrived at Old Town just before sunrise and carried the bedraggled white Ma up to her house. Next day she had a raging fever which kept her in bed for over a week.

While Mary was working at Old Town, Edgerley had been making more expeditions up the rivers. He had reached Atam a hundred and sixty miles above Duke Town but he went down with fever shortly after he arrived there. His crew got him back to Ikotana, but a rope of his hammock snapped during the night and he fell heavily and injured his back. The crew carried him to his canoe and got him back to Duke Town but he died on arrival.

Doctor Hewan, who had replaced Doctor McKenzie, now also collapsed. He was to die the following year. And now Mary Slessor collapsed too. Another tornado had ripped the roof off her house and she had been drenched again. Her temperature soared and stayed high. The mission brought her back to Duke Town but her fever got worse and worse and it seemed that she too would die. Luckily the monthly steamer had arrived and the mission decided to send her home. It seemed her only chance of surviving, although it was doubtful if she would last the voyage.

There was, however, a last minute hitch. Mary had rescued another pair of twin babies a few weeks before. But their family was determined to remove the curse of the devil baby and while Mary was away they had tricked her girls into letting them have the boy and had killed him. Mary was afraid that they would get the girl and kill her too, so she had kept the baby with her at Duke Town. Now she announced that the baby must go to Scotland with her. Her colleagues argued but she insisted. In her run-down state she wept when they explained just how impossible the idea was. In the end, probably to humour a dying woman, they agreed to let the baby go.

This was a most important decision for both of them. For this baby would be the woman who would be her friend and helper, would be for years her only companion in the forests, would be her nurse through countless fevers, and would watch beside her as she died. She would be Jean – 'wonderful Jean'.

7. THE LONER

When she arrived in Dundee in May 1883 Mrs Slessor, Janie, and Susan, helped their Mary from the train for the second and the last time. She had recovered well on the voyage but her legs were still a little shaky. She was delighted with the twin snuggled up in her arms, so shining, and serene and serious. The baby was an immediate hit with everybody. Mary had her baptised in the Wishart Memorial Church and named Jean Anna Slessor after sister Janie. Until she grew up, Mary called the baby Janie too.

When she was well enough to begin the inevitable lecture tours, Mary of course took little Janie with her – from now on they would rarely be separated. Masks, head-dresses, and drums were nothing compared to this beautiful baby. The money came pouring in. For there in Mary's arms was part of what it was all about. But for the mission this baby and hundreds of others would be dead.

The two of them were such a success that when Mary reported at the beginning of 1884 that she was fully fit and ready to return to Calabar, The Foreign Missions' Board asked her to postpone her return in order to make more tours. It pointed out that without more money and more recruits the mission could not continue.

In December 1884 the Board asked Mary if she would accept a transfer to Creek Town. Both Miss Johnstone and Miss Edgerley were ill. Mary reluctantly agreed. She would be sorry to leave her Old Town people, and her African way of life. But at Creek Town she would be with the Goldies and it was of course Eyo's town.

Before she could sail back however a series of disasters hit the family. First her sister Janie went down with tuberculosis and the doctor said that she needed a warm climate if she were to survive. Mary, in desperation, suggested to the Board that she should take her sister back to Calabar with her. But she gave up the idea when it pointed out to her that Calabar, although certainly warm, was hardly the place for an invalid. Her mother too now became ill. It seems that she also had caught tuberculosis in the slums. Mary had to ask for her sailing date to be postponed so that she could take Janie and her mother down to a house which had been offered to them through a friend at a place called Topsham in Devon.

They had only been a few weeks in Devon however when Susan died suddenly in Dundee, and Mary went back to bury her sister and to close up the house. She decided now that she could not leave her invalids and it began to look as if her work in Calabar was over. But her mother was adamant. 'You are my child given to me by God, and I have given you back to Him', she said. Mary decided however to stay on in Devon until they could look after themselves, or she could get someone to come and nurse them. Because she was no longer lecturing she had refused to go on accepting her home allowance from the mission. So when her mother recovered she took a job as a nurse at Exeter Infirmary, and reported to the Board that now she could go back to Calabar.

In October 1885 the Board announced that it had arranged for her to sail the following month. But by now her mother was ill again and a Dundee friend had to come to the rescue with an offer to look after her until she recovered.

Mary was most reluctant to leave, but her mother insisted that she must. As usual Mary prayed about the problem and the Lord must have insisted too because on the day appointed she sailed from Liverpool.

The ship neared the Coast. It was December and Mary was thirty-seven. She had had plenty of time on the voyage to look back over the nine years which had gone by since she first sighted Africa. Then she had been worried about going to live among 'an entirely different class of people', and among black 'savages'. Now she was only impatient to get away from the comparative civilisation of the Calabar towns and into the forests. Then, she had known nothing about the Africans except that they had cruel habits which needed to be changed. Now she could talk to them as easily as she could talk to the folk in Dundee. She liked them and they seemed to like her.

Now, although she did not know it, her training for the work which she was to do was almost finished. First she would have three years in Creek Town during which she received from King Eyo her knowledge of Calabar laws. Then she would be off into the bush and for the next twenty-six years the Calabar towns would rarely see her.

During the two and a half years in which Mary had been away several young Scots and two Jamaicans had joined the mission. She found that it had seven ordained missionaries (one of whom was an African), four men teachers, and now that she was back, four women teachers, as well as its other African staff. And the mission no longer needed to worry about all the hours spent in paddling up to Ikonetu and Ikorofiong, for the children of Scotland had raised over a thousand pounds to provide it with its own steam launch.

Using the new launch – 'smoking canoe' the Africans called it – James Luke, Thomas Campbell, and two of the new men, Ezekiel Jarrett and John Gartshore, had gone up to Umon and persuaded the tribe to have an African teacher and to let the mission negotiate for a station for another at Ikotana further up the river. Until then the Umon, who still exacted tribute from all canoes passing their town, had refused to let the mission set up a station beyond them

With the new launch, the new progressive spirit coming from the young recruits, and the establishment of The Oil Rivers Protectorate by the British, it looked as if the Efik blockade of the rivers was at last about to be broken. The British had been forced to declare the Protectorate because in 1884 Germany had annexed the neighbouring territory of the Cameroons, until then, like Old Calabar, a sphere of British influence. Consul (later Sir Harry) Johnston was now based at Duke Town but even so, as Sir William Geary the Gold Coast Attorney General wrote, 'the Crown failed to set up any administration. It was a paper Protectorate, only exclusive of foreign powers. There was no revenue, no government, no police force, the Consul had no executive power . . . The system was still the old Consul and gun-boat régime . . . The futile powerlessness of the Consul is illustrated by a despatch from Mr Johnston that . . . there was no means of putting his decisions into force when resisted.'

Johnston was trying to establish free trading on the rivers. But he reported that when he tried to get beyond Umon to Atam the tribe drove him back with 'a hail of slugs', and he was chased down the river by cannibals 'bent on eating' his Krumen. Later the Enyong tribe blocked the river above Itu, but the Efiks

Trading canoes on the Cross River

declared war on them, opened it again, and burnt an Enyong town. The situation was almost as chaotic as before.

In Creek Town Mary found that she was expected to board with the Goldies. She promptly announced that she had no wish to do so but wanted to live on her own as she had at Old Town. The mission however was not in favour of this because it did not have enough houses for its new staff, and it did not want Mary to find her own accommodation either.

Just why the mission objected was not explained. But in January 1885 the Foreign Missions' Board, in reply to Mary's suggestion that she should build a little house for herself and her sister Janie, had recorded its decision that 'It is not expedient for an agent of the mission to live in such a house.' It looks as if both Edinburgh and Calabar had decided that Miss Slessor had gone far enough in her experiments at living as an African and that she was beginning to lower the dignity of the mission in the eyes of other Europeans. Mary however got her own way, for later the minutes recorded that she was living in Miss Edgerley's old house.

This seems to have been the first record of a dispute between the presbytery and Miss Slessor. It would not be the last. It shows that if Mary was ever a timid, meek young woman — which is highly unlikely — she was so no longer.

She wrote long letters home and waited impatiently for news of her invalids, half dreading what she would hear. But the first steamer of 1886 brought good news. Her mother and her sister were in much better health. Mary wrote back: 'I was hardly able to wait for my letters and then I rushed to my room and behaved like a silly body as if it had been bad news. It brought you all so clearly before me. At Church I sat beside the King and cried quietly into my wrap all the evening.'

As Mary sat weeping beside the King her mother was already dead. She had collapsed and died at the beginning of the year. On the evening on which she heard of her mother's death Mary conducted her evening service as usual and then went to her room and cried most of the night.

Three months later she heard that her sister Janie was dead too. Now there was no longer any 'home'. She wrote to a friend: 'I who all my life have been caring and planning and living for them am left as it were stranded and alone. There is no one to write and tell my stories, and troubles, and nonsense to . . . Heaven is now nearer to me than Britain and there will be no one to be anxious about me if I go up country'.

Considering what comparatively trifling incidents Mary would take in later years as signposts from God, the sudden sweeping away of her family would for her have been a clear sign. 'Okoyong' had nagged at her over the years as once 'Calabar' had done. She knew now what she must do. She made formal application to the mission to be allowed to go and live with the Okoyong.

But Miss Edgerley and Miss Johnstone were both due for leave and there was no-one to take over their work except Mary. The Okoyong would have to wait. The mission was probably glad to be able to delay a decision.

1886 was a bad year for Calabar. The crops failed and hundreds died of starvation. Mary wrote to a friend, 'If I told you what I have seen of human sorrow during the past months you would weep until your heart ached'.

Now that the Consul lived at Duke Town, King Eyo was consulting her more and more about the British, and she could always go to Eyo for advice about her own relations with the Africans.

At the other end of the social scale, she made a new friend: a blind slave. 'She is so poor that she has not one farthing in the world but what she gets from us – not a creature to do a thing for her, her house all open to rain and sun, and into which the cows rush at times – but blind Mary is our one living, bright, clear light . . . The other day I heard the King say that she was the only visible witness among the Church members in the town, but he added, "She is a proper one." Far advanced in spiritual knowledge, she knows the deep things of God. That old hut is like a heaven here to more than me.'

Towards the middle of 1886 Mary returned to her attack on Anderson and Goldie about her going to the Okoyong. At the beginning of the year they had still been entirely against the idea, which is not surprising. Even after Mary had lived with the Okoyong for years the mission would never allow another of its women to live alone among them.

Both veterans had firsthand experience of what it was like to live among the old customs when women were flogged to death for trivial offences, branded with smouldering sticks like cattle, and dragged screaming to be buried with a chief. They knew, as Goldie had written, that the old customs 'still prevailed' among the Okoyong. And, after Mary had been living with them for five years, an experienced missionary wrote that if any man had interfered in one of their riots as she had done the week before 'he would have had his throat cut.'

Why then did Anderson and Goldie change their minds and decide to let her run appalling risks? Perhaps she simply nagged them into doing so. Certainly she would have made their lives a misery if they had refused to let her go. But more likely she managed to convince them that this was the work which the Lord was demanding of her; all the missionaries had of course a strong sense of vocation otherwise they would never have been in Calabar. What is clear is that the Slessor willpower was already beginning to dominate her colleagues and that they, like the Africans, realised that she was a female agent with a difference.

Goldie wrote: 'They [the Okoyong] are rude men and the young man sent among them at one time soon lost courage. This place is Miss Slessor's choice and it is the place where she could do most good.'

Anderson wrote that there would have to be preliminary meetings with the tribe to make sure that she would be safe. He must have known however that with such a drunken, reckless, tribe as the Okoyong there would be no guarantee of her safety. But in a land where fevers had killed so many of his colleagues and already twice nearly killed Mary herself, where was safety?

In July 1886 the mission made formal application to the Board in Edinburgh for Miss Slessor to go and live with the Okoyong. It had not yet definitely decided to let her go but it knew that it would be as well to allow plenty of time to get a decision on such an unusual matter. It was in fact eighteen months before the Board would agree to the move.

Meanwhile Mary made three visits to the Okoyong with a group of her colleagues. But although she reported that some of the chiefs seemed to be in favour of letting her join them, 'as a body they were not very enthusiastic'. For each meeting they and their men were fully armed and they clearly had no faith in the missionaries.

Mary however was most impressed with them. 'Like all isolated peoples they are conservative and independent. They are brave, almost fierce, war-loving, and as reckless of their own lives as they are of others' . . . Physically they are a far higher type of man than the Calabar people . . . the nose is higher, the mouth and chin finer, the eyes fearless and piercing'.

In June 1888 the Board at last agreed that she could go and

join the tribe. But she had no firm decision from the mission on whether she could go, or from the tribe on whether she could come. She decided therefore to leave her colleagues behind and go alone to the tribe to fix things once and for all. She wrote to a friend asking for prayers for the success of her visit, 'Pray in a business-like manner, earnestly definitely, statedly'.

Eyo lent her his personal canoe as he had done for her Ibaka journey. This time the crew were not anxious to go to a tribe with which the Efiks had been swapping heads ever since the war of 1867. Eyo still refused to bury a slave alive so the Okoyong still considered the tribes to be at war. The crew must have had great trust in Mary's *ifot* because they eventually agreed to go.

For her journey Eyo had a carpet and cushions spread in the cabin and also suplied a paraffin stove so that Mary could make tea and heat a tin of stew. Unfortunately her cup was left behind and when one of the crew went to wash out the tin it slipped and sank in the river. The crew would have thought this a bad omen, and Mary had to make do with a saucer.

She went to a place called Ekenge, probably because the earlier palavers were held there. She wrote that she made the visit 'quite alone . . . I often had a lump in my throat and my courage threatened to take wings and fly away . . . though nobody guessed it . . . I decided that Man could do nothing with such a people and to leave it all to God.' Even in later years Efik crews would not go up to Ekenge unless Mary was with them. Now they put her ashore at the landing place and then waited in the river out of gun-shot range.

Ekenge was a few miles north of Adiabo and the landing place was in a creek off the Calabar River. On the walk up the narrow path, which she would get to know so well, she had plenty of time to wonder about her reception. Before she reached the town the first sentries stepped out of the bush and stopped her. She had been expecting this but the sentries themselves must have been surprised to see a lone white woman walking towards them. One of them took her on to the next sentries who took her to Chief Edem's yards.

Edem and most of his chiefs could speak Efik because it was one of the Aro trade languages and these friends of theirs ran a slave route through their territory. Mary therefore needed no interpreter at the palaver which was held as soon as he was able to call together the council of the Ekenge branch of Egbo over which he presided. The Okoyong like the Efiks had borrowed the basic idea of the Order from the Ekoi tribe and had developed their own version of it.

Mary told the council that she was now ready to join the tribe if they were prepared to let her do so. The council was at first split on the issue but it finally decided that she could join them, at least for a time.

Why the Okoyong changed their minds about having a missionary was never explained. But at this time the more intelligent among the chiefs must have realised that their tribe was going downhill fast. Mary was hopelessly overworked during the fifteen years which she spent with the tribe and never seems to have collected statistics on it. But in 1932 a British officer, Major Sealy King, wrote an official report on 'The Okoyong Clan'. By then their territory had shrunk to about fifty square miles and their numbers to just over five thousand. He reported that, when Miss Slessor had gone to join them, the tribe had been quarrelsome and proud of their fighting qualities; that they had taught their young boys to stand up to hard knocks in mock battles and to pain by branding them with tribal marks from wrist to elbow; that all the fighting among themselves and with other tribes and the poison bean trials had killed off so many of their people that they had been forced to buy in more and more slaves from the Aro to keep up their numbers; that their obstinate refusal to make peace with the Efiks had cut them off from trade; and that in their isolation the 'drunken revelry' which Goldie had mentioned had become a habit.

In Mary therefore, with her 'God' and 'Book', the Okoyong probably saw the protection and the help which their hated enemies the Efiks had enjoyed for forty years. To them there would have been less risk in accepting a woman because, whereas a white man might try to take over control of the tribe, it was unthinkable to them that a woman should try to do so (and since she was a mere woman she could always be sent packing!) Although they looked on women as second-class citizens the mother of the head of the House often had great influence over him and it was probably this kind of influence they were prepared to accept from Mary.

When Edem told Mary that the council had decided that she could join them for a time she promptly asked for a piece of land for her house and school. Edem took her to a strip of bush near his own yards and said that she could have it. He agreed that it

D

would be sacred ground, a place of safety for all people, and that no one would bear arms on it.

Mary then asked to be taken to the village of Ifako, which was friendly with Ekenge. From this request it seems that Ifako must have been represented at earlier palavers otherwise Mary would not have known of its existence. Edem however said that Ifako was holding a celebration and all the chiefs would be drunk; Mary had better wait until the next day. He would give her a hut to sleep in.

She must have received a promise of safe conduct for her Efik crew because she walked back to the river and fetched them – or at least some of them – and held evening service with them in the yard outside her hut, while the Okoyong crowded round to watch. Again it says a lot for their confidence in Mary that Eyo's men had agreed to go with her. They knew that, without her, their heads would have been on poles outside the town's palaver house in no time at all.

After the service Eme Eta, the sister of Edem, came to talk to Mary. Their mother was dead and Eme – who was a rich widow – seems to have taken over the influence of the chief's mother in the affairs of the tribe. She and Mary talked well into the night and Mary wrote that she was sure that Eme would become her friend and would soon believe in the gospel. She was right about the friendship, but wrong about the conversion. Neither Eme nor Edem became Christians.

When a tired but happy Mary decided to get some sleep she found that the hut was not exclusive to herself after all. 'I am not very particular about my bed these days, but as I lay on a few dirty sticks laid across and across and covered with a litter of dirty corn-shells, with plenty of rats and insects, three women and an infant three days old alongside, and over a dozen sheep and goats and cows outside, you don't wonder that I slept little. But I had such a comfortable quiet night in my own heart.'

At sunrise next morning she was wakened by the sound of shooting and went out to see what was happening. Ekenge warriors with guns and swords were running past the yard. One of them told her that two women had gone to a spring and been fired on. She went with them while they searched the bush, for they seemed to be pleased to see her, but the attacker had gone.

The incident was a warning to Mary not to stray outside the stockades until she had been accepted by the other villages in the area.

This was a time when, as one of her colleagues, J K McGregor, wrote: 'Every village had a feud with its neighbour . . . even when going to the springs for water the women took their lives in their hands. Besides the spirits that were supposed to dwell in the bush and molest people, any tree might have behind it a foe of flesh and blood.'

Later in the morning Mary went on to Ifako, which was about two miles west of Ekenge. Its chiefs were now sober but not over-pleased to see her. When however they heard that Ekenge had given her land they too agreed to give her some and that it would be sacred ground.

By the time she had walked the six miles back to the landing place it was late afternoon and the tide had turned. About half way to Creek Town they ran into a rain storm and with the tide too strong for the paddlers they had to shelter in a bay for two hours. While they waited for the tide to slacken Mary watched some crabs fighting round some rotten tree stumps and thought how like the Okoyong they were. Later a human corpse floated up to the canoe.

It was nearly dark when they got under way again and Mary tried to get some sleep. She heard the paddlers telling one another to be quiet and not to wake Ma. With the pleasant thought that once more they were looking after her she did eventually fall asleep and only wakened as the watch-fires of Creek Town came in sight.

She reported to Anderson and Goldie that the Okoyong had agreed that she could go and live with them for a time and that she proposed to move to Ekenge with her orphans as soon as possible. News of her plan spread quickly through the Calabar towns and most of her friends were horrified. Even a group of traders came from Duke Town to try to dissuade her. 'The Okoyong don't need a missionary', one of them said, 'they need a gun-boat!'

Eyo too was against her joining the Okoyong. He, of course, knew at first hand, just how bloody their customs were. However when he failed to get her to change her mind he agreed once more to lend her his personal canoe and crew for the journey. The date which they fixed for it was 4th August 1888. It was a day which she would remember for the rest of her life.

Mary on leave in 1884

8. THE SHAPE OF COURAGE

It had been a hard day. As she stood in the mud at Ekenge listening to the sobbing of her orphans and the drumming, screaming and gunfire coming from Ifako, Mary began to feel that her friends had been right and that she had made a terrible mistake. In her first report to the mission from Ekenge she wrote: 'The tribe seemed so completely given over to the devil that we were tempted to despair.' When she was lonely and in danger she often wrote 'we' instead of 'I'. It was as if she was trying to convince herself that she was not, after all, alone.

But the first thing to do was find shelter and to make a fire to warm the children, dry their clothes, and cook a meal. She asked the women to find her a hut and they took her to an old one. The thatch was leaking and there was no door and no window, just a hole in the wall. The women brought her wood and a pot of embers with which to start a fire then they left her. She got the fire going, undressed the children, rubbed them down, and hung up their clothes to dry. Her boots were caked with mud and soaked through so she took them off. She began to cook the meal

After the meal she wondered whether she should risk leaving the children alone and go back for Mr Bishop and the boxes or wait in the hope that he would realise that something had gone wrong and come with some of the crew. She decided to wait.

It was several hours later when she heard a shout and went out to find Mr Bishop with one of the crew ploutering through the mud. He told her that the rest of the men had refused to come. They said that they were too tired. Luckily a paddler who had been up to Ekenge with Mary on her last visit, had agreed to guide him. But neither he nor his guide had enjoyed walking through the forest at night.

Mary thanked him and the crewman and explained that, because of the funeral celebrations, she had not been able to get the Okoyong to carry up the boxes. She took the two men back

to the hut. The fire was a poor one. The floor was muddy. The
naked children were shivering. Without dry clothes and blankets
they would all get fever. The 'Carrots' temper blazed. So the
crew were too tired. She would give them tired! She tried to get
her boots on again but her feet were too swollen. She asked Mr
Bishop to look after the children and set out barefoot. He
probably tried to stop her but he might just as well have tried to
stop a hurricane. As she splashed back through the lanes she
met an Okoyong boy who offered to go with her and carry her
lantern. She was grateful for this because she needed both hands
to manage her long, soaking, mud-caked skirt.

In the alluvial soil down by the Calabar rivers there are few
stones but her feet were badly cut that night by the twigs and the
sharp prickly leaves which the Okoyong women used to smooth
their clay walls and benches. In later years she hardened her feet
until they were as tough as any African's but after this barefoot
walk to the river and back she had to hobble about for several
weeks in canvas shoes.

When she reached the creek she found the canoe moored out
from the bank for fear of the head-hunters and the leopards. The
crew were asleep inside it safely tucked up under a canvas cover
which made it look like a stranded whale. She soon shattered
their sleep by wading out up to her breasts and bashing on the
canvas. With a mixture of ridicule and flattery she got them into
the river and hauling the canoe ashore. Then, in spite of their
fear of the Okoyong, she got them to load some of her boxes on
their heads and set off up the path. Ma Slessor, they knew, was a
very special woman who was backed by all the power of the
white man's God. There was just no knowing what terrible
things Ma, when in a temper, might bring down on them. Ma
herself, who had already walked eight miles through the mud,
was having great difficulty in keeping one damaged foot going
ahead of the other.

'Had not Mr Bishop come with us', she reported, 'I don't
know what I would have done . . . The next day was the Sabbath
wet and miserable. Miserable because it was a wet and idle one.
Only a few women and children were left in the town and we did
not think it prudent to go to the place of revelry for many
reasons'.

The next day was also the twelfth anniversary of her first sailing from Liverpool to Calabar. For most of these twelve years
her great ambition had been to get out into the forests to bring a

new way of life to the Okoyong. Now she had achieved the first part. To achieve the second she would have to live for years as a forest African among all the stink and cruelty of a primitive township.

On the Monday – no work was of course possible on the Sabbath – Mary and Mr Bishop between them persuaded the crew to begin carrying up the rest of the gear. Because of her cut and swollen feet she had to stay in the hut while Mr Bishop looked after the work at the river end. She had been given many parting gifts by her friends, including a portable organ for when she was able to start services, and she had a door and two window frames for when the Okoyong built her a hut. So it took the crew until the Tuesday morning to bring everything up from the river through the mud. Then they made a half-hearted attempt at putting a door and a window into the old hut, worried no doubt that the Okoyong would return any minute from Ifako. On the Wednesday morning they thankfully departed for Calabar with Mr Bishop.

Mary wrote: 'In the forenoon I was left alone with the mud and the rain and the general wretchedness of flitting, with a gap round the window frame and more round the doorway. I looked helplessly on day after day at the rain pouring down on the boxes, bedding, and everything.' The hut was so small that to get room to move during the day she had to put most of the boxes outside. It was a grim beginning to her stay and that it was entirely her own fault that she was in such a mess was no consolation.

It was several days before Edem and his people began to trickle back from Ifako and Mary was able to reflect on her situation. She knew that before she could begin to tackle their old bloody customs she would have to try to establish the same relationship with the Okoyong as she had with the Efiks, who were well-behaved compared to this tribe. The Efiks knew that she was in every way a friend who would walk miles to treat their sick and injured. They also knew that she would face up to dangers which few warriors and fewer women would face alone. To the Efiks she was a very special person. But the Okoyong did not know she was special. She must not get herself killed before they found out. If she vanished without trace they could always claim that she had been killed by leopards or head-hunters. In any event the British had no troops in Calabar so there was nothing they would be able to do to avenge her death. She had put herself beyond the reach of any law but Egbo's.

When Edem and the other chiefs returned they were not feeling their best and did not go out of their way to welcome her. Edem did transfer her from the tumbledown hut into which the slave women had put her, but unfortunately he insisted that she must move into one of the huts in the yard reserved for his wives. It was Okoyong protocol that important guests be housed in one of the chief's huts, so as long as she was a guest and not part of the tribe she could not refuse.

But Edem and his people did not stay for long. 'Immediately the people came back a palaver came up and off they went for another week of rioting. On the way back from that a free man died so another week was lost. So during this time my mission work was mostly of a nature of cutting back and felling trees to get a few conveniences.' She did her cutting on the piece of land near his huts which Edem had allotted to her. The first thing she would have done was dig a latrine for herself and the children. The Okoyong used the bush as both latrine and rubbish dump.

The palaver which 'came up' was over a skirmish with intruders in which the free man died of wounds and several other warriors, slave and free, were wounded.

When the people finally returned from their funerals and their fighting, the boy who had gone back with Mary to the landing place was accused of breaking the customs of the tribe by remaining in Ekenge and taking no part in the Ifako celebration. Mary, who spoke no Okoyong at this time, did not know of this. Although she saw the boy in the middle of a circle of chiefs near a pot which was heating on a fire, she did not realise what was happening until she saw him forced to hold out his hands and a chief ladle boiling oil over them.

Mary was furious and demanded to know what the boy had done. The chiefs told her that he had broken Egbo law. But it may have been that those among them who had opposed her coming to the tribe intended the boy's punishment as a warning both to her and to the people as to what would happen to anybody who took up with her newfangled ideas. There was nothing Mary could do except, seething with anger, give the boy a dose of laudanum and put ointment on his hands. These were soon so badly skinned and blistered that to move his fingers was agony.

Mary found that for the first few days she was as big a source of entertainment to the women and the slaves as she had been at Ibaka. The women crowded into Edem's yard to watch this strange new being. But although Edem's senior wives considered it good manners to keep close to their guest by day, she managed to convince them that she must sleep in her own hut at night with only her children. As at Ibaka too she found that most of her day was taken up with treating the sick and injured among the women, the slaves, and the children. The free men however did not come near her and Edem himself avoided her. It was clear that as far as the chiefs were concerned she was very much on trial and that some of them still thought that she should never have been allowed to come to live with them.

Edem's sister, Eme Eta, however, as Mary had hoped, quickly became her friend. Mary described her as, 'a noble woman according to her lights' and, later, as 'my almost sister'. Eme's husband had died a few months before and she had been one of the wives suspected of causing his death by *ifot*. The witchdoctor had placed the suspected wives in a circle, cut off the head of a white cock, and thrown the headless bird into the centre of the circle. It had fluttered round and round until its muscles stopped twitching and the wife at which the stump of its neck was pointing was then judged to be the guilty one and executed. When Eme was declared innocent she fainted. After only a few weeks in the widows' mourning shed she had, through Edem's influence, been allowed to return to Ekenge.

Eme told Mary that her narrow escape had sickened her of the old customs which she had earlier accepted without question like everybody else. But she warned Mary not to try too soon to interfere in the ways of the tribe. If she did, she might be killed. To the Okoyong life was cheap. At recent funeral celebrations for a dead chief four wives had been strangled, eight slave men, eight slave women, ten young boys and ten young girls. Over twenty other men and women who were suspected of *ifot* against the dead chief were forced to undergo the poison bean trial and all had died.

So Mary did not interfere when a number of women condemned to take the poison bean were chained in one of Edem's yards. They were left there all day under the blazing sun with no food or water and some of them had babies at the breast. Mary decided to cook them a meal. When at sunset she went to give it to them she found that their guards had left them – perhaps to get a meal themselves – and that some of Edem's wives were taking water to the prisoners while others kept a lookout. To interfere with Egbo prisoners was a capital offence so Edem's sands of people, that have set *them-selves* against me round about.

7 Arise, O LORD; save me, O my God: for thou hast smitten all mine enemies *upon* the cheek bone; thou hast broken the teeth of the ungodly.

8 Salvation *belongeth* unto the LORD: thy blessing *is* upon thy people. Selah.

PSALM 4.

To the chief Musician on Neginoth, A Psalm of

5 The fool... sight: thou ... quity.

6 Thou sha... leasing: the... bloody and ...

7 But as f... thy house i... mercy: *and* ... toward thy l...

Extract from Mary's Bible

women were risking being flogged to death. Mary was pleased to see that the Okoyong women were neither as cruel nor as callous as they were made out to be.

She was beginning to understand the men better too, 'notwithstanding that Calabar hates and fears them, and possesses the entire monopoly of trade and the protection of Britain . . . they [the Okoyong] keep their position proudly and defiantly.' But because of their isolation she had to admit that her chosen tribe were heavy drinkers. 'To give an idea of the drink traffic here would baffle my pen. There is nothing like it anywhere I have ever been. I have seen about five shillings worth of legal trade done here with Calabar and I have seen barrels of rum and boxes of gin by the score. *Everybody* drinks. I have lain down at night knowing that not a sober man and hardly a sober woman was within miles of me.'

Meanwhile, as the weeks went by, Mary was finding her surroundings more and more trying. 'I am living in a single apartment with a mud floor and that not in the best condition. Moreover it is shared by three boys and two girls and we are crowded in on every side by men, women, children, goats, dogs, fowls, rats, and cats all going and coming indiscriminately.' It is doubtful if, without Mary's conditioning in the slums, any white woman could have endured the life which she was now living.

'Try to push your way through the crowd and the exhaling odour from that naked congregation almost paralyses you . . . you feel conscious of it permeating the whole surface of your body.' This is how, in the 1880s, Consul T J Hutchinson described a short visit to a Calabar market. Since Mary was living among humans and animals in a primitive township it is probable that at this time, considering all the difficulties of taking a bath, she sometimes smelled pretty badly herself.

The total lack of privacy was beginning to weary and depress her. She needed peace these days to talk to her God who was her guide in everything, and even at night when the door was closed the little hut was too crowded to give her this.

She had by now developed the habit of silent prayer which she had once told James Logie she found so impossible. In the same letter to Thomas Hart in which he described Mary's river bathing, the orphan Daniel Slessor described how she would stand in clearings in the forest looking up at the stars. 'She was praying to God for help, strength, courage, and resource. At these moments you can imagine Ma as far away from her surroundings. We [her orphans] used to look upon her then as a spirit. Her blue eyes fixed steadfastly above . . . her lips moving . . . Oftentimes Janie would think "Ma is gone" . . . with tears she would approach and say gently "Ma, are you with us?" '

But at this time to go into the bush at night was dangerous because of local enemies and the leopards which scavenged round the town. So Mary simply had to find a way of getting rid of her hangers-on by day. She managed this by going, after she had finished her morning dispensary, to her piece of land and hacking away at the bushes and small trees and pestering anyone who insisted on going with her into hacking away too. This soon got her peace in which she could pray without distraction.

Gradually the free men of Ekenge began to accept the white woman. Nothing dreadful had happened to the town since she came so perhaps their own gods had no objection to the introduction of the white man's God. For her part Mary had to admit that trying to teach Christianity to the Okoyong was very much an uphill struggle. Even after she had been living with them for fifteen years most of the Okoyong, like Edem and Eme, simply included Mary's God among all the rest and worshipped hers in her way and their own in their way. She found that their religious customs were very like those of the Efik. The Okoyong too were surrounded by gods, spirits of the dead, devils, and of course witchcraft. And, they too, having such an uncertain future, tended to live for the present in a happy-go-lucky way, unless depressed, drunk, or raging. They were a much livelier tribe than the Efik however and their behaviour was, to say the least, unpredictable, as she soon began to realise.

The women, children, and slaves, who came to Mary for treatment obviously received benefit from it. So more and more free men began to come to her too. They found that – although she had a nasty habit of punching them in the stomach to make them swallow the pill they were hoping to put with their other charms – her medicine worked well. But she was still no more than tolerated by the chiefs.

Then, after she had been a month with the tribe, Mary made the breakthrough which she so badly needed. 'I got a patient in one of the wives of the chief [Edem]. He had bitten her during the orgies at the funeral feasts and the native faculty [witch-doctors] having done their best without avail he begged me to take the case in hand.' The bite had festered, and was extremely painful, and the poison was spreading along the woman's arm. Mary's poultices and disinfectants succeeded where the witchdoctors had failed, Edem and his wife were grateful, and the rest of the chiefs most impressed.

'From this my fame spread far and wide, for the lady is of gentle birth and every trifling act of courtesy, I have since found, was retailed and appreciated, proving that, with all their faults, they are not insensible to kindness . . . After this I had many visitors from the interior towns some of whose names were familiar as the terror of Calabar, but everyone was gentlemanly and gracious, everyone laid aside his arms at the entrance to our yard, and everyone gave us an invitation to spend a week or two at his place.'

The Okoyong 'gentlemanly and gracious'? Not many people in the Calabar towns would have believed that! Nor would many Victorian Britons have described the wife of a chief of an obscure forest tribe as 'a lady of gentle birth'. But on this point at least Mary was correct: the family trees of the Okoyong chiefs went back a long way even though, until Major Sealy King attempted to draw them up on paper, they existed only in the memory of the tribe.

But, as if to confirm just how unpredictable they were, no sooner had Mary described the good manners of the tribe than she found herself at the receiving end of some very bad manners indeed. Members of the Ibo tribe, because of their fine physique and intelligence, were the most expensive slaves, and one of the Ekenge chiefs had bought a beautiful Ibo girl from the Aro and made her one of his concubines. She, however, fell in love with another slave and went to his hut to persuade him to run away with her. He, knowing the awful penalities, refused, quickly left his hut, and went to his work, while the girl went into the forest and hanged herself. But she had been seen going into his hut and he was accused of enticing her by *ifot*.

Mary attended his trial and when the chiefs, sittting as the Egbo Council, sentenced him first to be flogged and then executed, she protested that the sentence was manifestly unjust. What else could the man have done but quickly leave the girl? But, the chiefs argued, he was not to be killed for that, but for bewitching her.

It was morning, they were sober, and they seemed now to have accepted her. She had saved the lives of the girls at Ibaka

and now, angry at the injustice of the sentence, she decided to
try to save the slave. What evidence was there, she asked, that
the slave had bewitched the girl? The chiefs were clearly
amazed. Here was an outsider – and a woman at that – daring
to question their judgement. They began to get angry and to
shout at her. They did not need evidence, they said, it was
obvious that the slave had bewitched the girl. It was not obvious,
said Mary; a court of law could not condemn a man to death
without evidence. At this, not only the chiefs but the watching
freemen too leapt up in rage. Everybody began to shout, and the
more they shouted the more excited they became. They waved
guns and swords at her, the dust flew, and as they pressed round
her the men began to push one another aside to get into the front
line. The proceedings were rapidly developing into a riot.
'Things', Mary wrote later, 'got critical.'

She knew from Mrs Sutherland and Louisa that to show fear
was the best way to get herself killed. But although she was surprised at the explosion of anger which her interference had
caused she also knew that if she backed down now her chances
of guiding the tribe to a better way of life would be gone. They
would despise her and she might just as well return to Creek
Town. She had unintentionally staked everything on the
outcome of this confrontation. So she stood her ground and the
angrier they got, the angrier she got. She stood silently in the
middle of them and glared at them. Now the chiefs faced a
woman with red hair and blazing blue eyes who was defying
them. This was something right outside their experience. How
could it be happening? This could be no mere woman.
Gradually, as they realised that their shouting was making no
impression on her, they calmed down. This situation needed to
be thought about. Were they faced with the power of the white
man's God? The chiefs resumed their seats and condescended to
argue the case with the outsider. In the end they compromised:
the slave would be flogged but not executed. As at Ibaka Mary
thanked the chiefs for listening to her and for their clemency.
Face was saved all round.

This was a most important event for Mary. The Ekenge
branch of Egbo had recognised that she was not merely a
medical worker and teacher in the tribe but that she had the
power to influence their decisions. Fortunately she had not
chosen a religious custom for her first interference in their
affairs. If she had chosen at this time to defy their gods and the

spirits of their ancestors they might well have killed her. Their religion had been so bound up with cruelty for centuries that in obeying its demands they could behave like sadistic monsters. From now on however it would be more difficult for any man to kill her. They knew now that she had very special *ifot* indeed.

But it was a hollow victory. To teach her that their judgements were not lightly to be interfered with, the chiefs chained the slave to a post in a yard behind her hut and put sentries on the gate to make sure that she could not get to him. They then had him flogged there every day for three days during which they gave him no food and no water. Through the mud wall of her hut she heard by day the slash of the whip and the screams of the slave and by night his moaning and the rattle of his chains. When he was nearly dead they let her go to him and eventually she nursed him back to something like his former self.

The screams and moans of a tortured man were not the only sounds which Mary heard through the walls of her hut. Edem, like everybody else, was often drunk by sunset. Sometimes he held celebrations in the women's yard for important guests from other towns. They were invited to take their pick from among the slave girls. Some of these girls were willing and some unwilling, but either way Mary dared not go out of her hut because of the romping of the naked men and women.

On these nights she sat and read her Bible by the light of her lantern. She scribbled notes in the margins and tried to drown out the sounds of struggling and mating by reading aloud. Then, when she lay down to sleep, she recited aloud the psalms which she knew by heart:

> The Lord is my Shepherd
> I shall not want
> He leadeth me by green pastures.
> Yea even if I walk
> In the valley of the shadow of death
> I shall fear no evil
> For thou O Lord art with me.

Of these nights she wrote, 'If I did not know that my Saviour is near me I would go out of my mind.'

Three of her Bibles are preserved in Dundee museum. Every blank space is covered with her scribbled notes. In one of them she wrote, 'God and one are always a majority'.

The women weavers of Dundee, who so often had to be the breadwinners for their families, had a reputation for being tough and formidable personalities — a reputation which has endured to this day — and when Mary went to Ekenge she was already a formidable personality herself. But underneath her toughness she had a loving nature. From now on she would keep this side of her nature mainly for her children. For while she lived for several months next to Edem's hut in the middle of his harem and surrounded daily by cruelties of one kind or another, she developed a core of steel off which problems and opponents would bounce. Ekenge completed the conditioning of Mary Slessor.

9. BIRTH OF A LEGEND

Mary had never expected life with the Okoyong to be anything but hellish at the beginning and, although at this time it was even worse than she had expected, she was careful not to let the people see that she was upset. She carried on with her work as if the torturing of the slave had never happened. One of her greatest needs was to get out of Edem's yards and into a place of her own. But when she asked him if his people would now build a hut for her, he waved her away. It was not the building season yet, he said. It would not come round for some months yet. He seemed to be finding his missionary an embarrassment.

The first rush of patients to her dispensary was beginning to lessen now, so she decided that it was time to introduce the Okoyong to 'Book'. She asked Edem for permission to open her school and for a yard in which to hold it and this time he was agreeable. He said that she could have one of his own yards.

To begin with, everyone wanted 'Book'. 'There was such a crowd that I could not count them . . . The school here is held in a Big Man's yard in the evening. Then the wives and slaves can come. They make a motley crowd bound [slave] and free, male and female, young and old, all crammed into the shed. The master [Edem] and his sister [Eme] who can claim a pedigree few can claim in this land are hustled by the slaves bought but yesterday and there is a great deal of merriment and good nature and a great deal of earnestness in their struggle to master the alphabet and the multiplication table.'

She was teaching them to read and write Efik, since this language would be most useful to them for communicating with the other tribes, and European arithmetic which would be useful for trading. 'The routine is the same at Ifako only there we hold a short service of evening prayers to finish with . . . The distance between Ekenge and Ifako in good weather is about twenty minutes, in wet owing to mud and ruts it takes thirty minutes.'

The ruts were not of course caused by wheels, for there were none, but by the flow of water during the torrential rains. Even though the journey was a short one Ekenge provided Mary with an armed escort on her way out and Ifako one on her way back. The Okoyong were always careful to guard their people. Sealy King reported that the head of the House had an escort of forty warriors wherever he went.

Mary was soon proud of how quickly her Okoyong pupils were learning. Within a few weeks she was writing, 'Some of the lads and men are already spelling words of two syllables.' With their introduction to the mysteries of 'Book', Edem, Eme, and some of the chiefs at both Ekenge and Ifako saw progress towards the new life which they had hoped Mary would bring to them and her stock rose again. She wrote that whereas to begin with the Ifako chiefs had seemed surly and uninterested, they were now more friendly towards her than those of Ekenge.

It was just as well that she was popular with the people now, for she found herself once more in confrontation with the chiefs and creating what she took to describing as 'the usual uproar'. Although in the case of the slave she had set a precedent, this time when she interfered in the town's affairs she was in greater danger because it was evening and most of the chiefs were drunk.

A slave who had done work for a young freeman, to be paid for in food, demanded the food from the young man's wife. But it was against the law for a wife to give food to a man in her husband's absence – it was held to be a promise of adultery – so the girl refused. The slave however declared that he was starving and threatened her. She was afraid, so to get rid of him she gave him a small piece of yam. Unfortunately somebody saw her do this and reported her to the Egbo council which found her guilty and sentenced her to have boiling oil poured over her belly.

The chiefs managed to keep the trial secret from Mary and the first she knew of any unusual event was when at sunset she heard drumming and saw the people gathered in the market place. She went to find out what was happening, heard a girl screaming, and pushed her way through the crowd. In its centre lit by flaring torches she found masked Egbo men tightening the cords which tied the spread-eagled and terrified girl to stakes driven into the ground. She must have known that the moment for the oil had come and was writhing her naked body against the pull of the cords. The oil was boiling on a fire nearby and a

Mary in the 1890's

Jean

masked man was ladling some of it into a pot. It was a scene
which would have daunted the bravest of people: the ring of
seated chiefs, the masked men grotesque in the flicker of the fire
and of the torches, the laughing, drunken, warriors, the screaming, the drumming, and the sexual excitement and anticipation of
the spectators. It is at least possible that if Mary had known
what she was going to find she would have thought it wiser to
stay away. Of course it would have been wiser, because the
crowd were so excited that if one of the Egbo men had attacked
her they could quickly have changed into a mindless mob.

But as she stood inside the circle and the chiefs saw her, it did
not occur to Mary to turn back because at the sight of what was
happening to the girl her 'Carrots' rage took over once again.
She walked out and got between the fire and the girl. What a film
sequence it would have made. The hush as everyone stared at
the small white woman. Then the explosion of chatter as the
crowd babbled their amazement. At this point anything could
have happened if the masked man with the ladle had not taken
matters into his own hands and set up a contest which distracted
the crowd. He began to swing the ladle round his head and to
caper towards Mary. She stood and stared at him. It was the
weight on the cord in the slums all over again. But this time the
stake was her life. The ladle whistled nearer and nearer her head.
The crowd looked on in silence. The Egbo man dodged from
side to side, his eyes staring at her through the holes in the
mask. He had the choice of striking her with the ladle or of
retreating. Mary stared back at him. He retreated. Mary walked
towards him on her way to where Edem was sitting and he
almost fell over himself to get out of her way. Such a show of
power from a mere woman astounded the crowd. They had
never seen anything like it before. They broke up into groups to
discuss the event, while Mary pleaded the girl's case with Edem,
who must himself have been a very surprised man. The girl's
punishment now became a trivial matter compared to this ex-
hibition of the power of the white man's God and the chiefs
allowed Mary to take the girl into her own custody pending
further consideration of her case. In a few days, in typical
Okoyong fashion, 'the palaver was forgotten' and the girl slipped
quietly back to her husband. But the first episode had been
recorded into what was to become the legend of *Eka Kpukpro
Owo*.

Mary, exhausted by the nervous tension, would have prayed

with extra fervour that night. She wrote to a friend that God was protecting her in an amazing way. Since she was a highly intelligent person she must have seen the implications of what had happened. Certainly she believed from now on that the Lord had given her power over the forest tribes and she used that power whenever necessary. She had been living under great strain for several weeks and the discovery of it must have cheered her up.

Because she never doubted that she was living in the presence of God and that he was guiding her in the special work for which he had shaped her, she found it easy to understand the religious feelings of the Efiks and of the Okoyong. The plane on which they met was very much a religious one. With such an intensely religious people only the power and the teaching of a new God had any chance at that time of altering the bloody ways in which they worshipped their old gods and which brought such cruelty into their lives. Mary Slessor was just as convinced as the other missionaries that to convert the Africans to following the teaching of Christ was the greatest gift which she could bring to them and she found many aspects of their own religion abominable. But at root, without the cruelty, magic, and superstition, Mary Slessor's belief in her God was the same as the Okoyong belief in an omnipotent, omnipresent, *Abassi*. This was the main reason why she began to fit so quickly into the Okoyong community. It was also the main reason why, over the years, she was able to develop such a deep understanding of the African mind.

There were other lesser reasons why Mary began to fit so well into the life of the tribe: the jumbled poverty in which she had lived as a child, and a highly developed sense of humour, of the ridiculous, and of fun, like theirs. Like them she could find great pleasure in the simplest things.

Although the proceedings were in many ways farcical she found great pleasure in the evening services which she now began to hold in both Ekenge and Ifako. Her services in each place were held in a chief's yard and the congregation spent as much time fending off children and livestock as they did in listening to her talks. In any case they found it very difficult to understand the new element which Jesus of Nazareth had introduced into religion and which, before them, the Jews, Greeks and Romans (whose religions at one time had also included human sacrifice), had found such difficulty in accepting; which indeed few men have ever fully accepted. God was not jealous and vindictive but loving and forgiving? He wanted to see a kingdom of peace, justice, and brotherhood on Earth? All men — even women and slaves — were equal in the sight of God and must be loved? It was all much too confusing for them.

But there was one part of the proceedings which they really did enjoy. 'The singing is of the simplest kind but it is a great attraction and they are loath to let us go even when the sun is setting.' Mary had translated some rousing English hymns into good rousing Efik, and for some reason, perhaps because she was homesick, or perhaps because to begin with it did not much matter what the tune was, she set these to good rousing Scottish tunes. This is how 'Sweet Rothesay Bay', 'The Rowan Tree', and 'Scots Wha Hae' came to be sung in the forest in several different keys and to the accompaniment of a drum or two and Mary and the children (and anyone else who could snatch one) on tambourines.

Mary Kingsley described the first attempts of forest congregations at singing European tunes as being like frantic braying: 'Never noticed mission had donkey . . . but they have and its off in an epileptic fit . . . Oh! . . . It's morning service!' At Ekenge, the Okoyong had loud, deep, voices and they were enjoying themselves. People for miles around would have known that powerful 'devil-making' was going on and would have been careful to keep away.

During September Mary had several bouts of fever but she managed to shake them off without having to go back to Creek Town. School settled down to never less than a hundred children in the daytime and thirty adults in the evenings at both Ekenge and Ifako. When school ended towards sunset, more people packed into the yards at both places for the singing round the fires and torches which blazed and smoked to keep away the mosquitoes. Then on the way home with her escort, Mary watched the fireflies dancing in the clearings. If only she could persuade Edem to get his people to build her a hut where she could live away from his drunken orgies she was beginning to think that she could be happy with her tribe. But Edem still put her off with excuses, and the thought that perhaps the people would never accept her and that she would have to trail back defeated to Creek Town, worried her. Eme kept telling her to be patient. She was sure that one day the tribe would accept Mary. It would just take time.

Meanwhile Mary and Edem were beginning to understand

and to respect each other. She hated his drunken bouts and lectured him on them even more severely than she lectured the rest of the tribe. When he was in a drunken rage and Eme was having extra trouble in protecting his wives from him Mary now began to help her. Soon the wives became used to the spectacle of the small white woman fuming at their chief and shoving him away from them. Next day he sometimes seemed to be grateful to her and sometimes he sulked. But gradually a friendship was building up between the Okoyong chief and the Scottish missionary.

The first time Mary noticed it was when he saved her life on the night when the tribe's 'Amazons' invaded the town. These were bands of women warriors, all born in the same year, who did not merely drag away the dead and wounded but themselves fought in battle. They may have had some religious significance, for Egbo gave them special protection and in consequence the towns and villages were afraid of them. When there was no fighting to be done they descended in force on these communities, ate, danced, and drank, at their expense; and then moved on leaving the women terrified and the men exhausted. One of these bands had heard about the white woman at Ekenge. White women were rich; they would get dash (presents) from the white woman.

When Edem's lookouts warned him that the Amazons were on their way, he told Mary to stay in his yard and placed his own bodyguard on the gate to keep the women out. They arrived at night, shooting off their guns, shouting, and waving swords and torches, their naked bodies covered with designs done in yellow chalk. They demanded to see the white woman. She must give them dash. Mary would have gone out and faced them. But Eme had arrived by now and, being twice Mary's size, had no difficulty in showing her that out she was definitely not going to go.

The Amazons were furious with Edem and threatened to break in and take his missionary. But he pacified them with a gift of rum and they went off to find other amusements. Edem and his men stayed sober and guarded the gate all night. Mary was most impressed.

Although chiefs from other places which were friendly to Ekenge and Ifako had been coming to see Mary and to invite her to visit their communities, Edem was against her making any long journeys. All paths were dangerous, he said. Mary took his advice until a delegation came from a village a day's march away on the Cross River side of the forest to tell her that their chief was dying and to ask her to come and cure him. They were poor people but they had brought her dash of four brass rods and a bottle of gin to persuade her to go with them. Mary asked what the bad thing was which was killing their chief but she could get no sense out of them about it. All they knew was that she could cure him by her medicine: a simple faith which she did not share.

Edem and Eme were entirely against her making the journey. She would have to cross several creeks and some of the paths were swampy. And if she failed to cure the chief there would be uproar; accusations and counter-accusations of *ifot* would fly, and in order to save themselves some of the people might accuse her and if they did she would be poisoned.

But the delegation were people who were close to the chief and who were obviously afraid that when he died they would die too. So Mary asked for time to consider the problem, prayed about it, and decided that she must go. Edem however refused to let her do so until the village sent a proper escort of warriors to guard her on the journey. The delegation promised that they would come back with one the following morning.

It was raining heavily when the women of the delegation arrived next day with the escort, and it went on raining. For what was probably the last time in the forests, Miss Slessor was dressed in the proper mission uniform and carrying an umbrella. First the umbrella caught in the bushes and ripped. Mary threw it away. Her helmet fell off soon afterwards and was abandoned. What with the mud and the wading her long skirt was slowing her and everybody else down. She took it off and one of the women put it in the calabash which she was carrying on her head. Next Mary's boots which were soaking and heavy with mud also went into a calabash along with her stockings, and a barefoot, bareheaded Miss Slessor in a knee length petticoat found that she could now keep up with the rest. In later years people criticised Mary for going barefoot and bareheaded and wearing very little. But on this journey she proved that Victorian paraphernalia had no place in the bush.

At the village, she found the people keyed up for the killing which would follow the chief's death. They seemed to have accepted that he was going to die and many of them with him. Mary was very much a last resort.

The chief was barely conscious. She made his wives take away the charms and sacrificed chickens from round his bed and by doing so laid herself open to charges of killing him. Strangely enough she never reported what was wrong with him, or if she did then the information has been lost. She gave him medicine and spent a sleepless night wrapped in a filthy blanket beside one of the fires in his yard, watched by his bodyguard and his wives. The question in all their minds, including Mary's, was 'By this time tomorrow will I too be dead?'

But in the morning the chief's condition had improved and Mary made some soup for him and dosed him again. In a few days he was out of danger. The people were amazed. Mary's medicine beat all medicine. Much to her embarrassment his senior wives, some of whom would certainly have been killed, came weeping and knelt in front of her. They told her that since she had saved their lives they would always be her children and she their mother. All the people announced that they wanted 'God' and 'Book' and she promised to try to find an African teacher for them.

She had a large escort back to Ekenge and she had to wait at each of the two villages through which they had to pass while the people were told about the wonders of the white Ma. She had great power. They had seen it and they knew. One of the villages had not been too keen on letting her pass through on her out-ward journey because they thought she might upset the spirits. But now both villages welcomed her and said they too would be her children and she promised to be their mother.

When she got back to Ekenge Mary had a bout of fever which took her several days to shake off. Meanwhile word about the wonderful powers of the white Ma went out all over the Okoyong territory. She was going to bring big new protection for the tribe. So now Mary began to be accepted not only by Ekenge and Ifako and the chiefs who had visited her there, but by all the Okoyong.

Living at Ekenge however was like sitting on a case of dynamite while drunks pottered round lighting matches. Edem went down with a painful abscess on his back. When Mary's poultices had no effect on it he called in the witchdoctor who produced a bag of nails, gunpowder, shot, eggshells, and other odds and ends out of the abscess and declared that some of his women were operating witchcraft against him. Soon a number of women both slave and free were chained to posts in his yard pending a decision on which of them should be forced to take the poison bean.

Mary argued but neither Edem or Eme would listen. The pain was even worse and the witchdoctor had taken an even bigger crop of devil-things out of the abscess.

In the end Edem got so angry with Mary that he ordered his slaves to carry him to one of his farms, took his prisoners with him, and put a guard on her to prevent her from following him.

Then somebody told her that the African missionary at Adiabo had a good charm for curing this bad thing and Mary sent a message asking him to come up and treat Edem. Unfortunately the messenger told the missionary that somebody's soul was troubling the chief and, since he was an Efik and witchcraft was clearly in the air, he decided it would be wiser not to get involved. His sister however decided to take the risk and her poultices succeeded where Mary's had failed.

When Mary questioned Edem about the prisoners he assured her that they had all been released. But when she persisted he said that nobody had been hurt. One worthlesss slave woman had been sold to the Inokon, that was all. He did not say that the Inokon were cannibals. But Mary knew that already and relations between Edem and his missionary were distinctly strained for a time.

The 'smokes' came and went. A powerful chief from across the Okoyong territory – whom Edem described as 'savage' – came to visit her with a large group of his warriors and they carried off a man from a village which was under Edem's protection while on their way home. Ekenge and Ifako prepared to go to war, school and services stopped, and Mary had to make a long journey to plead with the other chief for the man's release, obtained it, and restored what in Okoyong terms passed for peace.

In the Scotland of Mary's childhood New Year had been a greater festival than Christmas. Families and friends made a special effort to get together to see the old year out and the new year in. On December 31st 1888 Mary felt especially lonely. She had been with the tribe now, living in Edem's yard, for nearly five months. School had made progress and they still sang her hymns with grisly gusto. But she was depressed and dissatisfied with how little success she was having with converting the tribe. As if to excuse herself she wrote in a report to the mission, 'It will be the truest economy to husband my strength for the house-building. I am entering on the third year of my term and I am not as strong as I was three years ago'.

There was still, however, no sign that the Okoyong were ever going to build her a house. One day they seemed to accept her and the next she seemed to be a stranger again.

She encouraged herself by writing: 'Christ was never in a hurry. There was no rushing forward, no anticipating, no fretting over what might be. Every day's duties were done as the day brought them and the rest was left to God . . . There is a perpetual Spring: a Spring down here for the body and one coming on for the whole man. We are journeying on towards fullness of life not towards death. We are journeying towards the East and the sunrise not towards night.'

Then one morning at the beginning of the new year Edem sent for her. She found a crowd of people on her land clearing away the trees and bushes. Edem told her that they were going to build her the finest house Ekenge had ever seen.

Now she knew that, at last, she belonged to the Okoyong.

Ekenge: The house Charles Ovens built for Mary, who can just be seen at the window

10. PEACEMAKER

For the next few weeks Mary was, 'architect, clerk of works and chief labourer'. Because at this time Calabar wood was thought to be either too soft to last or too hard to saw, the mission still imported frame houses, and Mary was hoping that soon it would be safe for a carpenter to come up from Duke Town and put one up for her. Meanwhile she would have her huts and store sheds round three sides of a square and leave the other side for the frame house. She wanted a kitchen-cum-living room, a room for herself, one for the boys, and one for the girls. So she measured out four huts each twelve paces long and six wide.

The Cross River tribes made their huts by digging in thick branches with forked tops as the main central supports and shorter ones as side and corner supports. To these they lashed a framework of thinner branches, piled mats woven from palm leaves on the frame and lashed them down to form the thatch, and then lashed branches down over them to stop them blowing away. So that the roof came right out over the walls to make a shady verandah, they built them a pace or so inside the line of the side supports. The walls were of wattle and clay: two rows of sticks through which thin branches were laced and then clay packed through them. The weaving of the mats and the 'mudding' of the walls was women's work and they also made clay benches to support the foot of the walls and provide places for sitting and sleeping. The men built the framework.

The building of Mary's huts was a great event for the village. Up to now she, with her dispensary and school, had been doing things for them. Now they were doing something for her. So many people arrived to lend a hand or to give advice that for the first few days the site was considerably overcrowded. But because it was community work in which she shared it brought her closer to the people and confirmed her acceptance by the tribe.

When the tallest of the men, standing on each other's shoulders, had finished building the framework, Edem ordered fires to be lit to drive out the insect life from the branches and dry out the sap. The fires were to burn all night and Mary was a little worried that the frames too might go up in smoke. But Edem assured her that the slaves who were going to keep the fires burning would also keep them under control.

Mary helped with weaving the mats and mudding the walls and making the clay benches and other furniture. Because of a shortage of nails and tools it was easier to make it from clay which was also proof against the ravages of the white ants. The women built a clay fireplace in the living room for her and a clay sideboard which had hollows scooped out of the top to fit plates, saucers, and cups. This was the most important piece and the women took great care over it. They stained it with vegetable dye and polished it until it shone. They also made her a special table for her sewing machine. Unfortunately this had rusted up solid during the rains but she intended to take it back to Duke Town for repair.

When everything was finished and her belongings had been moved in, everybody had to come and admire the final result of their work. Mary was delighted and called the huts 'my caravan'. To the pride of ownership was added the pride of achievement. It was at Ekenge that she learned to be not only a builder of bridges between sections of the human race, but also a builder of huts. To get away at last from Edem's orgies seemed like heaven. She soon found however that cows, sheep, and other livestock took the open end of her yard as an invitation to come into the shade and she had to build a fence across it to keep them out.

To prevent Ifako from feeling neglected she had decided to build her church-cum-school there. But its chiefs seemed to have lost interest in her affairs. Then one morning a young freeman came to tell her that they wanted to see her. She was surprised to find her site at Ifako already cleared, branches and clay piled on it, and a large number of people waiting to start work on the building. Since it was to be a sacred place no slaves, they told her, would be allowed to work on it.

After consulting the chiefs, she decided that the building should be thirty paces long and twenty-five wide and that two huts should be attached to it for her to live in when necessary. Over a thousand mats would be needed for the roof so she asked a man who had Okoyong blood and could therefore risk trading with the tribe to take a note to King Eyo asking him to help out by sending mats up to the Ekenge landing place. Eyo agreed, and for several days lines of free women walked the six miles to the river and then walked back with piles of the mats balanced on their heads. When the roof was on, the women pounded and smoothed the floor, made and polished benches across the building for the congregation, and stained and polished the walls.

Neither Mary nor the Okoyong had ever built a church before and they were delighted with it. Of course it had no doors or windows but nobody worried about that.

When Hugh Goldie had heard that Eyo was sending up mats, he asked for boxes of second-hand clothes from Scotland to be taken up with them. The boxes, Mary found, were filled with children's clothes. They gave her an idea: she would open the church with a children's service. She knew that the tribes enjoyed dressing up for ceremonies: the men taking part in their Egbo processions wore elaborate masks, turbans, feather headdresses, and silk jackets trimmed with ribbons. The children would dress up for the service.

The parents of Ekenge and Ifako were perhaps disappointed that only the children could dress up but they supported the idea enthusiastically. Mary shared out the clothes between the two communities and when they ran out helped the women to sew simple smocks for any other children who wanted them.

When the great day came the parents were mostly 'dressed in their own clean skin', but 'Each child was radiant in some sort of garment. We made a happy and proud company . . . and certainly a magnificent show of colour . . . I think it was the best show of their appreciation of the gifts that not one of them was unwashed . . . To most of them it was their first experience in the shape of covering and to most of them it was not less a novel experience to be clean . . . Indeed I don't know whether the mothers or the children were the most proud; for every mother who had an adornment added it to the rest; for all matted hair was cut or shaved off and all sores were dressed and clean, making the children look as different from what they had been as possible.'

Probably the one who was most proud was Mary herself. For even the sores were 'dressed and clean', a situation which she had been trying to bring about for months. Fancy dress had its advantages.

Now that she was accepted by both communities, Mary decided that it was time to move on from 'God' and 'Book' to 'Trade'. 'Several chiefs have expressed a desire to have glass windows since they saw my poor little sash and everything I have they declare they must get. The clock and the organ and the sewing machine they can't get tired of. The same people come and wonder and admire over and over again, and they bring people from far and near to see.'

She saw clearly that as long as the menfolk had only drink, fighting, and sex on their minds, she was unlikely to be able to lead them towards a better way of life. By encouraging them to get, by trading, the type of goods which she had she could raise their standard of living and eventually, she hoped, break down their isolation. And if they could be persuaded to go to Creek Town to see the way in which the Efik now lived this would be an even better encouragement to them to change their own ways. But when she suggested to the chiefs that they should begin trading with the Efiks, they laughed and replied, 'We do, Ma, we trade in heads!'

To get them to risk a journey to Creek Town was clearly going to take time. Meanwhile she sent messages to some of her Efik trader friends asking them to bring goods like pots and pans, mirrors, clocks, tools, chinaware, cloth and other useful articles to trade for the Okoyong farm produce which she assured them was good. She assured the traders too that they would be under her protection and quite safe.

The replies were explicit but disappointing. She had to be joking. On no account would any of her friends risk their lives by coming within a mile of the Okoyong. It was one thing for a few 'small' men of Okoyong blood to trade gin and rum and guns to them. It was well-known that they had a craving for all three. But legitimate trade was not possible.

Mary wrote home sadly to a friend: 'Calabar people are so frightened of them [Okoyong] that to ask any of them to come to see us is to bring a volley of abuse or laughter down on your head. They would as soon think of going to the moon as going to Okoyong.'

But Mary was not in the habit of giving up, so now she wrote to King Eyo. He had often agreed with her that the old tribal quarrelling was outdated and a menace to the prosperity of the area. Now was his chance to help her work against it. Would he send a formal invitation to the Okoyong chiefs of Ekenge and

Ifako to visit him and hold a trade palaver, and at the same time give them a guarantee that they would not be harmed? She would lead the Okoyong delegation herself.

Eyo promptly sent the invitation. But the Okoyong chiefs, while agreeing that it was a good idea, said that they would need time to discuss such a dangerous thing. Mary had to leave it at that for the time being.

She sent to Hugh Goldie for more boxes of clothes and worked hard at persuading the mothers to wash and brush up their children every Sunday to go to church, and showed them how to mend the clothes which she had given them.

The next step was to work on the women. Many already wore a 'Mother Hubbard' smock like hers when they felt like it. This was loose to let air flow round the body and rather like a long sack tied round the middle. Mary's own ones were much patched and darned and faded. Now she selected a smart blouse and skirt for herself from the boxes, for her own clothes had gone mouldy in the rains, and distributed the rest of the women's clothes among the mothers of the children.

How about the mothers being as smartly turned out for church as the children? Soon the Sabbath turnout for church was even more colourful. It was not that Mary now gave two hoots for nakedness. 'Clothes', she wrote 'never fail to give self-respect.' The sooner she could get the Okoyong women to stop looking on themselves as slaves, playthings and breeding mares, and wean them away from the gin, the sooner life would improve for them and for their children.

Not everyone would have agreed with her about the clothes, but then not everyone had ever attempted what she was attempting. And not one in a hundred of the critics would have gone naked themselves. Nakedness was good enough for blacks but not for whites.

The little family had settled down in their new house. Janie was now seven and not quite so wild, Annie was toddling, and to Okon and Ekim Mary had added another boy, probably to save him from starvation. At meal times they all squatted on the floor round the cooking pot with Mary and ate with their fingers African-fashion.

Meanwhile Mary worked away at the alcohol problem. Did the Okoyong really think it was sensible to be fuddled half their lives? Did they really enjoy feeling ill every morning? She was making some progress with the women, but the men were a

E

more difficult problem, although one lesser chief did come to her and boast that he had not been drunk for three whole days.

She knew that she would make no real progress until she had got them trading, and returned to the attack about this with Edem. As usual he put her off with excuses, so she simply settled down to pester him and the other chiefs as well. They endured this for a time and then announced grimly, as men who had made the most momentous decision of their lives, that they had borrowed a canoe from a 'small' trader, collected some of their best produce, and tomorrow they would load it and be ready to go.

Next morning after she had fed the children Mary set out for the landing-place with Edem. When they arrived the canoe was already piled high with yams, palm kernels, maize and a sample barrel of palm oil.

A big crowd had gathered at the landing-beach, most of whom were convinced of course that the chiefs were going to their deaths. Tearful farewells were said and, amid wailing, the canoe was pushed off the mud before the delegation embarked. But the Okoyong were farmers and warriors and not boatmen, and the canoe promptly turned on its side and sank.

Oh well. The River God was against the journey. They could not go against the River God.

Mary said it was nothing to do with the River God. They did not know how to load a canoe. She got hold of the 'small' trader and asked him if he had a bigger canoe. He had. Right! He must get it . . . quick . . . and supervise the loading of it.

The small canoe was hauled up, the produce was rescued, the big one loaded, and the chiefs went back to be embraced by their wives. Mary shouted to them to hurry up since the tide would soon be turning. They came out from the crowd, but now they were armed to the teeth.

No, oh no! said Mary. This was a peaceful trade delegation not a military expedition – no arms were to be carried.

Not carry arms? An Okoyong never went without his arms. What sort of men did she think they were? How could they defend themselves if they were attacked?

Mary explained patiently that they would not be attacked, and in any case they would not be able to defend themselves against the whole of Creek Town.

No, but they could die fighting in proper Okoyong manner.

Mary said there was no question of dying or fighting. King

Eyo was her friend. He had promised they would not be harmed. Did they think she would be asking them to go with her if they would be harmed? Did they not trust her?

Yes, they did, but she was not King Eyo and his Efiks.

They argued for nearly an hour, and then Mary noticed that half the delegation was missing. Where were the other brave heroes she asked? This brought a laugh from those who were not going anyway. But only Edem and one other chief would get into the canoe with her.

With only three passengers the trim of the canoe was wrong and the load had to be shifted. Mary was having great difficulty in keeping her temper and when, as the bags were moved, she saw swords hidden underneath, she exploded in good old-time 'Carrots' rage.

They were old women . . . (and one sword whistled into the crowd) . . . they were cowards! . . . (another sword) . . . imbeciles! . . . (another sword) . . . babies! The crowd scattered right and left until she ran out of swords and of epithets. But three of the chiefs did not run far enough. She saw them, yanked her skirt up above her knees, jumped out of the canoe, grabbed them, and pushed them forward ordering them to get in.

So five chiefs, and a missionary with a wet skirt, set out for Creek Town.

King Eyo did her proud. He was courteous and he was kindness itself. He praised their farm produce. He pronounced that their palm oil was of good quality. He was very generous when it came to bartering. He took the Okoyong chiefs on a tour of Creek Town and showed them over his own house and took them into his storeroom where goods of all kinds were piled.

Hugh Goldie invited them to evening service and the King gave an address. He took for his text 'To give light to them that sit in darkness and in the shadow of death; to guide our feet into the way of peace.'

The King for his part made arrangements for his traders to call regularly at Ekenge landing-place, and agreed to provide the Okoyong with canoes until they could get some of their own.

The Okoyong on their part agreed not to raid Calabar farms in future, and not attack Efiks travelling along their borders. Edem explained that he could only speak for the chiefs of the area round Ekenge and Ifako, but he was sure that the rest would also want to trade once they saw the goods which the delegation were taking back with them.

Mary took the chance to visit Duke Town and make an oral report to her colleagues. She told them that it was now 'quite safe' for them to visit her at Ekenge. There was, however, no great rush among the missionaries to do so.

When she returned with the chiefs there was an even bigger crowd to welcome them at the landing-place, for the big talk-drums, the bush telegraph, had beaten out the news that they were on the way back. These drums had a range of about seven miles depending on their size and, by relaying simple messages from one to the next, they could cover over a hundred miles.

The chiefs were embraced by their wives. The goods were unloaded and admired. A long procession of Okoyong marched back down the path, and as they went they talked of the intrepid five who had braved the dangers of Creek Town, and of their wonderful Ma who had arranged it all.

Back in Ekenge she gave the children presents from Duke Town and sat with them and told them the story of the journey and answered their questions.

In the yards of each of the five chiefs who had gone with her, fires blazed until long after midnight, as they too told their stories to their people and answered question after question about Creek Town and the house of the great King.

At sunrise Mary, who had slept late for once, was wakened by a babble of voices and by spades thumping into the hard ground. She went out to find a chief giving orders to a crowd of men, and asked him whatever was the matter. Instead of answering he shouted to the men to listen and began a speech in praise of her. Even King Eyo had listened to her, and all men had honoured her. It was good for them to have her among them, and they must do everything in their power to deserve this honour. He had seen how the houses were built in Creek Town. Now they would build their Mother a house which was really worthy of her.

It was at this time that the Okoyong began to call her '*Ma Akamba*'.

When Mary's first report from Ekenge appeared in the *Missionary Record* in March 1899, a carpenter called Charles Ovens was back home in Edinburgh on holiday from America. The holiday was coming to an end and when he went to say goodbye to an old lady who was a friend of the family, she showed him the part of Mary's report about the church at Ifako: 'It is a beautiful building though neither doors nor windows are put in as we are waiting for a carpenter . . . and if only there were a house built any other agent could come and take up the work if I fail'.

The old lady said to Ovens that in Mary there was a brave lassie if ever there was one. He was a carpenter. What did he want to go back to America for? Why wouldn't he go to Calabar and help the Lord's work and this brave lassie?

Ovens had knocked about the world a good deal but as a young man he too had wanted to be a missionary. Now he read Mary's report and the comments of the editor on the past history of the Okoyong, decided that she was indeed a brave lassie, got some references from ministers who knew him, applied to the Foreign Missions' Board, was accepted, changed the labels on his luggage, and sailed for Calabar.

Meanwhile Mary, who had been under great strain for months, now took a bad bout of fever and collapsed. When she had partly recovered she tried to go on working but after a few days had to give in and go back down river with her 'family' for a complete rest. She must have been very ill and life in the primitive township sheer hell before she would have decided to leave her tribe just when she was beginning to make progress with them.

She recovered quickly at Duke Town and while she was convalescent she met a new recruit called Charles Morrison. He had joined the mission to take over the training of the African teachers. He wrote poetry and was working on a novel at this time. He seems to have been rather a delicate, sensitive, man and a loner like Mary.

The two loners got on well together. They both loved books. And when Mary went back to Ekenge they wrote to each other.

She wrote that she 'got a great welcome' from the Okoyong. The return of any valued member of a tribe to a township usually creates quite a celebration. None of Mary's descriptions of her welcomes have survived but one of James Luke's has: '. . . We found a seething mass of excited and joyous people . . . Through the midst of a happy, dancing, cheering, crowd we were led to a palaver shed.'

The house had made little progress in her absence. It was to be built on the lines of the Old Town house but the Okoyong had never built a two-storey house before. It really needed the attentions of a skilled carpenter for as yet Mary could not cope with putting in doors and windows and making stairways. This

Mary with Mr Ovens and Mr Bishop

deficiency in her missionary skills was however about to be removed: the man who would teach her had arrived at Duke Town.

Charles Ovens breezed into the mission. During the weeks in which he worked at Duke Town before going up to Ekenge he could talk about nothing but the wonders of America. When he came back from Ekenge he could talk about nothing but the Okoyong and the wonders of Miss Slessor. It is a tribute to his own toughness and adaptability that after only a few weeks in the mission he was able to stand up to the extraordinary world, part nightmare, part fairy tale, part knock-about farce, which was life with the Okoyong.

Photographs show him to have been a stocky, bearded man, not much taller than Mary herself, who favoured a round, flat-topped, wide-brimmed hat rather than a sun helmet. Like Mary he had a strong sense of humour, a habit of taking life as it came, and a good singing voice. He was an ideal companion for her among the rough, volatile, people of Ekenge and just the tonic which she needed as her strength gradually ebbed away and her need for an extended rest became more and more obvious.

Mary moved the boys out of their hut to accommodate Charles Ovens and cleared one of the store sheds for them. On the evening of his arrival they sat round a fire in her yard and sang all the old Scots songs which they could remember. The Okoyong crowded round to listen to 'Loch Lomond', 'The Eriskay Love Lilt' and 'Auld Lang Syne'. Mary said later that the tears were running down her cheeks at the end. The reaction of the Okoyong was summed up by Tom, who became Ovens' assistant: 'I don't like these songs. They make my heart big and my eyes water.' But since Mary and Ovens and Janie often sang together in the evenings and the people always came to listen perhaps they did like having their 'hearts big' after all.

Ovens would have been pleased to find that Janie spoke English fluently with a nice homely Scots accent, for of course he spoke no Efik at this time. She became his interpreter when he was working at Ifako and Mary was busy with her dispensary and other work.

If he had any reservations about Mary's 'beautiful building' he kept them to himself, and with the Okoyong and Mary herself helping, both the church and her house made good progress.

His work and the visit of the chiefs to Creek Town triggered off a spate of house building in the area which pleased Mary because it kept the men off the drinking and fighting. Then, just as she seemed to be making real progress at last, disaster struck.

Etim, who was Edem's eldest son, was one of the men caught up in the house building. He was out in the forest cutting the main supports for his new roof when a heavy branch fell and struck him on the back of the head and neck. Boys came running to tell Edem and Mary, who was working with Charles Ovens at the time.

When they got to Etim he was unconscious and Ovens improvised a stretcher. He could not understand why everybody, including Mary, looked as if the end of the world was at hand until she explained to him that, if Etim died, his death would most certainly be attributed to someone using witchcraft against him, and torture, poison bean trials and strangling would follow unless she could find some way of preventing it.

When Etim recovered consciousness she found that his spine had been damaged and that he was paralysed from the waist down. She nursed him for nearly a fortnight while he drifted in and out of consciousness and the people became more and more excited. Accusations and counter-accusations of witchcraft multiplied, and Edem drowned his sorrows, and his people their fears, in gin.

Mary must have realised that Etim was beyond help, for she made no effort to bring up a doctor from Duke Town. She knew that this would be merely to risk the stranger's life since he would certainly fail to cure Etim, and might then be blamed for his death. She warned Ovens not to go out into the village except with her because the people were on the verge of panic and anything could happen.

Once again Edem returned to the ways of his ancestors. One morning Mary found Etim propped up with his father shouting into one ear, and his uncle Ekpenyong into the other, while a witchdoctor blew smoke and pepper into his nostrils to bring him round, and his mother and the other wives screamed and beat drums to drive away the evil spirits. In the middle of these activities the patient died. Immediately the witchdoctor announced that the village near which Etim had been working had been responsible for the witchcraft which had caused his death, and Edem's warriors rushed off to get prisoners from it.

Meanwhile Mary undertook to see that Etim was dressed in a style befitting his rank for his entry into the spirit world. She dressed the body in a shirt with collar and tie and a suit from one of the boxes of clothes, wound a length of fine silk round the waist as a cummerbund and another piece round the head under a tall black top hat to which she added red and blue plumes. Edem's wives then placed the body in an armchair in their yard under a large striped umbrella. They tied the whip and silver-mounted stick of a chief to his hands, and Mary placed a mirror in front of him so that he could see that he had been dressed in proper style.

She explained to the mystified Ovens that she was hoping to prevent the killing of a 'retinue' to go with Etim into the spirit world, by making certain in other ways that he would be accepted as the son of a chief even without a retinue.

The chief's wives now placed, on a table beside his body, the skulls of enemies whom Etim had killed in battle, and his swords and guns and other prized possessions to be buried with him under the floor of his hut, as was customary.

Etim's mother had collapsed with grief, but Edem came and viewed the body. He seemed to be satisfied with these preliminary arrangements, but Mary was left in no doubt that he regarded them merely as a preliminary. The people were then admitted to the yard, and to Mary's relief, were clearly most impressed. They could never have seen such a beautiful corpse before.

Mary remembered that Hope Waddell in the early days in Calabar had used a magic lantern show to damp down an explosive situation. So she sent Tom, Ovens' assistant, off to Creek Town with a note asking for the lantern and slides to be sent up.

Now the dirges for the dead man began and Edem's warriors returned with their prisoners.

Ovens wrote: '. . . The yelling seemed to me like fiends. Then there are about fifty men all armed with swords and guns. There are twelve people in chains, three mothers with infants and some young men brought from the next village. If Miss Slessor or I leave them they will be put to death.'

Mary asked him to make a coffin for Etim as part of her plan to make the funeral as impressive as possible and a retinue unneccessary. But then they saw a witchdoctor preparing the poison beans in the yard where the prisoners were chained.

Ovens wrote: 'We saw them begin to ground the beans so Miss Slessor told them that we would not let them do what they proposed. By this time they were nearly all drunk and running about with their guns loaded and swords in their hands. However they did not frighten us, we sat up night and day till we got all the prisoners free. It was a terrible time for us. We had the last two prisoners in our hut for 21 days.'

Mary took the night watches and Ovens took the day. Edem was drunk most of the time and so furious with her that he refused to listen to any arguments.

Chiefs from outlying areas were now beginning to arrive with their warriors for the funeral and they were impatient to get on with the celebrations. Already there was 'the usual uproar' and things were getting 'critical'. It would have begun to look as if she must give way or face the likelihood of sudden death for both herself and Ovens. The number of impatient, drunken warriors was increasing all the time and any one of them, in a fit of rage, could put an end to the interfering white woman with a slash of the sword in his hand or pressure on a trigger.

In one shouting, screaming palaver the chiefs claimed that if none of the prisoners were guilty then the poison bean would not hurt them. And at this point Mary's knowledge of native customs came to the rescue. If people were guilty then if they took the *mbiam* oath, that would kill them. The chiefs agreed that this was so. Very well, they would accept that all the prisoners should take the oath and, if guilty, die. Mary knew that unlike the *esere* mixture the stinking *mbiam* liquid, which was spread on the lips and tongue before the oath was taken, was not poisonous.

All the prisoners except three took the oath, survived, and were released. Two of the others, a free man and a free woman, disappeared and Mary thought that they had been released too. Edem announced that the other, a slave woman, must die. Etim must have at least one slave to go with him into the spirit world.

When Mary refused to let him kill even a worthless slave woman he was almost frantic with rage, and threatened to drive her out of the town and burn her house and all her possessions. The slave woman herself was so terrified at all the yelling and sword-waving that she begged to be beheaded and have done with it. But Mary Slessor simply stood in front of the prisoner and refused to let anyone near her.

She would never be nearer a violent death than she was at this moment. Eme almost certainly saved her life by going forward and kneeling in front of Edem and pleading with him to let the slave be taken and locked up in Mary's yard. The woman was so loaded with chains that she could not possibly escape and a palaver could be held later to decide her fate.

By now, with the visiting chiefs joining in the threats against Mary, perhaps even a drunken Edem could see that he was in danger of losing his missionary, for he agreed. And Mary managed to avoid any definite decision about the prisoner until after the funeral.

Next day two missionaries arrived from Duke Town with the magic lantern and the Okoyong saw pictures of cities and ships and horses and carriages which they had never dreamt existed. They called the horses 'the white man's cows' and the carriages 'the white man's cowsheds'. Such an amazing, wonderful event more than compensated for the lack of a retinue and only a cow was sacrificed to go with Etim.

After the two missionaries returned to Calabar Mary found that the other two prisoners had not in fact been released.

She managed to get the man released immediately and the free woman moved into her yard. It was these two women, one free, one slave, whom Ovens referred to as being with them for twenty-one days before Mary finally had them freed.

Meanwhile, after the funeral, the warriors of two of the visiting houses started to fight against each other on their way home. Several men were killed and wounded, a village was destroyed, and the Egbo Council for the whole of the Okoyong tribe had to be called in. This created panic among the Ekenge slaves. They packed into Mary's yard for sanctuary as soon as they heard the 'Big Egbo' drum. The Egbo men however made no attempt to enter Mary's sacred ground and, after a few hours, withdrew from Ekenge. But they shot or beheaded any people they could find from the village accused of bewitching Etim and slaughtered its livestock. Edem's warriors too were caught up in the prevailing lust for blood and, during the next few days, shot down any strangers, men or women, whom they found in the bush. Men with whom, before Etim's death, Mary had been laughing and joking turned overnight into manic killers. That the Lord should so protect her that these men put up with her interfering ways was, to Mary, a never-ending source of wonder.

It was two months before the tribe settled down again and Ovens could get on with his work. No wonder that stories about Mary Slessor and her Okoyong took over from his stories about America.

In December 1889 Mary completed her four year term and
was due for leave in Scotland, but since nobody could be found
to take over from her she refused to go. She knew that the
Okoyong would go back completely to their old habits if they
were left to themselves for a year.

It was not surprising that none of her women colleagues were
anxious to take over, for to live as a primitive African was no
part of the duties of a female agent. Mary, as she put it, 'drudged
on'.

11. ROMANCE AND RECOGNITION

The Calabar mission had begun to make real progress at last. While its Miss Slessor was opening up the Okoyong territory it had established Ezekiel Jarret at Ikotana above Umon, James Luke at Emuramura, and John Gartshore even further up-river at Unwana nearly one hundred miles above Duke Town. But this advance was soon halted by death, sickness, and shortage of staff. Jarret died. Gartshore collapsed and was invalided home. Luke too collapsed and was sent home and forbidden to return for at least five years.

Dr Rae – the latest of a succession of medical missionaries the rest of whom had either died or been invalided home – wrote, 'An under-manned mission in such a climate means a high death rate.' And he underlined the accuracy of this statement by dying himself after only eighteen months in Calabar.

There was nobody to take over Unwana or Emuramura but Andrew Porteous took over Ikotana until he too died of fever.

Throughout 1890 Mary eked out her own failing strength by taking short rests at Duke Town or Creek Town. Sometimes she and the children arrived unexpectedly and there was no mission accommodation for them. But this did not worry her. Any hut would do.

At Duke Town she met Charles Morrison again. She had to spend several weeks there recovering from an especially bad bout of fever and for the first few weeks, while she was in hospital, he used to go and read to her. Their friendship grew. Perhaps she was thinking of him when she wrote, 'What a strange thing is sympathy. Undefinable, untranslateable, and yet the most real thing and the greatest power in human life. How strangely our souls leap out to other souls without our choosing or knowing the why. The man or woman who possesses this subtle gift of sympathy, possesses the most precious thing on earth.'

When she returned to Ekenge she had to add to her routine of

school, dispensary, and services, palavers which went on for
hours and sometimes for days. The chiefs had begun to make
regular visits to Creek Town and were seeing for themselves the
proper way to behave. Instead of fighting over their disputes
they now began to take them to her for arbitration. During all
the hours in which she had to sit listening to arguments about
witchcraft, wives, divorces, dowries, slaves, livestock and land,
she sustained herself by chewing home-made toffee and tried to
keep her patience by knitting. She called these informal tribal
courts her 'knitting palavers'.

She could no longer make long journeys so the tribe had to
come to her: 'Every chief, more or less, has been under my care,
or some of his people have been, and they have expressed in
various ways their appreciation of my services . . . No white
need fear to go anywhere now.' But Hugh Goldie was of the
opinion that 'Miss Slessor's influence over the Okoyong is hers
and hers alone.' And although Charles Ovens had nearly finished
her house and she had a proper guest room there is no record of
her having had any white visitors at this time.

Ovens himself went down with fever. He was too ill to travel
so Mary had to nurse him at Ekenge and this did not help her
own health.

Her letters gave her friends in Scotland little idea of the risks
which she was running with the Okoyong. But when Charles
Ovens went back to Duke Town to recuperate, his letters home
described their adventures together at Ekenge. One of his letters
was printed in the *Record*. It told how she had stopped a battle
by getting between the rival warriors and defying them to pass
her; how she disarmed drunken warriors who wandered into her
yard and, when in a temper, took them by the arm and slung
them out of it; how she slapped, like naughty children, chiefs
who hesitated to take her medicine. But, although his pictures of
life at Ekenge helped to make her famous in Scotland, they
hardly encouraged any of her colleagues to offer to replace her
until she recovered her health.

In April 1890 the Annual Report of the Women's Foreign
Missions Committee stated that: 'Miss Slessor has been labour-
ing at Okoyong with extraordinary courage and perseverance.'
In July Goldie was minuted as saying that only a man could
replace Mary at Ekenge and he asked for a volunteer from
Scotland who would not mind 'roughing it for a time'. But in
spite of this understatement nobody volunteered.

By October it was clear that Mary simply could not be allowed to work on and that she would have to take leave whether she liked it or not. Help came from a surprising source. A trained nurse called Margaret Dunlop who had looked after Mary at Duke Town offered to replace her at Ekenge. Margaret must have been a remarkably courageous young woman because she had only been about a year in Calabar, had no experience of out-station life, and had only begun to learn Efik. If the situation had not been so desperate the mission would never have considered her for such a post. It had decided that she would not be allowed to live alone with the Okoyong and to delay her transfer until a companion could be found to go with her. But this does not seem to have been explained to Mary. If she had known that her tribe were to be left with no missionary for months at a time she would almost certainly have refused to leave them.

In November Margaret went to live with Mary at Ekenge to get experience of the primitive life and to get to know the Okoyong. Edem and the other chiefs, who knew better than anyone just how ill their *Ma Akamba* was, promised to behave themselves and to help their new missionary.

Mary booked a passage home on the December steamer and was packed and ready to leave Ekenge when messengers came from an outlying House with a desperate plea for help. One of their young chiefs had shot away part of his hand and had died. His brother had blamed his death on the chief of a bigger House and had attacked and injured the man. Now there was to be a battle between the Houses which their small one would almost certainly lose. Would *Ma Akamba* please come and stop the battle?

Once again Mary found the simple faith of her people in her powers both flattering and embarrassing. Edem, Eme, and Margaret were in no doubt that her answer should be a quick 'No'. She would have to walk for at least six hours to get to the area, Eme said, and in her bad state she would never get there at all. But, once Mary had made sure that it was to be a real battle and not more of a war game, she decided that she must go to prevent villages from being destroyed and innocent people killed. Edem said that if she must go, he would give her an escort and the Egbo drum of the Ekenge branch to take her as far as the boundary with the next House. She could then ask for its drum and an escort to take her to the battle area. It would be dark before she got there and the drum would prevent her from being shot by mistake.

But the head of the next House refused to give her either drum or escort. He sent her a message to say that no battle was planned and that, even if there had been, a mere woman could not stop it. Mary sent back the reply that in judging the power of the woman he had clearly forgotten the power of the woman's God. She decided that, with the messengers to guide her, she would go on. She hoped that her lantern would show who she was and prevent her from being shot. Soon, for her, the circle of leaves which the lantern lit and the endless ribbon of path would have taken on an unreal quality as her legs grew weaker and weaker and her fevered eyes kept losing focus.

When she reached the first of the townships which was supposed to be going to war, it was in darkness and she thought that she had indeed come on a fool's errand. Then a group of warriors, stripped and painted for battle, seemed to materialise round her out of the ground. They gave her such a fright that she shouted at them. When they heard her voice they crowded round her and asked why she had come to them in the night. She told them she had come to stop them killing one another and demanded to be taken to their chiefs.

The chiefs agreed to postpone the battle to give her the chance to settle the dispute peacefully. She could have a hut to sleep in and they promised that their women would wake her at sunrise.

The women did indeed wake her as promised but the warriors had already left for the battle. The women showed her which path to take and begged her to 'Run, Ma!' It was however all she could do to walk. She heard the warriors moving in the bush, but when she called to them they ignored her. They belonged to the bigger House whose chief had been attacked and were in no mood for arbitration.

Eventually she came to the first village of the smaller House. Here a group of warriors who were also painted up for battle blocked her way. They ignored her greeting and she was walking straight at them when the chief whom she had cured after making her first long journey from Ekenge pushed his way through them and greeted her. Thanks to him she was able to arrange a palaver in which, after hours of argument, the smaller House agreed that their man had been in the wrong and to pay a fine. The bigger House demanded that part of the fine be paid immediately in gin. This too was agreed.

Since some of the warriors of both Houses were clearly itching to set about one another Mary tried to postpone the
payment. Once the gin circulated anything could happen. But
she was exhausted and nobody would listen to her. However the
cases had to be piled up for counting and at this point her knowledge of tribal custom came to the rescue once more. If the
clothes of an Egbo official were spread over any article to touch
it was held to be an attack on the official himself. If this worked
for Egbo it could work for *Abassi*. W P Livingstone wrote,
'Divesting herself of as many garments as possible she threw
them over the stuff.' Since by now Mary was known to wear
very little there cannot have been many garments but they were
enough. The warriors were furious but they dare not touch the cases.

It would have been an interesting scene: the sick, bedraggled,
presbyterian female agent facing up, half-dressed, to a crowd of
yelling, painted, warriors who could so easily have killed her and
taken their gin if, by now, she had not been as special to them as
the tallest of their tall trees and the most magic of their magic
groves. To be there defying them this sick woman must be
protected by the spirits and therefore no-one in his right senses
would attack her. No-one did. And no-one, in a world of cruelty
and of killing, ever would.

When eventually they had calmed down a little one of the
chiefs pointed out that it was customary to taste the gin to make
sure that it had not been watered. Mary had to agree that this
was indeed so. They could taste one bottle out of each case. She
may have lost one or two bottles, but at last all the cases had
been lifted on to heads and she had gone back with them to the
township where she had spent part of the night. There she had
another sleep and then, somehow, made her way back to
Ekenge.

The steamer had already arrived at Duke Town and Margaret
had sent her luggage down by the mission launch. Next day,
seen off by a large crowd of Okoyong, Mary set off for Duke
Town herself with Margaret.

There Charles Morrison asked Mary to marry him and she
agreed provided that he could join her at Ekenge. She explained
that this was the work which her God had chosen for her, and
that if Charles could not share it with her then no marriage was
possible. They decided therefore to keep their engagement secret
for the time being. But in Scotland she had her photograph taken
wearing his ring.

In January 1891 she landed with Janie at Plymouth so that she could go to Topsham to see the graves of her mother and sister. A doctor advised her not to risk the hard Scottish winter so she stayed in Devon until he decided that she was fit to travel. By then it was July.

In Scotland she stayed with a friend, Mrs McCrindle, at a country place near Edinburgh. Even by then she had not completely recovered. She complained of all the noise and bustle of the cities which she had to visit on the inevitable lecture tours: 'This country has too many things. It is always in a hurry. I lose my head.'

Thanks to Ovens and to the reports of other missionaries home on leave the name of Mary Slessor was now well-known in Scotland. People crowded to her lectures. But she hated all the publicity and fuss. She had not recovered her nerve on platforms and could often only manage a stilted address. She knew that her audiences were disappointed and became even more nervous.

In September she broke the news of her engagement to the Board and asked for Charles to be allowed to join her at Ekenge, pointing out that she could no longer continue to run the station alone. The Board was, to say the least of it, surprised. Morrison was only twenty-five and she was nearly old enough to be his mother. Was she really serious or was this merely the passing fancy of a middle-aged woman who was suddenly looking for a little ordinary happiness? Doctors had been worried about whether Morrison's health would stand up to the Calabar climate. The primitive life at Ekenge would probably kill him. On the other hand to struggle on alone would probably kill one of the Board's star missionaries. In the end it ruled that his work of training African teachers was too important for him to be spared from Duke Town until someone with equal qualifications could be found to replace him.

Mary wrote to Charles to give him the bad news that their marriage would have to wait. She wrote to a friend, 'If God does not send him up there he must do his work and I must do mine where we are placed. If he does not come, I must ask the Committee to give me someone, for it is impossible for me to work the station alone.'

The following month she wrote an appeal for an industrial training centre at Duke Town. She pointed out that young Edgerley, shortly before his death, had written that there was a

Mary wearing her engagement ring

need to provide employment for the young Africans whom the mission was educating. She went on: 'There is an idea around that our [Calabar] wood is unworkable. Would it be like God's ordinary way of working to make hundreds of miles of unworkable wood? . . . Our natives with a sixpenny matchet or an ordinary hatchet make canoes, paddles, doors, tables, seats, bedsteads, sofas etc . . . If we could teach the natives to manufacture . . . it would utilise the materials at our hands; it would elevate our people, and it would give a profit to the Church.'

She pointed out that there was a great demand now in Calabar for goods of all kinds. Tradesmen could be brought in as teachers and, 'Each tradesman could manage his own department, live in his own compound with his own men, influence them, educate them and have stated days on which he could accompany them either by boat or on foot to the villages and hamlets all round.'

For once the Mission Board acted promptly and the Hope Waddell Training Institute, which would train thousands of young Africans over the next sixty years, was the result.

In January 1892 Mary had a bad attack of influenza and the Board's doctors suggested that she should go south to Devon to recover from it. She could sail back to Calabar in February as scheduled but from Plymouth instead of from Liverpool. She took her mother's old sideboard back with her as a 'keepsake'.

She must have been glad to leave the cold rainy shores of Britain. She was fifteen years older now than the shy, tongue-tied, young woman who had first felt the warm breath of Africa on her cheek. She had heard men and women screaming as they were killed and women whimpering as they were raped. She had delivered babies and watched men, women, and children, die. She had nearly died twice herself and had known all the waking and sleeping nightmare of fever. But she knew now that she had within herself a power over the forest Africans which had been given to few white men and to even fewer women. She had become in fact what she had dreamed of being.

Over there in Africa was more fever and more pain and more fear; for the reputedly fearless Miss Slessor did not exist; she would have to have been an idiot. When a colleague had commented on her courage she had said: 'Courage is only the conquering of fear by faith.'

When she arrived back at Duke Town at the end of March

1892 she found that she had just missed seeing her friend King Eyo again. He had died on March 26th. Mrs Goldie, Mrs Cruikshank and Andrew Porteous had also died.

A Mr Deas was now at Ikotana and a Mr McKenzie at Unwana. McKenzie died just after Mary arrived and a Dr Fisher took over at Unwana. There was nobody at Emuramura where a huge cesspool swarming with mosquitoes near the village was making life almost unbearable.

The mission had placed an Efik teacher with the Akunakuna tribe and one with the Ebom, but after a few months once again tribal violence drove them out and they refused to return.

For the next ten years this would still be the pattern; fevers would disable or kill the mission's white staff, and violence would drive out its African staff. The overworked Scots who were left were sick men and women and the great dream of using Africans to bring Christianity to their fellow countrymen remained just that.

While she was getting acclimatised again before rejoining her wayward tribe, Mary had a few weeks at Duke Town with Charles Morrison. But he was ill with fever and in April the mission doctor ordered him home.

He wrote to Mary from Scotland that the Board's doctors had ruled that he must not return to Calabar, but must be posted to a country with a dry climate. Later he wrote to say that he had resigned from the Foreign Missions altogether.

He wandered off to America where he had relatives. There all his manuscripts were destroyed when the log cabin in which he was living caught fire. Soon afterwards Mary heard that he was dead.

She seemed completely to dismiss him from her mind. But during her 'gypsy' years which followed she gave or threw away or lost most of the few things which she possessed. Two of the half dozen keepsakes which she clung on to through all those years were the battered copies of *Eugene Aram* and *Sketches by Boz*, in each of which they had signed their names side by side. 'When you have a good thing or read a good thing or see a humorous thing and cannot share it, it is worse than bearing a trial alone.'

She would work alone, except for Jean, for the rest of her life. For the next twenty-three years no missionary would be found who could keep pace with the expendable Miss Slessor.

Meanwhile the Duke Town which Mary had known had

ceased to exist, for in 1891 the British had at last moved in and taken over the administration of the area. Civilisation backed by bullets and bayonets had arrived. The new consulate building and the new barracks where three hundred troops were stationed dominated the town. The stinking river front had been cleaned up, some of the narrow tracks had been widened into streets with proper drainage, and soon steam launches, each with thirty soldiers and a Maxim machinegun, would be patrolling the rivers.

Sir Claude Macdonald, the new Consul-General, had been stationed at Duke Town for over a year and he of course had heard all about Mary Slessor and her adventures with the Okoyong. He was in process of appointing vice-consuls to supervise the running of the native courts in the various parts of his territory and he asked Mary if she thought that the Okoyong were ready to receive one. She quickly assured him that they very definitely were not, whereupon, to her amazement, he offered her the post. An ex-mill-lassie a British vice-consul? It would have appealed to her sense of humour but at the same time she would have been highly honoured.

She would have wanted to know how much interference she would have to put up with from officialdom and whether she would still be able to tackle her problems in her own way. Macdonald would have been able to reassure her on this point because his instructions were, 'It is not advisable that you should interfere unduly with tribal government, the chiefs should continue to rule their subjects and to administer justice to them, but you should keep a constant watch to prevent injustice and to check abuses.'

At first her colleagues were none too keen on a lady missionary sitting in judgement on all the sordid affairs of a misbehaving tribe. But she was in the middle of them anyway and finally they agreed. So it was Vice-Consul Miss Slessor who went home to her tribe. She does not seem to have realised it, but she was in fact the first woman to be appointed to such a post in the whole of the British Empire.

She wrote that once more she 'got a great welcome'. It would have been more of a riot than ever for the Okoyong may have been afraid that she was never coming back. They had it seems, in their own eyes anyway, behaved themselves and kept their promises to Mary.

Her own diaries for this period have not survived but some of the diaries of Elizabeth Hutton, who joined the Calabar mission as a young girl in March 1891, are preserved in the library of Edinburgh University. The first two − written in a round schoolgirl hand which after her first bout of fever becomes as much a scrawl as Mary's own − give some idea of what Mary's ruffians were up to in her absence; for Elizabeth went up to Ekenge with Margaret Dunlop, after she had been only a month in Duke Town.

On 22nd April 1891 she records that eight Krumen rowed them up the Calabar River. They landed at Ekenge beach and walked up the path where the foliage was, 'so dense as to exclude the sky'.

At Ekenge, 'Imagine our surprise to find that part of the house had fallen down . . . Had a very refreshing sleep in spite of the rats which abound here . . . The garden is quite open to the forest so we are at the mercy of the leopards . . . Ma Eme is very rich . . . but kind to missionaries . . . Edem is a cruel man he has quarrelled with his steward and cut the man's arm very severely in three places . . . Miss Dunlop pleaded to be allowed to dress the wounds.'

At Ifako, the people are, 'Not very attractive . . . they seem bent on fun . . . Was at a palaver where twelve chiefs all jabbered at once . . . How they understood one another I could not make out . . . The chief of a neighbouring village is a very wicked and lawless man.'

After only a month at Ekenge the girls went back to Duke Town where Eme visited them. That must have been quite an adventure for her. On 11th June they went back to Ekenge which Elizabeth now described as 'this outlandish place'.

The grave of a mother of a chief had cracked open and it had been decided that this meant that she was calling for a sacrifice. The chief chose a slave boy to be killed but the boy escaped and took refuge in Mary's yard. True to their promise the tribe left him there.

Ekenge was visited by, '. . . a very powerful tribe and there was drinking, drumming, and dancing, all night.' Afterwards Eme took her sister to the girls, '. . . her husband had bitten her arm, the cruel monster, it is an ugly wound.'

A few days later the son of a chief died at Ifako and they went there to make sure that there were no ritual killings. There were, 'men with swords and guns . . . about fifty women groaning and wailing . . . In the midst was a chair on which the boy was seated . . . His body was dressed in a cloth of bright colours and he had a feather head-dress. There were lots of gifts on his knees, and on his coffin a bottle of gin, a dish of food, caps, whips and walking sticks.' Next day, '. . . what with people rushing to and fro the noise is dreadful . . . the neighbouring chiefs have gathered . . . they are greeted with shooting . . . The place is swarming with people . . . Crowds of men armed with guns and swords . . . singing and dancing . . . drinking and quarreling . . . women fighting . . . men and women behaving like beasts'.

It would all have been dreadfully familiar to Mary. But at least the girls were able to get away from it all into her 'caravan', which was more than Mary was able to do during her first months with the Okoyong. If the tribe did kill a retinue they kept it secret. Perhaps they buried the boy Etim-fashion.

Next Eme amazed and disappointed the girls by accusing two men of bewitching some animals into eating a pile of her yams. She demanded that they should take the boiling oil test to prove their innocence. In this test if the oil was sufficiently hot and was poured quickly enough, and the palms sufficiently moist and sufficiently angled, the oil bounced off harmlessly. But since these conditions rarely prevailed the test was usually an agonising experience. However on this occasion the girls 'prevailed on Edem' to stop the test.

After a month the girls went back to Duke Town. Elizabeth wrote, 'How I wish I did not have to return there but could get a place where . . . I could do proper work.'

On their next visit they were taken up-river by a crew of Efiks who in Mary's absence flatly refused to carry their baggage up the path. This was Elizabeth's last visit for at the end of it the girls were delighted to hear that Miss Slessor was on her way back from leave.

Margaret Dunlop wrote that she was glad to be done with the Okoyong because 'they boasted of their lawlessness and even came drunk to church.'

When Mary did get back to Ekenge the house which had not been lived in for several months was in an even worse state: 'You would hardly believe that it is so much work to repair a place . . . I have not been washed and dressed till night time since I came back'.

A mission carpenter had come up to help with the work: 'He said as we sat at my bench one day, "What would the braw folk of Edinburgh think if they saw you just now?" . . . referring to my bare feet and very unconventional dress. He sat on the ground as I did so I just said "What would they think if they saw you?" . . . a woolen garment and some unmentionables on his understandings. He looked as much a tinker as I did . . . He is the man for our place . . . It is splendid to have people who can sympathise with your inclination to shout "Hallelujah!" sometimes.'

But the 'Hallelujah!' shouting vice-consul was not always acceptable to the new British officials. One of them studiously ignored her when she was pushing a canoe into the water as he went by in a launch. Newly arrived from a land of impeccable ladies, the poor man was probably embarrassed at what she was not wearing.

Soon her Ekenge circus was in full swing again. School, dispensary, services, palavers, fights, and riots. A chief had bought a new wife who was beautiful but sad. Mary discovered that the people who had sold her had first disposed of her husband to cannibals and sold her son into slavery.

To help her to get to the source of trouble before the bloodshed began Mary and Eme arranged a code. When Eme sent her an empty gin bottle for medicine it meant that devilment was afoot and Mary must stand by.

Her hair had grown while she was in Scotland. Now she cropped it even shorter. She hardened her feet until she was able to do without shoes altogether. She shortened her cotton dresses to above her ankles. And fully fit and in sparkling form she was ready for anything. Now at forty-four she was at her peak. Her hair was bleached golden by the sun. Her body was hard and muscled from all the manual work and marching. And she could go down the bush paths as fast as most Okoyong.

James Lindsay, who was in charge of the mission's new steam launches came to stay with her at this time and reported that she always went barefoot and bareheaded: 'What she lost in outward respectability she more than gained in mobility and usefulness. She kept herself untrammelled in the matter of dress that she might be ready for any emergency. In the case of a sudden call at night she was literally ready to leave at a moment's notice.'

As for the Okoyong, they were glad that their *Ma Akamba* was no longer ill. But her new health had its drawbacks. They could not understand how she usually knew beforehand what they were up to. This became another of her magic powers.

To settle a long-standing dispute between two Houses which kept breaking out into fighting, she called a palaver of all the chiefs in the district. It went on well into the night and, when finally she found an acceptable compromise, the 'braw folk of Edinburgh' would have been even more shocked if they could have seen their female agent presiding over the taking of the barbarous heathen oath which was necessary to put an end to the dispute once and for all.

Inside a circle of half-naked warriors lit by flaring, smoking, torches, the heads of the two Houses wearing only loincloths knelt in front of her. The senior chief then cut the back of the right hands of the kneeling men. They clasped the hands in front of her and then corn, salt, and pepper, were laid on the cuts until the mixture was soaked in blood when each man sucked it from the back of the other's hand. This was an oath which Mary knew that they would not break and, like the *mbiam* oath, she would preside over the taking of it many times in years to come.

In recent years it has been customary to claim that no missionaries had any respect for native customs. But Mary Slessor was merely following the lead set for her mission by Hope Waddell himself. And she was by no means the only missionary to respect them. James Luke wrote this description of how a chief, who could not understand why the Christian God should allow a follower to have such a bad bout of fever, decided to see if his own gods would help: '. . . to save his white friend he had set his own machinery in motion . . . In imperious tones he ordered me to stretch out my hand. I did so. On the back of the hand he made a mysterious marking with coloured chalk . . . then standing there the priestly chief poured out the libation of wine and prayed – the heathen for the Christian who sorely needed prayer. I greatly respected the heathen chief at that moment . . . One other bit of common ground – praying ground; one other elementary principle of true religion – prayer for one another; and the heathen sought to improve the Christian's trouble by sacrifice.'

At Ekenge the weeks went by and the gin bottle went backwards and forwards. In trying to stop one fight Mary was accidentally hit with a stick and knocked down. When she recovered she found the man who had hit her, down in the dust, being beaten by the fighters of both sides. If she had not recovered he would have been beaten to death.

Then she heard that a chief had died in one of the border villages and that prisoners had been chained before being forced to take the poison bean. The trials were to be held in the forest to avoid the attentions of Ma. But, thanks to Eme, Ma had discovered the place.

The proceedings were about to begin when she arrived. James Luke wrote that by now she had: 'not only the colloquial phrases of the Efik but also the inflections, the guttural sounds, the interjections and sarcasms, as well as the quick, characteristic gestures that belong only to the natives . . . She could cut with it and make them wince, she could play with it and make them smile.'

Now she cut and they winced. But they did not know her except by reputation and they decided to sit her out. If they had known her they would have had more sense. After four days and four nights they gave up. During this time they very kindly made her a bed out of plantain leaves and lit fires to keep the leopards away from her, from the guards, and from the prisoners. Presumably they fed her too, although they would have dispensed with the usual courtesy of first showing her the meat with the fur on to prove that it was not human. She knew that the meat would be animal, for they were not cannibals, but she may have wondered if it were cat, dog or monkey. She was fond of all three when alive and she knew that the Okoyong were fond of them cooked.

She said afterwards that the leopards had been her main worry. When she wakened in the night she had occasionally seen their green eyes gleaming in the light of the fires from among the shadows in the bush.

A few weeks later she gave terrible offence to the whole tribe. A woman had given birth to twins and Mary, after trying unsuccessfully to have them taken immediately to Duke Town, had taken them out through a hole in the wall of the mother's hut and through the bush to her own house. She had done this because any door though which, or path along which, a twin passed was cursed for evermore.

When Edem heard that Mary had the babies not only in her own hut but in her own bed, he was most upset and said that he could never visit her again. He sent a message asking her to come and see him. She replied, 'I live in my house as I ever did.' He sent her his usual present of yams. She returned them. The people did not dare come near her and she ignored them. Dispensary, school, and services stopped. Life was just not the same for anybody. Then one of the twins died and perhaps the people managed to convince themselves that this must have been the devil baby, for the next day Eme came to visit Mary and everything thereafter went back to normal. But of course nobody would touch or even go near the remaining twin. Mary never seems to have told them that Janie was a twin too.

Just how strong the Okoyong considered Mary's powers to be, Mr Weir, a new dispensary assistant in Duke Town, discovered when he visited her towards the end of 1892. He wrote that they were having a cup of tea and a chat when Mary stopped in the middle of a sentence and said, 'Something's wrong!' Sure enough, within minutes, messengers came for her. Weir went along too and they found the daughter of a chief lying unconcious on a bench in his yard, her mother in hysterics, and the place full of people yelling that the girl had been bewitched. Weir examined her and said she seemed to have only fainted. The dust was flying and people were crowding round so he asked Mary to try to get them to stand back and let the girl get some air.

Mary stood up on the bench and shouted for silence. Then she drew herself up, tensed as if she were going to spring at them, and said '*Soi, wara do*!, ('Shoo, get out!'). To Weir's amazement everybody, chief, mother, wives, children, and visitors rushed for the gate and fell over one another to get out of the yard. He saw then that Mary was suddenly exhausted and trembling. She sat down on the bench and put her head in her hands. 'Now I'm done for this day!'

The girl recovered and another story went into the legend of *Eka Kpukpro Owo*.

12. PLAGUE

Now that the rivers were patrolled and the Okoyong were settling down, visitors began to come to Ekenge to see this Scotswoman who lived, dressed, and spoke like an African. The British even began to send some of their new officers and officials to learn at first hand 'how to handle the natives'.

Malaria was still a killer and a mystery. Europeans were so afraid of it and of the other fevers that when Sir Richard Burton was appointed Consul of the Bights he wrote that his enemies had arranged it to see him die.

Recruits received the following instructions: 'Always use quinine, mosquito nets and boots . . . avoid native quarters . . . they are a source of infection . . . wear wool next to the skin and a cummerbund after sunset to protect the kidneys from chill . . . By day always wear a sunhelmet and spine-pad and carry an umbrella . . . Always filter the water.'

Sir Harry Johnston himself denounced the bravado of Europeans who went out in the sun without an umbrella. But when the recruits with their escorts of soldiers arrived at Ekenge they found the great expert striding about bare-headed, bare-footed, with no umbrella, and wearing so little that one of her men colleagues refused to walk behind her because of the way in which her thin dress clung to her sweating body. She called them 'laddies' and offered them tea, and when one of them asked a little anxiously what kind of water filter she used, roared with laughter and said, 'Water filters were'nae created! They were an afterthought!'

She could out-march them all and they knew that in emergencies she sometimes made night journeys through the bush to Creek Town – an eight hour walk – which they would never have attempted even with an escort. She was one of the few people who could explain to them the peculiar ways and beliefs of the Africans. She gave these greenhorns firm knowledge to

145

stand on in a welter of mud, magic and mosquitoes, and they went back to Duke Town full of stories about her. Soon 'Mariolatry' was a word much in use among them, half joking, half in earnest.

One officer came back with a story of how, when he had toothache, Mary had been most sympathetic. As they went through a clearing she pulled the head off a plant and gave it to him saying, 'Here, chew this. It'll fix your toothache!' He did as he was told and, sure enough, the pain began to lessen. Later, he saw another of the same plant and pulled the head off it. But Mary was watching him. 'Na! Na!', she said casually, 'dinna chew another today or you'll die. It's poison you see.'

Another of the new men, T D Maxwell, who was a favourite of hers – she promoted him to 'dear laddie' – wrote of how when he first met her he was surprised 'most unreasonably' by her strong Scottish accent. The first time he saw her preside over the Okoyong Native Court she was sitting in a rocking chair with a baby in her lap and a lace shawl over her hair. He thought that the shawl must have been a concession to a stranger for he never saw it again. 'Suddenly she jumped up with an angry growl, her shawl fell off, the baby was hurriedly transferred to somebody qualified to hold it, and with a few trenchant words she made for the door where a hulking overdressed native stood. In a moment she seized him by the scruff of the neck, boxed his ears, and hustled him out into the yard telling him quite explicitly what would happen to him if he came back again without her consent . . . Then as suddenly as it had arisen the tornado subsided, and (lace shawl, baby and all) she was gently swaying in her chair again.'

The man had been rude to her and she had forbidden him to come back to court until he had apologised to her. He had hoped to use Maxwell's visit to ignore her ruling. Now he knew better.

To men who, as boys, had been taught to stand up to blows from clubs, Mary's slaps would have seemed more like gentle pats. But they were men of action; to them talk was cheap; action was respected. It may have seemed a little ironic to Mary that, after all the years of trying to 'better herself' to become a good missionary, one of her most useful qualities from now on would be the knock-about technique which she had learned as a 'wild lassie' in the slums.

But she never made the mistake of thinking that, because of

their physical toughness, the Africans were insensitive. She wrote to her Dundee friend Thomas Hart, 'You read the African aright in regard to his seeming reticence and stolidity in the deepest things . . . But never dream that he does not feel. He feels deeply but cannot express it in ordinary language.'

This seems all too obvious today. But in her day most Europeans looked on the Africans as half animal. To the trained, 'stiff upper-lip' British the yells of glee, the leaping about, the slapping on the shoulder of the happy African were as uncouth as his wailing, tearing of clothes, and rolling on the ground when in utter misery. And his outbursts of rage and violence were equally uncouth to them, although they could respect these. Mary spent many hours trying to explain to British newcomers that the Africans were really a friendly, hospitable people, who must not be written off as savages because of the old cruel customs which they had been conditioned from childhood to look on as right and proper. Some recruits understood. Some had to learn the hard way. Some never learned at all.

Soon however Mary had a visitor who understood very well. Mary Henrietta Kingsley who, complete with velvet toque, button-up costumes, and knee-high boots, had herself survived perilous adventures in the forests of Africa, arrived in Duke Town. She was, she said, 'in search of fetishes [African beliefs] and fish.' She was a niece of the writer Charles Kingsley, and a naturalist and anthropologist. When her book on West Africa was published she became recognised as an expert on African beliefs and behaviour, although she had spent fewer months in Africa than people like Mary Slessor had spent years.

Unlike Mary, who went her perilous way wrapped in the certainty that God was guiding and protecting her, Mary Kingsley went hers with a revolver in her handbag and a dagger concealed on her person in case things 'got too uncomfortable'.

At Duke Town of course they told Miss Kingsley all about Miss Slessor. So Kingsley wrote to Slessor and asked if she might call on her. When the visitor arrived at Ekenge one of the 'usual uproars' was in progress and her guide suggested that it would be prudent to wait until another day. 'I think not', said Miss Kingsley. 'Miss Slessor is expecting me.' 'Just as if', said the guide later, 'she were paying a call in Kensington.'

Miss Slessor was in process of rescuing twin babies who had been born in a nearby village. In her book *Travels in West Africa* Miss Kingsley described the event in her usual laconic style: 'I arrived in the middle of this affair . . . and things at Okoyong were rather crowded one way or another that afternoon. All the attention one of the children needed was burying, for the people who had crammed them into a box had completely smashed the child's head. The other child was alive and is still a member of that household of rescued children all of whom owe their lives to Miss Slessor . . . She [the mother] was subjected to torrents of violent abuse, her things were torn from her . . . and she was driven out as an unclean thing. Had it not been for the fear of incurring Miss Slessor's anger, she would at this point have been killed with her children and the bodies thrown into the bush . . . Miss Slessor had heard of the twins arrival and had started off barefooted and bareheaded, at that pace she can go down a bush path. By the time she had gone four miles she met the procession, the woman coming to her and all the rest of the village coming howling and yelling after her . . . Miss Slessor took charge of affairs relieving the staggering woman of her load . . . and they started back together to Miss Slessor's house in the forest clearing, saved by the tact which, coupled with her courage, has given Miss Slessor an influence and a power among the negroes unmatched by that of any other white.'

Since Miss Kingsley was an agnostic and not given to admiring missionaries in general this was high praise indeed. She had seen what a wonderful thing it was for an Okoyong in trouble to know that to reach Miss Slessor meant safety.

Mary Kingsley spent several days at Ekenge with Mary and described them in her book as 'some of the pleasantest days of my life'. She summed up on Miss Slessor: 'this very wonderful lady . . . Her abilities both physical and intellectual have given her among the savage tribe a unique position and won her among many, white and black, a profound esteem. Her knowledge of the native, his language, his ways of thought, his diseases, his difficulties, and all that is his, is extraordinary, and the amount of good she has done no man can fully estimate . . . This instance of what one white can do would give many lessons in West Coast administration and development. Only the type of man Miss Slessor represents is rare. There are but few who have the power of resistance to the malarial climate, and of acquiring the language and an insight into the negro mind, so perhaps after all it is no great wonder that Miss Slessor stands alone as she certainly does.'

The two Marys wrote to one another for years until Mary

Kingsley went to South Africa during the Boer War, where she nursed Boer prisoners, caught enteric fever, and died. 'The type of man' Miss Kingsley represented was rare too. Mary Slessor wrote of her, 'Richly gifted in humour she could see all their [the Africans] follies and foolishness, but she never under-rated them as a race, and there was no sting or contempt in her joke or her laugh, and what is more uncommon even among missionaries, she respected their religious beliefs however foolish and never either ridiculed or laughed at them.'

This was a presbyterian missionary writing in 1900. The quotation hardly fits the picture so dear to modern writers of a narrow-minded bigot.

It was as well perhaps that Mary Kingsley was unable to stay longer at Ekenge for, shortly after she left, the whole district erupted once more in rage and violence. Ekenge and Ifako fought a battle against two other Houses and won. A group of women were blamed for causing the trouble and herded into a stockade to be executed. W P Livingstone wrote, '. . . a band of men were proceeding to murder them. Mary came on the scene and held them at bay.' Whether they were strangling the women, beheading them, or clubbing them to death he did not say. He took most of his material from Mary's reports and letters to friends. This must have been an event about which Mary had no wish to go into detail.

Her people must have been very determined to kill their prisoners because they refused to let her arbitrate. Once more she had to sit them out, and this time there was no Charles Ovens to help her. She guarded the women all that day and through the night while her girls passed her food and cups of tea through the stockade fence.

The next afternoon a tornado blew up, her roof blew away, everybody was drenched, and the guards left their prisoners chained. The girls told her that her clothing and bedding and theirs was soaking and that the tinned milk for the babies was running out. Under her embattled circumstances the only place where she could find more food and more clothing was Calabar. But no messenger could be trusted to go quickly enough through the rain and dark, or even to go at all, so she decided to slip away and go herself.

Clutching her lantern and no doubt praying her 'Daniel' prayer she walked down the muddy paths to Creek Town. She arrived there at four in the morning and knocked up Mary

F

Charles Ovens with helpers

Johnstone who refused to let her start straight back to Ekenge but made her lie down for a rest while she got her a fast canoe and crew to take her up the Calabar with the clothes, the milk, and the tide.

In one way it was lucky that it was a rainy morning, because when the wet, bedraggled Ma had once more splashed her way up the muddy four mile-long path, she found that the guards had not yet returned to the stockade and she had not been missed. When they did return they found her sitting beside the prisoners as before.

When the men from the crew, who had carried the milk and clothes up from the river for her, told the men of Ekenge what she had done, the chiefs must have realised that they had no chance of beating their astounding Ma, for after the 'usual uproar' the prisoners were released and returned to their village. Mary however paid the penalty for her forced march. Two days later she went down not only with fever but with dysentery.

A medical missionary who had worked for years in Central Africa, Dr Laws, was one of the deputies who had been sent out by Edinburgh to look into the feasibility of Mary's suggestion of an industrial training centre. When he heard of her illness he volunteered to go up to Ekenge to look after her. One of the mission staff went with him as guide.

As usual the coming of the white men was passed on ahead of them by the talk-drums and when they reached Mary's house they found that she was at her door to welcome them, clinging to a table for support.

Laws promptly ordered her back to bed. She gave him a long, hard, stare but did as she was told. Laws had not met Mary before and could not understand what was amusing his guide, until the man told him that it was years since he had seen Miss Slessor 'taken charge of', and that she must be feeling really ill or she would quickly have told him not to dare to give orders in her house.

When Mary recovered and Laws returned to Duke Town he found that he was famous as 'the man who made Miss Slessor do as she was told'. He wrote to a friend: 'She is a bit of a character. What a Salvation Army lass is to the Church at home, Miss Slessor is to the mission . . . I could not commend her as a pattern to others but she has saved lives as no other man or woman would have dared to do. Had a man attempted to do what she has done in the recent riot, he would have had his throat cut.'

He was an experienced man, and to be fair to him, he also wrote in his official report: '. . . few women or even men could stand the isolation which she endures'. But it is interesting to compare his patronising views with those of Mary Kingsley and of British officials. He clearly saw no future for foreign missions in identifying themselves as closely with 'the natives' as Mary was doing. Events however over the coming years would show that it was only by so doing that Christianity itself would have any future either among 'the natives' or among anyone else. Mary Slessor was ahead not only of her time but of Dr Laws. Fortunately for the mission, four of the greatest of the women missionaries to Calabar, who came after her, did take her 'as a pattern'.

Now, so great indeed was Mary's isolation that she even got her days mixed up. Charles Ovens arrived one morning to start work. Mary welcomed him but seemed surprised. 'Whatever are you doing, arriving on the Sabbath?'

'Sabbath?' said Ovens, 'It's Monday!'

'Oh losh no! . . . Ah weel you'll just hae twa sabbaths in one week. I was whitewashin' yesterday.'

Even Hugh Goldie, that precise scholarly man, began a letter a few weeks later with, 'I am at Okoyong and am not sure of the date.'

When she was tired and had fever she had days of complete depression. She wrote on one of these days, 'I cannot pretend to work this station; the school work is simply a scramble at the thing . . . I cannot overtake it. It is because I am not doing it efficiently that I am grieved.' And she was even more depressed when one of her favourite orphans, whom she called Susie, was scalded with boiling water through the carelessness of one of the older girls. Mary sat up all night nursing the child. But Susie died and Mary wept, 'My heart aches for my darling . . . Oh the empty place, and the silence and the vain longing for the sweet voice and the soft caress and the funny ways . . . Oh Susie! . . . I feel dreadfully lonely and have made up my mind at the next [Presbytery] meeting to ask for a companion.'

But even if anyone had been prepared to join her, they could not have been spared from the other stations. So Mary wrote an appeal to the *Record* for recruits. The Okoyong needed, '. . . consecrated women who are not afraid of work or filth of any kind, moral or material. Women who can wash a baby or teach a child to wash and comb as well as read and write . . . Women who can take it all to Jesus and there get strength to pull on under any circumstances. If they can play Beethoven and paint and draw and speak French and German, so much the better but we can do without these latter accomplishments if they have a loving heart, willing hands, and commonsense. They will not need fine English for there is none to admire it. I would gladly welcome any warmhearted woman from any sphere if she would come to me.'

But nobody came.

Fevers, like Eme's empty gin bottle, came and went. Sometimes she simply had to go back to Creek Town for a rest. But when her colleagues suggested that she should leave Ekenge until she had recovered completely she refused to hear of it.

In 1895 she sent a long report on her work to the Foreign Missions Committee. It was, she wrote, impossible to talk of church membership because no ordained minister had been available for any length of time but several of the tribe now said that they believed in Christ and followed him. 'Raiding, plundering, and the stealing of slaves has almost ceased. Any person from any place can now come for trade or pleasure.' She gave full credit to the Lord for protecting her during her early years with the tribe, and for the fact that in those years '. . . armed, drunken, passion-swayed, men should give chivalrous homage to a woman.' Considering the bloody reputation of the Okoyong, the Efiks would have been inclined to laugh at the idea of 'chivalrous homage', but that in the end was precisely what she did receive from those men, according, as she would have said, 'to their lights'.

She went on to report that killings at funerals were a thing of the past and so too were the roving bands of 'Amazons'. It was a rare thing now in Ekenge and Ifako to see a woman drunk. Twins were still a problem but she was usually called in to take them away before they were injured. People were now actually sitting in her yard while twins were being nursed near them and one or two women had even touched a twin.

Chiefs were now sending their girls and boys to her for training. But since the station 'is manned year after year by the magnificent total of one individual' it was impossible to expect many conversions.

The report was published in the *Record* but it brought no help.

Mr Bishop, the friend who had risked going to Ekenge with her on that rainy night seven years previously, died in July. In August she heard that William Anderson, now over eighty, was returning to Calabar, 'to lay my bones beside my dear wife and among my people'. He had retired, and had returned to Scotland but had found that, after forty years in Calabar, it was no longer 'home'.

Hugh Goldie, now over eighty himself, was looking forward to seeing his old friend again. But he went down with another of his countless bouts of fever. He said, 'I am afraid that I shall not see Mr Anderson again on this side of the river.' He was right. The bout was his last. The mission buried him beside his wife at Creek Town and hundreds of Africans, weeping and wailing, gave him a spectacular funeral.

Mary, of course, had come back to Creek Town for the funeral, and two weeks later she had to leave Ekenge again. She was so ill that she simply could not go on. The mission doctor ordered her to have a complete rest if she wanted to survive.

William Anderson arrived back in Duke Town at almost the same time as Mary. He received a tremendous welcome when he came ashore. In the book which she and her husband, William Marwick, wrote about the Andersons, Elizabeth Hutton described how the mission staff had to form a cordon round the old warrior to prevent him from being crushed by all the excited people who had come to meet him; how he had been carried in procession up the path to Mission Hill; and how although he had to go to his room and rest after all the excitement, crowds of people sat round Mission House just to be near him.

Next day Daddy Anderson – 'Daddy-O' Mary called him – went to sit beside the stricken *Ma Akamba* dozing in her bed. She was too ill to talk so he just sat and held her hand. She was his link with his dead wife and he her link with Dundee and with her family. The two of them were the sole survivors of the Scots who had been with the mission when she had joined it nineteen years earlier.

By the middle of November Mary was up and about again and Eme, Edem, and some of the other chiefs came to visit her. They brought messages from her people who, they said, were missing her badly. So a month later, fit and in sparkling form again, Mary went back to Ekenge and to the customary welcome. But she had hardly settled in when a message came saying that Daddy Anderson was dying and was asking for her. She immediately commandeered a canoe and hustled the paddlers into bringing her tearing back to Duke Town.

As his brain faltered the old warrior was worried about his sins and Mary had to encourage him. She prayed with him and sang hymns for him and talked about all the people they would meet, along with Louisa, on the other side of the river. He could no longer hear well so she knelt beside his bed, put her head on his pillow and spoke into his ear.

That night she took her turn at watching beside him. Anyone who looked into his room after midnight would have found the old man asleep and Mary kneeling beside him, a very crumpled 'tornado': two warriors together.

William Anderson died the following afternoon. He got his wish and was buried with Louisa. Once again it was a spectacular funeral. Mary did not grieve for the pale shadow of the big, tough, man she had known. She was quite certain that he had rejoined Louisa and his friends, just as she was certain that they and her family and Charles Morrison would be waiting for her too. Half beliefs were not for Mary Slessor.

By the middle of 1896 she found that the tribe was moving away from the Calabar River nearer to the Cross which, now that the British had opened it to all the tribes, was more than ever the main trade route. A new market had opened at a place called Akpap about three miles beyond Ifako and six miles inland from Ikonetu. As the land which they had been cropping became exhausted the tribe had been clearing new ground near Akpap and some of the farming settlements near Ekenge were becoming deserted. Mary decided to move with the tribe. She left behind some of her brightest pupils to run the schools at Ekenge and Ifako.

The mission agreed to build her a frame-house at Akpap and a hut and store at Ikonetu where the old mission house was in ruins. Mary knew however that it would be several years before her new house materialised at Akpap so she took over two disused huts there and moved in with her orphans. The huts were swarming with cockroaches and were a favourite haunt of rats, but she was used to coping with these. The move brought her back into the centre of the tribe and, of course, back into the centre of its endless disputes. To help her deal with these the British agreed that the Native Court be moved from Ekenge to Akpap.

Then smallpox hit the Cross River tribes and with them the Okoyong. Mary sent for lymph to Duke Town and began vaccinating. Hundreds of the tribe came for this new *Ma Akamba* magic. With only Janie, now fourteen years old, to help her, Mary went on vaccinating for hours each day until the lymph ran out and she had to wait for a new supply. After a few days she was told that there was no more to be had and Charles Ovens and a new recruit, Mr Alexander, found her, so exhausted that she could hardly stand, scraping with a penknife the pus from the arms of people whom she had already vaccinated and using it to vaccinate others.

The tribe was dying in hundreds and the panic stricken people were beginning to run off into the bush and leave the villages to the dead and dying. Next Mary heard that the epidemic had spread to Ekenge and that Edem was among the infected. She left Ovens and Janie at Akpap and went back to her old house and 'caravan' at Ekenge and turned them into a hospital. Soon it and her yard were packed with people who had staggered their way to her in the pathetic hope that she would cure them. But as the pile of dead in her yard grew, and they realised that not even *Ma Akamba* could cure them of this terrible thing, Ekenge and Ifako also panicked and soon they too were deserted except for the dead and the dying.

When the last of her patients had either died or gone away she went to Edem's hut where she had been nursing him and found him lying dead. She rested there beside him, just looking at the man who had protected her and to whom, almost certainly, she owed her life. There would be no retinue, no skulls of enemies, and no fine clothes to go into the grave with Edem. To him to lie there waiting for the scavenging leopards, rats, birds, and ants, would be the ultimate disaster, the ultimate shame. She must bury Edem.

But she was exhausted and there was no one to help her. Somehow she scratched him a grave under the floor of his hut and, as was customary, buried his sword, gun, and chief's staff and whip with him.

Afterwards, because of the scavengers, she had to get away from the village. It was near sunset. She could hardly walk. And she had no lantern. Akpap was five miles away. It was as well that the leopards had no need to hunt that night.

Ovens had gone back to Duke Town. When he returned to Akpap with Alexander the following morning they found Mary still asleep. She was lying fully dressed and filthy on her bed. She told them about Ekenge.

A few days later Alexander went there to get some timber from her old house for her new one. He found the house and the village still deserted, still full of the dead. The people never returned. Soon the bush crept back over Ekenge and over Mary's first 'beautiful house'.

By the end of the year she was due for leave once more but no one would take over from her. She 'drudged on'.

Chiefs were now beginning to come to her from beyond the Okoyong territory. Even some of the Aro from across the river came to see her when they were on their slaving expeditions. Probably they thought that anybody who could change the ways of their old mercenary friends was worth seeing. Mary told them that she would like to go over and live with them for a time. They said that she would be most welcome. But it is doubtful if she would have been for these cannibals had too much to hide.

The frame-house had still not arrived but Ovens came up again to repair her huts. She found him accommodation in an old hut near her own. It had no windows and when he went to wash one morning and grabbed what he thought was his sponge floating in his basin, he found it was a dead rat. Life anywhere near Miss Slessor was always unpredictable.

When he finished patching up the huts Ovens went back to Duke Town and Mary had a lonely Christmas and New Year. On 31st December 1897, Hogmanay (that great Scottish festival), she wrote to a friend: 'This is the last night of the year, tho' one has to be reminded of the feast since there is no outward sign of it in our bush home.'

Three of the babies she had rescued the previous week had 'gone up higher': 'I felt so utterly depressed I had to keep working to keep my spirits up at all . . . I keep very good health. It is only after a walk for a twin or some extra spell of fatigue that I get fever and I am thankful to say that I have recovered easily from every attack . . . It is want of sleep I daresay that makes me susceptible, for I get very little sleep with babies to nurse. But with it all I am as well as I would be in Britain, so if no help comes I shall just go on until I feel I must give up.'

She was making cots for her orphans out of the cases in which her supplies of tinned milk arrived. The sick babies she slung in little hammocks near her bed with pieces of string from the bed to the hammocks so that when a baby cried in the night she could rock it without getting out of bed. Her sleep was always being interrupted and she could never get enough of it.

Early in the new year the frame-house at last arrived and Charles Ovens with it. But he had hardly started work when Mary had an even worse bout of fever and had to agree that now it was time to give up for she could not even walk. At Duke Town she was ordered, and carried, on to the next steamer for Liverpool. Ovens was left to look after Akpap.

Her orphans were distributed around other stations, but she was so worried about her four girls – Janie who was fifteen, Mary who was five, Alice three, and Maggie sixteen months – that she decided to take them all with her. Neither she nor the girls however had any clothes either warm enough or fit to be seen in polite society. Luckily boxes of second-hand clothes had just arrived from Scotland and they were fitted from these. 'It will be trying to get back to the home kind of life and of language . . . I shall just want to find a place to hide in: away from conventionalities and all the paraphernalia of civilisation.'

Her friend Mrs McCrindle met the train at Edinburgh. When an African baby was handed out, people were mildly interested, but when an African girl got out and another and another, everything stopped and passengers, porters, and cabbies, gathered round to stare. Whoever could she be this thin, sallow, foreign-looking, woman who had such a strange family? Then the word went round, 'It's Mary Slessor . . . Mary Slessor!' And Mary Slessor was glad to get away and 'hide' at Mrs McCrindle's home.

She must have been on the verge of a complete nervous breakdown. She was terrified of the Edinburgh traffic and refused to cross the streets by herself. If men were in the audience when she stood up to speak during the usual lecture tours, she asked them either to leave or to sit where she could not see them. At one meeting she lost her nerve altogether and ran off the platform.

At a reception for her in Glasgow she had to spend over an hour shaking hands. She got so upset that at the end of it all she could hardly speak.

She denied that her work was any more remarkable than that of the other missionaries, 'They all work as hard or harder than I do.' Then she went on to stun her audience by sincerely but casually remarking, 'I feel that my work there [with the Okoyong] is done, I can teach them no more. I would like to go further inland and make my home among a tribe of cannibals.'

What the Okoyong needed urgently she said was an ordained missionary. She wrote to the *Record*: 'If missions are a failure, it is our failure not God's. If we only prayed and had more faith what a difference it would make . . . In Calabar we are going back [backwards] every year . . . we get money . . . but not the men and the women.'

She brought money flowing in and the Committee wanted her to extend her leave. But she was so worried about her tribe which had no one looking after it that she refused. It was at this time that she said: 'If ye dinna send me back, I'll swim back.'

So in December 1898, just after her fiftieth birthday she and the bairns sailed back from Liverpool. They spent Christmas on board and everyone from the captain down made a fuss of them. Mary was interested in everything. She questioned the ship's officers about the engines and about navigation, and other passengers about the development of new roads, railways, and industries in West Africa.

The stories of her way of living and of dressing, of her amazing courage, and of her humorous way of looking at things, which officials had brought back from Ekenge, had been taken from station to station by other officials. When the ship called in at Lagos and other ports, and the British heard that Mary Slessor was on board, they all wanted to meet this woman about whom they had been hearing so much. Mary was surprised when their spokesman came on board to invite her to go ashore and visit them. Why did they want to see her of all people? The ship's officers explained that she was famous right along the Guinea Coast. But instead of pleasing her this news seemed only to upset her and she declined all the invitations.

13. 'WONDERFUL JEAN'

1897 had been a good year for recruitment to the mission and by April 1898 all the up-river stations were manned for the first time in four years. Dr Rattray and Mr and Mrs Simmers were at Unwana, Mr and Mrs Deas at Ikotana, and Mr and Mrs Marwick (Elizabeth Hutton) at Emuramura. And a new medical missionary, Dr Cowan, had arrived at Creek Town to replace Dr Rae.

But once again the climate, the fevers, and the overwork, destroyed the mission's hopes of expansion. Mr Deas died at Ikotana, Mr Simmers died at Unwana, and Miss Budge, Dr Cowan, and Mr McMillan died at Creek Town. Mr and Mrs Deas had to be invalided home, and a few months later Mr and Mrs Marwick had to go home too.

Because of these casualties the Board in Edinburgh banned further expansion up the Cross River and the Calabar Presbytery too gave up all hopes of expansion. Once again it was all it could do to cling on to its old stations in the Calabar towns, to Ikorofiong, to Akpap, and, after the invincible James Luke returned, to Unwana. The great dream was still a dream.

When Mary returned to Duke Town the mission had not recovered from all the deaths. She too was of course depressed by them and not even the welcome which the Okoyong gave her at Ikonetu beach seems to have cheered her up for long, because she wrote to a friend that, after such heavy losses, 'one does sometimes feel so very lonely'.

Charles Ovens had finished the new house but it had a corrugated iron roof and in the dry season she found it like an oven and in the wet the drumming of the rain got on her nerves. She often wished that she was back in her old mud huts. She had however converted these into accommodation for all the chiefs who were now coming to see her from as far away as a hundred miles. In one week she had deputations from four different

The frame house at Akpap

Mary's mud house at Akpap

tribes. They were looking for advice on how they could obey the new white man's laws without bringing the wrath of their gods down on them. The British had banned all the bloody customs of their religion by which they hoped to win the favour of the gods and please their ancestors, in order to win protection from evil spirits and from human enemies. Nothing terrible was happening to those who had abandoned the old customs. So they were losing faith in their old ways of worship and of consulting the spirits; losing faith too in their old oracles. The whole of their religious life was under attack.

For years the up-river tribes had been waiting for the white men from *Abassi* to come to them. What they would bring they had no idea, but they had heard that it was good. Now, at a time when they badly needed advice on how to consult their old gods in new ways, and on how to consult and please the new white man's God, they had heard of this white woman. It was said that she wanted nothing for herself, that she would walk miles to cure sick people and rescue worthless babies; that she was a messenger from *Abassi* who had magic powers and whom no man nor wild creature could attack; that she understood their ways and tribal laws. So they came to her in their bewilderment looking for advice from one whom they heard was a wise human friend and, perhaps hoping also to find in her a new oracle.

Mary therefore found herself once more in an impossible situation. The work load which she faced would inevitably shatter what remained of her health. To dispensary, services, school, walks to sick and injured people and to find abandoned babies, three-mile walks to Ifako, and six-mile walks to Ikonetu beach, she had to add endless palavers with a steady stream of chiefs, and the writing of replies to a steady stream of letters from Scotland.

Many of her letters were now headed 'Midnight', '3 am', 'Dawn'. Whenever she could not sleep or a sick baby roused her, she began writing letters or working. A visitor, hearing bumps in the night, got up herself and found Mary rebuilding a fireplace. 'I have nine babies and what with the washing and the school and the palavers, you can be sure that there are no drones in this house.' To her original 'family' she had added two boys, Daniel and Asuquo. Years later Daniel wrote that at this time she was always mending roofs or walls, gardening, sewing, cooking, or writing. 'She was never idle. She would become ill if she were idle, she would say.'

As at Ekenge, Vice-Consul Mary Slessor presided over the Native Court at Akpap in much the same way as she had once presided over her 'knitting palavers' in the days before Pax Britannica arrived to reinforce Pax *Ma Akamba*. She sat at a small table under a tree or in a palaver house with a tin of her toffee at her elbow – made with baking soda now to help digestion – and knitted away while she and the three chiefs appointed to the court listened to witnesses and accused. Serious cases of assault or theft had to be referred to the District Commissioner's Court, and the most serious cases, like murder, were passed on to the Supreme Court in Duke Town. The native courts tried to resolve according to native law and custom, cases of minor theft and assault, and tribal squabbles about dowries, wives, slaves, and witchcraft. Often there was little factual evidence on offer since witchcraft was nearly always involved. It was difficult to follow the rambling tales about how and why who had bewitched whom, and one hearing could last all day. There was so much lying to the court that Mary often made witnesses take the *mbiam* oath.

At Ekenge she had never kept records and never written down her judgements since at first nobody could read. But now the British expected her to do both. So, in the evenings, she had to labour to make sense in English of evidence that made no sense in any language. And since she was supposed to issue her judgements in writing, she handed them out on scraps of paper. Few of the accused could read them, but since they came from *Ma Akamba* many put them away carefully with their other charms. Sealy King was shown some of them in the 1930s, still in a place of honour.

Although her methods were unorthodox, they were effective, and the British did not interfere. They were only too glad to have a magistrate who needed no interpreter, understood African customs, and had a personal authority greater than anything they had yet achieved with their patrols and Maxim guns.

So great was her reputation among the Africans for fairness, that when a serious quarrel broke out between the Umon and the Okoyong, the Umon invited her to arbitrate, confident that she would not favour her own tribe. The difficulty of getting the Okoyong to accept the judgement of anyone else may also have influenced their decision. The Umon sent a canoe for her and they started out at dawn, the time of day which Mary liked best.

But her enjoyment of the sunrise was shattered when, as they took a short cut through a narrow creek, a hippopotamus attacked the canoe. The beast came at them with its huge mouth gaping and tried to get a grip on the side of the canoe. One of the bow men stuck his paddle in its mouth and it turned away. Next it came at them amidships where Mary was sitting. As usual when frightened she lost her temper, threw a cooking pot at the gaping mouth, stood up, cracked the beast over the head with a pole, and shouted 'Go away, you!' To the amazement of the crew that is precisely what it did. Ma even had power over the river beasts! They were so impressed that they told the story to their people when they reached home. This story too travelled along the rivers and along the bush paths into the legend which was rapidly building up around Mary Slessor all along the Cross and the Calabar rivers. Sixty years later the children along the rivers were still playing at miming the incident. Perhaps they still do. Mary settled the quarrel and visited several townships on the Cross River on her way home. She was particularly impressed with Itu, which is on the west bank of the river about twenty miles above Ikonetu, near the junction with the Enyong Creek. This creek was an important waterway leading towards the territory of the great Ibo tribe, millions strong. In the days of the slave trade the Aro had brought thousands of prisoners down it to be sold at the big Itu market. Now, because of its position at the junction of the two waterways, and because the river was tidal to beyond it and therefore their steam launches could reach it even in the dry season, the British had chosen Itu for a military base. Mary saw that the advantages which had made it a trade centre and a military centre also made it ideal for a mission centre.

The Itu chiefs had welcomed Mary to their town. They too were looking for advice and protection and they had asked her to come and start a school for them, taking her to a ridge away from the stink and the mosquitoes, from which there was a superb view of the river, and saying that they would give her a site on it for her buildings. Mary had made no promises but had said that she hoped to come back before long and start the school for them.

She saw a move to Itu as a first step towards realising her ambition to tackle the Aro themselves. She knew by now that they had almost a monopoly in the domestic slave trade, and that they were using the other tribes' fear of their oracle at Arochuku to add to their wealth. Just what use they were making of the oracle however she did not know at this time.

Back at Akpap, the more she prayed about Itu the more convinced she became that this was where she was to go. There remained however the problem of who was going to take over the Okoyong. She would have to wait and see what the Lord would do about that.

While Mary was working at Akpap Sir Ronald Ross had arrived in Lagos from the School of Tropical Diseases in Liverpool. He was about to transform life along the Guinea Coast by his discovery that malaria is caused by the bite of the infected anopheles mosquito. Leopards, snakes, crocodiles, and other creatures had always been recognised as dangerous and had been respected. But mosquitoes were just a silly nuisance. Now, at last, they were known to be the deadliest enemy of all. The mystery which had brought so much fear was solved. There was a known enemy to fight. The first priority was to deprive the mosquitoes of as many breeding grounds as possible near the towns. So the British pushed on with drainage and sanitation in them and also began draining nearby swamps. It now became an offence to leave containers about which would catch water and become a breeding ground for mosquitoes.

Meanwhile, in December 1889 Janie married 'my best scholar' but the marriage did not last long. Janie had, of course, to warn her husband that she was a twin. Thanks to Mary's teaching he was brave enough to defy the curse and marry her but when their first baby died he must have thought that this was the curse at work, for he left Janie. In her grief she returned to Mary, from whom until her marriage she had never been separated. Now that she was grown up Mary called her Jean. She was a strong and intelligent girl, totally dedicated to Mary, spoke English fluently, competed with Mary to have first look at the books, newspapers, and magazines, which Mary had sent regularly from Scotland, and must at this time have been the best educated of all the Efik women.

From now on Mary would become more and more dependent on 'wonderful Jean'. Working and often sleeping in wet clothes had given Mary rheumatism to add to her fevers. Her speed down the bush paths which Mary Kingsley had described was now a thing of the past. The leopardess was being caged and would soon have to adapt to an entirely different way of life. Jean began to take over many of Mary's chores and she nursed her Ma, taught in her schools, helped in her dispensary, walked miles to collect abandoned babies, dug latrines and gardens, laundered and cleaned. Without Jean in the years to come Mary would never have been able to achieve what she did.

When Mary was ill and exhausted now, it was Jean who stood between her and angry chiefs who had walked miles to consult her. 'You are killing Ma with your foolish ways', Jean would say, 'You will wait!' And that was that.

Mary still asked Jean to make long journeys to rescue babies, many of whom died because of earlier neglect. Some people thought these journeys just stupid because the babies often needed special facilities which Mary could not of course provide. But she was trying to convince the Africans, to whom life was cheap, that it was sacred, and once again she knew that actions might convince them but words never would.

Yet in spite of her emphasis on action, when a new recruit asked her what she should do to learn to influence the Africans, she got the reply, 'Do, lassie? Do? You don't have to *do*, you just have to *be*, and the doing will follow!'

When driven nearly to distraction nowadays by all that she was having to undertake, Mary added another piece of nonsense to the nonsense songs which she still made up for the children. She would stand with her eyes closed and repeat over and over again, 'There was an old woman who lived in a shoe. She had so many children she didn't know what to do.' And she went on repeating the lines until she had pulled herself together again.

In spite of the recent deaths, recruitment picked up for a time – perhaps because of Mary's visit to Scotland – and several of the newcomers came to see the famous Mary Slessor at work. They described how she would bathe four babies at a time in four buckets warming on her stove. Then when she had tucked the first four into their padded milk-cases proceed to bathe four more in the same way, chatting all the time to her visitors. They described too how their own sleep was disturbed by bawling babies, scuttling rats, acrobatic lizards, and cockroaches as big as mice.

One of the newcomers, Beatrice Welsh, who was to become one of the four great women missionaries who followed Mary, wrote: 'Miss Slessor radiated energy . . . she was busy from morning until well into the night, helping the sick, teaching, listening to all who came . . . She made the past vivid as she lived it again . . . her girlhood, her love of fun, her mischievious pranks . . . I can still hear her, still enjoy her wild indignations, still marvel at her amazing personality, her extraordinary vitality and energy . . . Evening Prayers were a joy although it was a little disconcerting to sing hymns to tunes like "Robin Adair" and "Sweet Rothesay Bay" . . . Her whole life was dedicated to bringing to the lost and forlorn the knowledge that God cared for them . . . She said that God very plainly led her in all her ways, in all her plans.'

Another recruit, a man, considerably taken aback by her shabby, scanty, dress, as most people were at this time, wrote of how she went barefoot and bareheaded. 'No, I would not like to see other ladies do that, but I would not care to see her different. It is easy to give a false impression of her. She is not un-womanly. She is eccentric if you like, but she is gentle of heart, with a beautiful simplicity of nature. I join in the reverence which the natives show her.'

She had another visitor. He arrived when she was up on her roof mending the thatch and feeling ill and bad-tempered because everything had been going wrong that day. When she saw him in his smart uniform, looking up at her, she snapped, 'Yes? What do you want?'

He raised his sunhelmet. 'If you please ma'am, I am your new District Commissioner. But I can't help it!' Mary was delighted, hooted with laughter, and slid down and made him tea.

She had still not received her instructions about Itu from 'up higher'. But in any case it was useless to think of moving on. New recruits might admire her, but the last thing they wanted to do was to go and live the primitive life which she was living. Indeed, even in 1904, when living conditions at Akpap had been greatly improved, two lady colleagues refused to go on living there. They complained at length about the 'insanitary conditions' and the lack of 'proper furnishings'. On receipt of their complaint the Board in Edinburgh minuted its regret that 'Two ladies were stationed at Akpap without adequate preparation.' It trusted that such a thing would not be allowed to happen again. It would have been useless for the Calabar Presbytery to point out that its Miss Slessor had worked there for seven years. By now everybody knew that Miss Slessor was a very special person in whose shoes lesser mortals could not follow.

Mary's attitude to Akpap was summed up in a letter which she wrote to a friend in 1898: 'The test of a good missionary is this, waiting, seemingly useless time . . . But in a home like mine

a woman can find infinite happiness and satisfaction. It is an ex-
hilaration and a constant joy!'

Constant joy to her, but constant strain on her body. A few
months later it rebelled again at being treated like an un-
breakable machine and she collapsed, was carried down to a
launch, taken to hospital in Duke Town, and made to spend
several weeks in bed. The doctor would have liked to keep her
longer but after the first few weeks she had grown steadily more
mutinous and it became clear that if he did not discharge her she
would discharge herself.

When she arrived back in Akpap the Aro chiefs still visited
her when they came across the river on their slaving expeditions
through the Okoyong territory. They too asked her advice about
how to handle their new rulers. But they did not take it. They
were still chasing out any officials who tried to contact them and
still raiding canoes passing by on the river. They were interfering
not only with Pax Britannica but with trade. And British
patience with them was running out.

Towards the end of 1899, when just over a hundred survivors
from a column of eight hundred tribesmen who had gone to consult the Chuku oracle, reached a British post, British patience
finally did run out. The survivors were starving and in a shocking condition. They revealed the secret of the oracle. For centuries the Aro had persuaded other tribes to make pilgrimages to
the magic grove near their town Arochuku where the oracle
lived. But Chuku was an angry god and levied huge fines on
pilgrims who could afford to pay, and, over the years, was supposed to have eaten hundreds of thousands of others, who had
in reality been smuggled out of the grove and into slavery. It was
this wealth obtained from fines and the sale of slaves which had
enabled the Aro to dominate the other tribes militarily, through
their mercenaries, and economically. And they were still doing a
thriving trade in domestic slaves.

The story told by the survivors was passed on to London and
the Foreign Office agreed that, since persuasion was useless with
these cannibals, force would have to be used. So over a period of
several months the Aro Expedition was assembled at Duke
Town with one hundred and fifty white officers and several thousand African troops.

The British were afraid that the Aro might seize missionaries
as hostages, so in August 1901, before the troops moved up-
river, the Governor ordered all missionaries to return to Duke

Town. Mary of course rebelled. She sent back a message that she would be fine and safe with her Okoyong. But the military were very much in control at this time and they simply sent an officer and escort to fetch her in a launch. The officer was polite but firm and Mary was furious.

She was offered a government house but declined it. She and the bairns would hardly have fitted into an official compound. It would have cramped her style and put off the African chiefs who, now that the expedition was moving up-river in steel canoes towed by launches, were coming to her again for reassurance on the government's plans for them.

She had not been to Duke Town for three years and after all her months in the forest she complained of 'the terribly bright sky'. She was beginning to suffer from eye strain and would soon have to wear spectacles ('Oh, losh . . . No!') because the print in her Bibles was getting to be too small for her to read.

She had found some quite respectable dresses in the 'boxes', but she disliked wearing shoes and refused to wear a hat. And she was soon tired of being looked upon as an eccentric: an object at which people came to stare.

Her rheumatism, on top of her fevers and the headaches which accompanied them, was making her bad-tempered. She fretted at the nonsense of having to spend so many weeks in Duke Town when there was so much to be done. She had been so used to queening it over the Okoyong that she resented any opposition to her plan for moving across the river. Some of her colleagues found her domineering. And while she could be witty and amusing with people who accepted her as she was, she could behave outrageously towards people who looked down on her. She deliberately went out of her way to shock them, called pompous officials 'Laddie', made fun of their helmets and umbrellas, and used the roughest Dundee slum accent on them.

Before the British takeover there had been no racial discrimination in Calabar. The Jamaican missionaries, like Mammy Fuller and young Jarrett, had always lived on an equal footing with the Scots. And the white sea captains and traders had always behaved with respect towards the African chiefs because their livelihood depended on them. But now, with the malaria mystery solved, as more and more government officials moved in with their wives, there were places where a black skin was not welcome. This Mary, like the other missionaries, resented. She went out of her way to upset some of the whites by her 'familiarity' with the Africans, not just with the chiefs, but with the slaves as well.

The weeks at Duke Town were unhappy ones for Mary. The British admire and respect a 'character' but only an established character and the road to recognition and establishment is often painful. In years to come Mary would be established. But not yet, for many of the newcomers had not met her before. She was ill most of the time and her behaviour upset some of the missionaries too. It was at this time that one of their wives called her 'that coarse woman'.

Operations against the Aro began in November 1901. They and their mercenaries had never faced machine-guns before and they were forced back on Arochuku and the grove of the great oracle. For several days and nights their talk-drums beat out desperate appeals to the other tribes to come to the rescue of Chuku. But none came, and in the end most of the Aro chiefs, priests, and warriors surrendered. Some however escaped into the bush where they attacked supply columns and messengers and any official stupid enough to travel without a strong escort.

James Luke wrote: 'What is sad about the Aro Expedition is that the town names in connection with it are nearly all unknown to those of us who thought we had a passable knowledge of Old Calabar. It is somewhat humiliating that after over fifty years of work as a mission the district on the right bank should be so little known to us.'

He could have added that if it had not been for Mary Slessor the Okoyong district on the other bank would have been equally unknown to them; and that now, too, Mary was the only white person who had held palavers with the Aro chiefs and had got to know them.

Mary, as soon as she heard of the Aro surrender, set off straight away for Akpap without asking anybody's permission.

What was for the Cross River tribes a massive show of British force had upset them all. What the British needed now more than ever before were people who could reassure the tribes about the government's wish for peace. What the Aro needed was someone whom they trusted, who knew them and understood their ways, and who could plead on their behalf.

Only Mary Slessor could do this. And she knew it. But she was trapped at Akpap by her concern for the Okoyong.

Some weeks later, with sporadic fighting still going on beyond Arochuku, Sir Ralph Moor came up-river to negotiate with the

Aro. No civilians were being allowed into the area so the Aro had to send delegations to Mary across at her hut on Ikonetu beach to get advice on how to handle the palaver. In this way she was able to reassure them about the intentions of the British and help to get them to accept Moor's terms.

Now, like the Itu, the Aro were anxious for Mary to go and live with them. They probably saw in her protection from the chattering machine-guns. There was some hope too that she might be able to do so, for Janet Wright, one of the Falkirk girls, had arrived in Calabar four years earlier. At Duke Town she had been able to have long talks with Mary, who was probably still her great heroine, and after hearing about the plan to cross the river and open up the other bank, she had volunteered to join Mary at Akpap to free her to get on with it.

The mission, no doubt surprised and pleased that at last somebody was willing to share Mary's primitive life and to put up with her eccentric ways, recommended the move. But in 1900 the United Presbyterian Church had combined with the Free Church into the United Free Church. All matters concerning the women missionaries now had to go through a Women's Committee before being considered by the main Committee. As a result it took even longer for the mission to get a decision.

As the months went by the anxiously awaited arrival became a family joke. Almost every day Jean would say to Mary or Mary to Jean 'Ah . . . but wait till Miss Wright gets here!'

Meanwhile delegations from the Itu kept coming over to Mary to ask when she was going to come and start their school. In January 1903 she decided that she could wait no longer, and in spite of the ban on further expansion, she hired a canoe and went up the twenty miles to Itu with three of her brightest young people, a girl named Mana and two young men, Esien and Effiom. She left Jean to look after Akpap.

The chiefs helped her to mark out a site for her school, huts, and yard, and work began right away with Mary and her 'teachers' helping.

She found that relations between the sexes were much freer among the Itu than among the Efik or the Okoyong, who in public kept their women very much in their place. Here the men and women worked side by side: 'Sparks of wit and satire flew with as much zest . . . as in a Galloway byre or market fairin' . . . It is such a treat for me . . . They were daffin' and laughin' as in Scotland'.

She thoroughly enjoyed her weeks in the town, working once more as chief architect and worker and no doubt as chief joker as well. British officers, supervising the building of their own centre, would have been amazed at seeing a white woman in a sweaty, grubby, dress, working barefooted and bareheaded among a crowd of Africans, talking and laughing like one of them and, apart from her fair hair and brown skin, looking like one too.

She stayed until the school building was finished and the routine of 'Book' established and then went back to Akpap. On the day she left, the beach was crowded with a mob of shouting, laughing, men, women, and children, all milling about and being thumped back by the chiefs. It was a real Ekenge farewell.

When a way had finally been cleared for her, the barefoot Vice-Consul made a triumphal progress to her canoe leading on a piece of string a goat which the chiefs had presented to her as a parting gift. She promised not to be long in coming back.

Her church now had a new mission station which it knew nothing about. It had cost it nothing and would cost it nothing. Soon it would have more. Her church would know nothing about them either, but then they too would cost it nothing.

14. 'MOTHER OF ALL THE PEOPLES'

At last, nearly two years after the mission had applied for her transfer, Janet Wright arrived, and soon, after fifteen years without mission help, Mary was writing, 'She is a right sisterly help-mate and comfort in every way. Things go as smoothly as a summer's day and I don't know however I got on alone. It seems too good to be true.'

Janet took over the school and the dispensary and quickly adapted herself to Mary's African way of working, in which time mattered little and schedules not at all.

Among her other qualities Janet had a good singing voice and sometimes after the day's work she and Mary and Jean used to sit under the verandah and sing the old Scots songs as once they had done with Charles Ovens. The Okoyong came to sit under the trees and listen and before they broke up Mary always brought them into the singing by switching to her Efik hymns sung to Scottish tunes.

But the smooth summer's day did not last long. In June 1903 Mary received firm confirmation of what the Lord wanted her to do.

On top of everything else she had been making regular journeys up to Itu to check on the work of her 'teachers'. Now with Janet safely installed, she decided to go and spend a week or so with them. She walked the six miles to Ikonetu beach and then had a nap in her hut – she was beginning to need these more and more – leaving her young Africans to watch for the launch. It ran a regular schedule up the river now calling in at all the main stations. But it had to be hailed at small places like Ikonetu. Somehow her youngsters managed to see it too late and Mary had to trudge back to Akpap.

To Janet's surprise – because what with her rheumatism, fevers, and headaches, she was short-tempered these days – Mary was quite cheerful about her wasted journey. 'God' she said, 'didnae mean me to go the day. He'll hae a reason.'

A view of the Cross River

The following week she set off again and this time watched for the launch herself. She was not in the least surprised to find no less a person on board than Colonel Montanaro, the commander of the Aro Expedition, nor to get an invitation from him to go on past Itu with him to Arochuku itself. He knew of course about Miss Slessor's influence with the Africans and had the sense to realise that this barefoot, bright, woman in the patched and somewhat sweaty dress, might perhaps provide the help which he needed to get the Aro to settle down. After lording it over the other tribes for generations they were sullen in their defeat and some of them were still fighting from the forests. As Sir William Geary wrote, 'They had lost the profits from the enormous fees charged for consulting their oracle . . . and were deprived of victims for sacrifice or disposal as slaves.'

Mary promptly accepted Montanaro's invitation although, because she had clothes stored at Itu, she had brought nothing with her. She confided to the mystified Colonel that now she knew why God had made her miss the launch the week before.

So, in the gleaming government launch and escorted by the Colonel and his staff in their spotless sunhelmets and uniforms and shining Sam Browne belts, Mary made her long awaited journey up the Enyong Creek. They gave her a chair on deck and Mary settled down to enjoy the journey, supremely happy because God was steering her in the direction in which for years she had been wanting to go. It would have made an odd picture: the impeccable officers gathered round a gypsy-like woman with whom no respectable person should have been seen associating.

But was this the woman who single-handed had tamed the 'savage' Okoyong; who could stop battles, out-shout chiefs, and stop riots merely by walking into the middle of them? The Enyong Creek was one of the most beautiful waterways along the Cross River. Lilies grew along by the banks and torrents of blossoms, scarlet, blue, yellow, and white, sometimes foamed down from the trees; reflected in the still, green, water they made a tunnel of colour. To Mary it was 'awful bonnie!' As they watched this laughing woman taking such obvious pleasure in her surroundings the officers must have wondered if she could possibly be the 'tornado' they had heard so much about.

There was another surprise coming to them. When they arrived at Amasu, the landing-place for Arochuku, Montanaro was met by the garrison commander and a guard of honour. Among the sullen Aro watching the proceedings Mary noticed some of the chiefs who had visited her and she went across to speak to them. They crowded round her in welcome and asked why it had taken her so long to come. They had grown old waiting for her, they said.

Montanaro was surprised to see her chatting away in the middle of the group and asked his interpreter what was going on. The man replied that Miss Slessor's friends were asking her to come and live among them.

Was it really true, Montanaro asked her, that she knew these men? 'Oh aye', said Mary, 'I ken them fine.'

She told the Aro chiefs that it would be some time before she could come to live in the area but that she would start a school for them if they gave their word that her African teachers would be safe. This they did. Next day, laden with presents from them, she went back in the launch.

She now had another problem: if she started a school at Amasu, which some of the chiefs and Montanaro would welcome, she would be faced with journeys not just twenty miles up to Itu, but another twenty miles up the Enyong Creek, and these alone would take between eight and fifteen hours paddling, depending on the amount of water coming downstream.

But she had been surprised to find how many towns were clustered in the forest round Arochuku, with about thirty thousand people living in them and probably as many living in the towns along the creek. Since God was clearly pointing her in their direction it seemed that it was her duty to go forward and that, as usual, Mary Slessor would have to manage as best she could. So a few weeks later she started the school at Amasu in an old palaver house which the chiefs had made available.

She could not always fit her journeys into the launch's schedule and fretted at the hours which she was spending in canoes. But not all were wasted. One day her canoe was intercepted by a messenger from the young chief of a town called Akani Obio. Would Mary go and start a school at his town? Of course she would. Soon her church had three new stations which it knew nothing about.

In August 1903, to mark the fifteenth anniversary of that 'miserable Sabbath' at Ekenge in August 1888, Mary at last persuaded the mission to send an ordained missionary up to Akpap to baptise some of the people and hold a communion service. Over two hundred Okoyong turned out for the service but somehow they had managed to get the ceremony of baptism confused with the *mbiam* ceremony. If, after being baptised, they broke God's laws, would they drop dead? Mary did her best to reassure them, but after much palaver among themselves, they decided that it was a dangerous thing and that they would like to see what happened to those who risked it before doing it themselves.

In the end only eleven people were baptised, mainly from Mary's own 'family'. Fortunately Mary did not judge the success of her work from the number of baptisms which it produced and was not downhearted. The hymns were sung 'with fervour', she wrote, and she was 'very happy'. What the presiding minister thought of the hymn tunes she did not say.

Janet Wright had begun to share the journeys to Itu and Mary had also taken her up to Amasu. She too saw the importance of Itu and the Enyong Creek. So with Janet in 'complete sympathy', Mary wrote a masterly summary of the new opportunities facing her church to the Calabar Presbytery, now called the Mission Council. The council had no power to act on it and therefore forwarded it to Edinburgh.

The Enyong Creek, Mary wrote, was the gateway not only to the Aro and Ibibio tribes but to the great Ibo tribe. Itu, near its mouth, was to be a military and administration centre, it should also be a main mission centre. Launches called there regularly even in the dry season, and there the up-river, down-river, and the Enyong Creek communications would converge. To free them to establish a mission centre at Itu with out-stations, she and Miss Wright would like to see an ordained missionary and his wife stationed at Akpap.

Now that the British were opening up the waterways and building roads, the mission should take a completely new look at its method of working and at its tendency to consolidate at certain points without reaching out to all the other hundreds of thousands of Africans.

I think that it is an open secret that for years the workers here have felt that our methods . . . were far from adequate to overtake the needs of our immense field, and, as the opportunities multiply and the needs grow more clamant, the question grows in importance and gravity. The fact that only by stated consecutive work can a church be built up . . . cannot be gainsaid, and yet there is an essential need for something in between, something more mobile and more flexible than ordinary congregation methods. The scattered, broken, units into which our African populations are divided, their various ju-jus, *mbiams*, and superstitions, which segregate even the Houses of any common village, make it necessary for us to pay more than an occasional visit . . . even if that visit results in a school or church being built.

Many plans suggest themselves, Church members organised into bands of two or three or four to itinerate for a week over local neighbourhoods; native teachers spending a given number of days in each month in the outlying parts of their districts; trading members of the church undertaking service in any humble capacity on up-river trading stations . . . in these and in many other ways the gaps may be bridged . . . and communication be opened without the material expense which the opening of new stations involves . . . It may be out of my province to speak of anything outside my own station, but insofar as I know, I am voicing the opinions of the missionaries who are now working up Higher.

What Mary was recommending was the plan of using Africans to bring Christianity to their fellow countrymen which the Jamaican Presbytery had drawn up sixty years earlier. This, because of the tribal wars, had not worked in the outlying areas before the British took over, but could work soon in the areas which they were beginning to police.

Then, although her ideas were framed as a recommendation, she proceeded to tell her church what she was going to do:

By the 2nd January 1904 I shall have been out five years and so my furlough would then be due, but as I have not the slightest intention of going to Britain – I am thankful to say that I do not feel any necessity for so doing – I propose to ask leave from the station for six months, during which time I should in a very easy way try to keep an informal system of itinerating between Okoyong (Akpap) and Amasu. Already, I have seen a church and dwelling house built at Itu, and a school and a couple of rooms built at Amasu. I have visited several towns of Enyong in the Creek . . . I shall find my own canoe and crew and shall stay at any given place any length of time the circumstances suggest, so as not to tax my own strength, and members of my own family shall help with the elementary teaching in the schools.

From Itu she would work along the Enyong Creek to Amasu where she would 'itinerate in an easy way' among the Aro and then go back down the creek to Itu. If, then, the mission would please send a lady to be a companion to Miss Wright at Akpap:

The three of us, I have no doubt could dovetail detail of the work so that no part should suffer and nor should any special strain be put on our health. We should like this to take shape before the end of the year as the people will be more get-at-able in their villages . . . But I am willing to change, and Miss Wright . . . any plan of ours in order to let any larger undertaking make way if it should be proposed.

This could only come as a shock to a church which had banned further expansion on the Cross River. In the first place, in spite of Mary's adventure with the Okoyong, women were still not used to break new ground. 'Itinerating' among the Aro, some of whom were still fighting, was dangerous and not woman's work. In the second place nobody had ever spent their leave in this way before. In the third place, if there was to be no expansion, what was the point of any survey? And 'by the end of the year' too, if you please. And what was all this about new buildings at Itu and Amasu?

Miss Slessor was now clearly in a state of rebellion. For her, the mills of Edinburgh had usually ground more slowly than those of God. As she saw it, she owed it to God, to the Africans, who were anxious for her to go to them, and to her old colleagues who, she was certain, were looking down on her work from 'up higher', not to let her mission and theirs miss the new opportunities which were opening up for it.

While her plan was under consideration in Edinburgh, she took Mr Wilkie, one of the senior missionaries, up to Amasu to see for himself the territory which was opening up and the number of towns in it. But on the day when he and his wife arrived in a launch to take her up to Amasu Mary was furious with her body for letting her down. She was so ill that she had to be carried to the river in a hammock slung on a pole. She hated this but she was going to have to get used to it. Since her plan was not supposed to 'put any strain' on her health, and she was not supposed to 'feel any necessity' for going to Britain, it was not a good beginning.

At Itu they camped in the church, for Mary's house was not yet finished. A new expedition into the Aro country was assembling in a camp near the town and the Itu asked the missionaries to stay to protect them until the main body of troops moved on. Wilkie therefore had plenty of time to travel to the farms and villages nearby and see for himself the roads which were being built and to hear the invitations to Mary from the local chiefs to go and live among them.

While they were at Itu Colonel Montanaro came to see them and promised his support for any missionary activities in the area under his command.

On the way to Amasu they spent the night at Akani Obio where the young chief Onoyom met them at his beach and escorted them to his compound where he had a European-style house. Wilkie was impressed by 'his fine face and courteous manners'.

Since it was the dry season they took a canoe for the rest of the journey but even so the water six miles below Amasu was too shallow for it and they had to walk the rest of the way. Mary was going to have to do this in the dry season for the next ten years.

The British were building a large barracks on a hill near the beach and here again they were pushing roads out into the interior. The towns round about were filthy and stinking but some of these too wanted *Ma Akamba*, 'God' and 'Book', in that order. 'God' and 'Book' were unknown quantities, but *Ma Akamba* was not.

Wilkie reported to the Mission Council that everything that Mary had written was true, the mission now had a great opportunity to move forward which it should not let slip and in his view Mary should receive its full support. From now on Wilkie and his wife became two of Mary's greatest friends.

Everything now depended on Edinburgh. How would the rebel be treated?

A less democratic church might well have insisted that even a famous missionary must toe the line. But one of the hallmarks of the Scottish churches has always been their insistence on the right of their members, not only to have an individual point of view, but to fight for it. What Mary was saying made sense, and the Foreign Mission Committee, with even less money to spare since the union of the two churches, decided to take her up on her offer. She could spend her leave on her survey, and she could start up new schools and churches, where the Africans wanted them, provided always that this did not call for additional expenditure by the mission. She would be paid her salary and nothing more.

This on the face of it was a very good bargain for her church. Its mission would expand its operations at no cost to anybody except the Africans and its expendable Miss Slessor. She, it seemed, was determined to go her own way and whatever happened to her would therefore be her own responsibility.

So Mary spent the rest of her life, in W P Livingstone's words, 'dragging a great Church behind her' into Africa.

But just when permission to make her survey came through her body broke down again and she was very ill indeed from overwork, fever and malnutrition.

It really looked this time as if she was dying and the white community in Calabar, which had come to look on its most famous 'character' as indestructible, was shocked.

For over a week she lay in bed in Duke Town, sweating and

tossing, delirious with fever. Then, completely exhausted, she lay for several more days unable to move or to walk.

When over two months later she was able to move about again, she wrote: 'I rose a mere wreck of what I was, and that was not much at the best. My hair is silvered enough to please anyone now and I am nervous and easily knocked up, and so rheumatic that I cannot get up and down without pain.'

The remark about her hair was a reference to a long-standing joke among her friends that she only went bare-headed to show off her beautiful hair.

The quick moving Ma, like Eme's gin bottle, was now definitely a thing of the past. The leopardess had been caged. And she did not like it.

Her friends did their best to persuade her to give up her survey and go home to Scotland for a rest. But now more than ever she felt that time for her was running out. There was no money available for an expensive expedition complete with a train of bearers and an escort. Because of the legend of *Ma Akamba* she was the only white person who had a chance of being able to travel at this time alone and in safety through the Aro and Ibibio territory, and the only one who could live the primitive life which this would involve. Once again the formidable Slessor will was locked on target and nothing could deflect it.

Up at Akpap Janet Wright was ill too. Her leave was due and Mary insisted that she should take it. The Mission Council therefore arranged that two women would go to Akpap to take her place.

Mary saw Janet safely off to Scotland and then went back to Akpap to collect her family, some of her belongings, and the records of her Native Court. After twelve years as its Vice-Consul she was going to have to resign this post in order to make her survey.

Back in Duke Town she hired canoes and crews and bought timber, nails, hammers, saws, chisels, and other tools to build her new schools and churches.

Before she left the High Commissioner 'commanded' her to attend one of his receptions. She had the temerity to refuse. She was, she said, 'not visiting'. She did not want a fuss and in any case she had no clothes fit to be seen in such illustrious company.

So the High Commissioner went to visit her instead. He listened to her plans and promised her his full support. He

Okopedi Market: Enyong Creek

realised that this battered little peacemaker was just what he needed among the Aro.

She found two other new supporters at Duke Town, J K MacGregor, who had come out from Scotland to run the Hope Waddell Institute, and Dr Peter Rattray.

MacGregor wrote of her: 'A slim figure, of middle height, fine eyes full of power, she is no ordinary woman. It is wonderful to sit and listen to her talking, for she is most fascinating and, besides being a humourist, she is a mine of information on Mission History and Efik customs.'

When he heard of her plans to use Africans to open up new territory, Dr Rattray wrote: 'Bravo! Uganda was evangelised by these means, and teachers could only read the Gospels not write or count. The Mission understood that its task was to spread the Gospel and all who could read taught others and spread the news.'

But some of her senior colleagues disapproved. They had become accustomed to seeing their carefully laid plans come to nothing because of fevers and tribal violence. How could one woman achieve what the mission had failed to achieve in fifty years? These elderly men were wedded to white stations properly established on sound foundations after careful planning. To them Mary was rushing in with half-baked plans which would certainly go sour.

But, like Mary, they knew that to push new recruits up-river before they had spent a few years in Calabar and come to terms with the climate and the fevers was, if not to kill them, then at least to destroy their health. James Luke and Mary were the only survivors of the group which had pushed forward in the 1880s. If, with no money to spare, the mission was going to move into the new territories, only Miss Slessor could do it.

'It seems strange to be starting with a family on a gypsy life in a canoe, but God will take care of us. Whether I shall find His place for me up-river or whether I shall come back to my own people [the Okoyong] again I do not know. He knows and that is enough.'

Her salary was now one hundred pounds per year, yet out of this, because of her primitive way of life, she had saved and would save enough to finance her plans. In later years she would have the help of donations from Scotland sent specifically to finance her work. But for now she was entirely self-supporting.

In her wandering life ready cash was going to be one of her

great problems. The local currency was still the brass hoops, the local people would accept nothing else, and it took five hoops to buy even a small chicken. Government officials usually had five or six of their bearers, out of their trains of fifty or sixty, carrying nothing but the local currency. Mary, with no bearers at all would be dependent on cashing 'chits' at government camps and on what food the Africans gave her. But when a friend asked her what she would do for money she again showed her serene confidence in her Lord. 'Money is something I do not understand because I've never had to deal with it. What's money to God? The difficult thing is to make men and women. Money lies all about us in the world and He can turn it on to our path as easily as He sends a shower of rain.'

On the day she left Duke Town in July 1904, one of her colleagues saw a number of battered trunks in her canoes and said, 'You are surely richer than usual in household gear.'

'It's cement powder', said Mary. 'There's nae bags and I'm needin' it.'

Cement floors helped to keep out the ants. When asked who taught her to lay them she said, 'Naebody. I just mix it and I stir it just like porridge. Then I turn it oot, smooth it wi' a stick and say, "Lord here's the cement, if it be Thy will please set it!" And He aye does!'

So with everything from money to cement in the hands of God, she went back to Akpap to hand over to the two women who were replacing her and to say goodbye for the time being to her Okoyong.

A great crowd laden with parting gifts came sadly to see her off. Mary too was upset and ran up such a high fever the night before that once more she had to submit to being carried down to her canoes at Ikonetu beach and up to her new station at Itu.

Within a month the women who had replaced her at Akpap had found the tough life all to much for them and had deserted their post, an event which underlines the sterling qualities of Janet Wright.

Jean had been looking after Mary's orphans while she had been at Duke Town and of course Mary had taken them to Itu. There the tribe soon brought her more. A few weeks after she had moved in there, a government doctor described the conditions under which she was living: 'A native hut with a few of the barest necessities of furniture, she was sitting in a chair rocking a tiny baby, while five others were quietly sleeping wrapped in bits of brown paper in other parts of the room. How she managed to look after these children and do the colossal work she does passes my comprehension.'

To be fair to Mary, she usually made better arrangements for her babies than that. There must have been a temporary shortage of milk-cases.

She reported that Mana, Esien, and Effiom, had 'done wonders' and that she already had a congregation of three hundred and fifty. Delegations were coming to her every week from the Ibibio towns nearby asking her to visit them and to start schools and churches for their tribe. They too were finding it as difficult to adapt to the new way of life as they were to the new roads which the British were building through their territory, and along the edges of which their people still walked in single file.

As more and more of the chiefs from the Aro, Ibibio, and Enyong tribes came to see her, a new name for her began to travel along the bush paths, *Eka Kpukpro Owo*. From now on, until long after her death, this was her name.

But when they saw this 'Mother of All the Peoples', they realised that she was a sick, tired, woman. How could they get her to come to them and bring the protection of the white man's God? They soon realised that what they needed was a 'spirit house' much bigger than the ones which they built as shrines to their ancestors. They came to Itu and studied her 'spirit house' there – which was also her school – and went back to their towns and villages and copied it.

Soon little mud churches-cum-schools were dotted round Itu and more and more messengers were coming to Mary to say that their Houses were now ready for her to come and bring 'God' and 'Book'. A government official was present when one delegation arrived to ask Mary to bring 'God'. He was rash enough to show his amusement and in consequence collected himself a lecture from her which went on for nearly half an hour.

But in spite of all the talk about the importance of training African teachers, none were available. So, although some towns had saved up money to pay for a teacher's keep, all Mary could do was send them one of her brighter young boys. It was surprising that in the thirteen years since the British had begun to open up the country the mission had failed to train the African teachers for the newly settled areas.

Mary 'itinerated' in the Itu area until the rains ended and then moved on to Amasu. In October she was living in a shed while the Aro rebuilt an old hut for her. 'The boys are putting in the long big sticks which make the walls. The ants and damp have made ducks and drakes of the place but with a new wall I shall be able to stay in it on my next visit, which will probably be a month hence . . . Little did I dream that I would mud walls and hang doors again. But the Creek is at the back door and we have bathing in the sunshine. It is a delightful holiday.'

She held her first service at Arochuku under a big tree. She put out a table and her helpers spread skins and mats on the ground for the people to sit on. Everybody hung back to start with but when some of the chiefs arrived followed by their wives a crowd gathered round. All the young people were naked and some of the women too wore only strings of beads and patterns of yellow chalk. But when, with the help of a few traders, she got a hymn going, 'Everybody joined in anyhow. There was not the least semblance of a tune. But sweeter music I have never heard.' Some 'braw folk' would have found the proceedings quite shocking and disgraceful. But of course, if the New Testament can be believed, a number of the 'braw folk' of his time found Jesus of Nazareth quite shocking and disgraceful too.

Now, in spite of sporadic fighting in the forests round about, Mary began to 'intinerate' among the Aro. This was a time when Geary recorded that a white official might have visited a town several times and have been received in a friendly way, 'but later the town will throw him out and attack the escort . . . till a strong punitive expedition enforces the authority of the Government.' Escorts were continually on the lookout for trouble, African messengers in government service were intercepted and killed, and a British doctor without an escort who lost his way was killed and eaten. Several other whites were attacked and wounded or killed but nobody attacked Mary Slessor.

This shabby woman, wandering barefoot through their land with her orphans, was so different from the other white people with their strings of bearers and their escorts that the Aro did not class her with them. When they met her shuffling through the dust or plodding through the mud, she was to them, as to the British, simply out of this world. She was now as sacred to the Aro and the Ibibio as their tall trees and their magic groves.

But there were of course no maps and, although she used a pocket compass to help her to find her way, she often got lost. One day when she was trying to find her way back to the Enyong Creek to catch the launch back to Itu, a group of excannibals met her: '. . . two men took charge of my bundles and bairns and led me to a bridge round a little way. Then one asked me if I had come with God's word. What else should I come with I replied . . . he said, "We have built a small church and we are longing for you to come and teach us, and we will build a small house for you." . . . But I could not let the chance of the boat slip. I shall however go back and stay a little with them next month and build.'

This was typical of her operations for the next ten years. She had no fixed plan, no schedules, she simply relied on her Lord to guide her and to provide for her.

In November the Mission Council invited her to its meeting in Duke Town to give an account of her recent work. So much a loner had she become that this was the first of its meetings which she had attended for six years.

She reported that the buildings at Itu were nearly finished and that she had teachers at Akani Obio, Amasu, Okpo, Odot, and Asang. In other places too the Houses had built mud churches-cum-schools and in them the people were struggling to learn to read with no-one to teach them. The shortage of teachers was her biggest problem.

In spite of the misgivings of some of its members, the Council gave her permission to continue her work for the remainder of what should have been her year of leave.

James Luke wrote to the *Record*, 'Where the Church has failed a single woman has stepped into the breach . . . But it is like scattering crumbs before a starving multitude.' The mission for which so many of her old friends had given their lives was now, in her, reaching out to more Africans than it had reached in fifty years.

Just now I am the feet of the Church, as it were, and I am to go with the shoes of Peace.

15. BAREFOOT INTO AFRICA

The British were building another military base at Ikot Ekpene in Ibibio territory about twenty-five miles inland from Itu. The New District Commissioner there was Charles Partridge, a Fellow of the Royal Geographical Society, who had served on the Cross River for three years. His book *Cross River Natives* was about to be published in London.

He quickly realised that in Mary Slessor, this white African, he had a priceless asset, and at Christmas 1904 he sent her a gift which began a friendship which lasted for the rest of her life. He kept all the letters which she wrote to him and they are preserved in Dundee Central Library.

Itu. January 1905.

Dear Mr Partridge,

I must write a 'thank-you' for such a huge pudding. We had nothing to differentiate last Xmas from other days except that five days sit among flies and dirt at Ikonetu beach and this will be such a treat. It is simply lovely! And what about the basin? Shall I keep that too? Or shall I send it on to you? For such a basin is in itself a big thing here. We had it (the pudding!) for breakfast tea and dinner and again for breakfast this morning . . . A plum pudding was always my weakness. It was always on the table on my birthday, (when I had a home and a birthday which is in the far past now.)

She went on to give him advice about the Ibibio who were no fighters, had suffered badly in the slave wars, and were looked upon by the British as unreliable. 'I have many true and intelligent friends among them', she wrote, 'and so shall you . . . I trust them and have patience with them.'

At Itu, while she was taking what she called a rest, Mary had a visit from Beatrice Welsh, who described the life which 'Ma' was living: 'We visited the women in their homes . . . From morning to night Ma was busy – often far into the night. One brought a story of an unjust divorce, another was sick, one brought a primer for a reading lesson . . . another had, he claimed, been cheated in a land case. All found a ready listener, though not all found their protestations believed in.'

Mary was most impressed with Miss Welsh. 'She fits bush life like a glove.'

Janet Wright had not yet returned to Akpap and the Okoyong kept coming across the river to Mary with their problems. 'They seem to think that nobody can settle their affairs but this old woman.'

Encouraged by Partridge, Mary began to move inland away from the creek. She started a school at Ikot Obong six miles from Itu because the Itu would not let the Ibibio attend their school. The British had plans to build a road connecting Ikot Ekpene, Ikot Obong, and Itu, but this was still several months away. So, on top of everything else, Mary had to walk the six miles to her new school along the old winding bush paths. In the present-day world of telephones and automobiles it is difficult to realise just how cut off from each other places were in those thousands of tree-covered square miles with their maze of inter-secting tracks. Many of Mary's letters to Partridge were written when he was only twenty-five miles away, but until the road went through and he got himself a bicycle she rarely saw him.

Walking inland from Itu to Ikot Obong and along the three miles to Okopedi beach to take a canoe up to Akani Obio, Amasu, and her small out-stations in between, was obviously going to be too much for the rapidly ageing Miss Slessor, so it was fortunate that at this time Itu was taken off her hands. The Mission Council, acting on Mary's report, had decided to build a medical centre there, and a Mr A Kemp of Edinburgh, who was a great admirer of her work, had put up the money to build and equip a hospital for it. He would like it, he said, to be called 'The Mary Slessor Mission Hospital', and to this the mission agreed.

Mary was amazed. 'It seems like a fairy-tale. I don't know what to say. It's a grand gift and I am so glad for my people.'

Dr Robertson, one of the medical missionaries, came up to run not only the hospital but the school and the church as well. Dr Hitchcock, who took over from him when he went on leave, described the killing workload which Robertson somehow managed to sustain single-handed for two years. The hospital was always crammed with patients. They came by the canoe-load down the Cross and the Enyong Creek at all hours of the day and night, and sometimes the wards were so overcrowded that even urgent cases had to be turned away.

But Mary had no sooner been relieved of Itu than the High Commissioner invited her to become the Vice President of the Native Court for the area. He proposed, 'A nominal payment of one pound a year and to hand you the balance for use in forwarding your mission work.' Partridge, as District Commissioner, was President, and he was so anxious to have Mary's help that he arranged to have the court moved to Ikot Obong where she was now living.

Mary had seen the new officials struggling with the native laws and customs and with interpreters, who were sometimes inefficient and sometimes bribed by one side to twist the evidence. Here again was a chance for her to use her fluent Efik and her knowledge of their laws to help the people. Soon she was involved once more in day-long palavers in an airless little courthouse and in writing up the records with the native clerk in the evenings.

Some of the cases were trivial, but some involved floggings and other assaults, poisonings, and general ill-treatment of wives, widows, and slaves. Even some trivial cases were difficult to resolve. One concerned whether or not a rejected wife should return her husband's marriage gifts, the most important of which, in his eyes, were a roll of cloth, three bars of soap, a bottle of lemonade, two reels of cotton, and a thimble.

Other officials soon began to send to her for help in sorting out their own difficult cases. One had been bogged down for two days in a dispute over land ownership before he called her in. She listened for a time to the witnesses and then asked one question, 'Which House first sacrificed on the land?' That settled the case because the facts were known and no one could dispute any longer that this House was the rightful owner.

Another official described how she had quickly settled a case on which he had been sitting for three days. She had then set about one of the witnesses with her rapier tongue. 'Having no knowlege of the language', he wrote, 'I could not tell what it was all about, but plainly the man looked as if his very soul had been laid bare and as if he wished the earth would swallow him . . . She combined, most happily, kindness with severity.'

In July 1905 one of the ordained missionaries, Mr Macgregor, came up with his wife to stay with her. He took the Sunday service for her in her stifling little church at Ikot Obong and felt exhausted afterwards. He was ashamed of himself when he found that she had held twelve services that day and that this had involved walking over ten miles.

The following week Mary went up to Amasu with him in his canoe, crewed by young men from the Hope Waddell Institute, who sang hymns in harmony on the way. 'It's years since I heard such singing' said Mary. 'It puts me in fine key for the Sabbath.'

They held services at Akani Obio, Asang, Amasu, and Arochuku. It was a hectic week, but Macgregor wrote that on the way back, in spite of pouring rain, she sat with 'a face glowing with spirit', a tarpaulin over her head, and as they neared Itu beach, suggested that they should sing a hymn. But his boys were too wet and tired. So she sang it herself – twice!

She was beginning to find Partridge someone 'to tell all my stories and troubles and nonsense to'. He sent her a copy of his book and she was embarrassed to find that she had been giving advice about the Africans to a man who had already written about them:

> The natives have seldom had an interpreter so absolutely truthful and free from prejudice . . . I wish you had let yourself go a little though in regard to Nature, colouring and the mystery of mysticism, or whatever you call it, of the forest. I am sure you have had times when the bush with its myriad voices has called to you and you have not found it monotonous or tiresome. The spell of it is very strong on me sometimes. Then there are the sunrises and sunsets, the face of the river and so on waiting for you to give them voice for some of us . . . Here is a new baby, up like a rocket and down like the stick . . .

She was living as crowded a life as ever: 'I seldom get anything written without interruption, and at night when I could do it, there is no accommodation for anything in our crowded domicile, except to lie down and read in bed.'

Her Okoyong remained and would always remain her favourite tribe but she had already decided that she was under orders to push on further into the forests and that she would not be able to go back to live at Akpap. With the help of the Ibibio she had built several huts round a yard at Ikot Obong. Now she went back to collect the rest of her gear and her mother's old sideboard from the house at Akpap, and to say a painful goodbye to 'her very dear people'. Janet Wright was back with them again now, with a new recruit as companion, Mina Amess.

Daniel Slessor has described the awful day on which the Okoyong said goodbye to *Ma Akamba*: 'It was a most pathetic

Mary's courthouse at Ikot Obong

morning . . . you cannot imagine a whole people so stricken and distressed; swarms of them came from distant villages with all sorts of presents including yams, plantains, goats, chickens, eggs . . . so plentiful that if all had been accepted there would have been no room in the mission launch . . . At Ikonetu as the launch moved away for Itu, the great wail went up like thunder, men and women were weeping. Ma stood on the upper deck waving emotionally . . . As the launch turned the bend she collapsed into a chair.' For a long time Mary sat weeping and would speak to nobody.

During the rest of the year she travelled between Ikot Obong and her stations on the Enyong Creek, walking the two miles to Use, then the three miles to Okopedi beach. From there she went by canoe to Akani Obio and Okpo and, in the wet season, to Asang, but in the dry she had to walk the last six miles. She found the walking more and more exhausting and had to submit more and more to being carried in a hammock. She used the long water journeys to recover, sleeping curled up in the bottom of the dug-out canoes.

She sent a description of the brighter side of one of these day-long journeys to a group of Edinburgh schoolgirls who had written to her: 'There will be Jean, Maggie, Alice, Whitie and two infants . . . all crushed up in a space four feet by two and flies will be biting and girls will be screaming and the canoe boys will sometimes be singing and sometimes quarreling and sometimes splashing us and one another with water . . . Then there will be an alligator to shout at and throw things at – if at a safe distance – then it will be a monkey, then a snake paddling across . . . and then a bump on a sunken tree, and we will all be thrown anyhow, and some of the boys, if punting, will be sure to go overboard . . . and then the screaming'.

She told them too about a crew of young Aros who seem to have been real Mary Slessor people: 'They paddled the whole day as if the sun were not beating down on them like a blazing fire. When we came up . . . we had such a heavy load of timber for building purposes that they could hardly get a seat . . . They pulled eight hours on end without stopping to eat a bite. About seven o'clock we all lay down, after holding worship in the canoe, and didn't they sing!' The young Aro and the tough little Scotswoman, so soon to be crippled with rheumatism, singing round the fire in the last year in which she would move about without pain. 'And then about 3 am the moon began to show through the mist and they jumped up and pushed off, and then for eight hours pulled and sang and laughed and shouted in their high spirits'.

At the end of 1905 Janet Wright and Mina Amess came up the river to celebrate New Year with her. As they were walking along from Itu to Ikot Obong they met a group of British surveyors who invited the three missionaries to have New Year dinner in their camp. 'Ma', they assured Janet, 'won't have anything in the house.'

Mary was pleased about the invitation but she felt that the occasion demanded something better than her old cotton dresses. There was nothing remotely suitable in any of her boxes of secondhand clothes except a dressing-gown. So she wore that and was in sparkling form.

But soon afterwards she was ill again. Partridge had been away and on the 24th February she wrote to him: 'I had fever right on two or three times a week during January and have only twice been able to walk to church this year. But this Saturday I took quite a turn for the better'.

She had been losing her temper too often in court, she said, and must be more patient. She did not go into detail but at this time an Assistant Commissioner wrote that one day she had risen up in wrath, snatched his own umbrella from a man who had been lying to the court, and begun thumping him over the head with it.

But she did tell Partridge that she had been nearly smothered the week before by the enormous mother of an accused man who was certain that her son was going to be executed: 'She hung on me, lay on me, hugged me for four hours and I could not get out of her embraces till I was nearly fainting. "Take me! . . . Take me!" she kept saying. "He is all I have!" . . . It was a bad day for me I can tell you . . . What a wonderful thing is a mother's love . . . Now tell me, where can I buy land for an industrial school and refuge for women who need help? I have the money.'

All through her years in Calabar she had been determined to show that the African women could run their own lives if only they were given the opportunity to do so. The women still did most of the work on the tribal farms and most of the selling in the tribal markets too. If they had land of their own they could be self-supporting. But they still had no personal rights as citizens. When the men to whom they belonged rejected them or died, even freewomen often starved or turned to prostitution. At this time Mary was supporting several unwanted women for whom she had built huts in her yard.

She had seen so much suffering caused by the entire dependence of the women on the men that it had become even more a burning issue with her. In one of her Bibles, against the passage where St Paul lays down rules for the subjection of wives to husbands, she scribbled in the margin 'Na! Na! Paul, laddie! This will no do!' And in a letter to Partridge she even recommended that the wives of a rogue of a chief who had been sent to prison, should be allowed, according to tribal custom, to make temporary 'friend' marriages until he was released. To her it was better than starvation for them and their children. Another example of how Mary Slessor recognised that African law and African custom were sometimes best for solving desperate African problems – she wrote: 'Women here can't stay single for years.'

Partridge approved of her plans for a women's settlement and he began to help her to look for a site for it. The road had reached Ikot Ekpene now so that he could cycle over more often to see her. Their surveys had, however, to be on foot. These showed him just how painful walking was for her nowadays, and he sent to England for a bicycle for her.

When it came she was delighted with it. 'It is the very latest pattern.' With a good deal of advice from onlookers and help from Jean and Dan, she learned to ride it, shrieking at first when she wobbled and laughing when she fell. Because of the ruts in the road her progress was not fast and on the first of her journeys Dan used to trot beside her, pushing when necessary and steadying her when she wobbled. 'It was my job to push Ma's bicycle up the hills. She was light and I could do it without strain. On the return journey the steep part continued for a long way. I would let her go and down she would fly, her hair flying out behind her.' It was even better than climbing trees.

Mary wrote to a friend, 'Fancy an old woman like me on a bicycle. The new road makes it easy to ride and I am running up and down . . . It is doing me all the good in the world and I will soon be able to overtake more work . . . I wonder what the Andersons and the Goldies will say when they see we can cycle twenty miles in the bush.' Her bicycle became her great joy. But often she was too ill to ride it.

The Women's Foreign Missions Committee had extended her

'leave' until April 1906. Then she was due to return to Akpap. The Committee's secretary wrote to her to remind her of this. She replied that although no people and no place was dearer to her than Okoyong, 'There is an impelling power behind me and I dare not look baçk . . . Whether the Church permits it or not I feel I must stay here and even go forward as roads are made. I cannot walk now, nor dare I do anything to trifle with my health, which is very queer now and then, but if the new roads are of the easy gradient of those already built, I can get four wheels . . . and set a box on them and the children can draw me about. I shall take the risk of finding my own chop [food] if the Mission decide not to go on. But if they see their way to meet the new needs and requirements, I shall do all in my power to further them without extra expense to the Church.'

Then, to soften the tone of this mutinous letter she added, 'This is not for publication; it is for digestion.'

To a friend she wrote: 'I am not over-enthusiastic about Church methods . . . I would not mind cutting the rope and going adrift with my bairns.'

The same 'impelling power' had taken her to Calabar and to the Okoyong. Then she had been an apprentice. Now she was skilled. By September she would have thirty years' experience behind her. Perhaps she was, as Mary Kingsley thought, the greatest expert in her field. Clearly neither what she had taken to calling 'my poor carcase' nor other people were now going to stop her trying to use her skills to help her beloved Africans in obedience to God. And she knew that what she had achieved or would achieve would never amount to more than the tiniest scratch on a huge surface.

The Committee cannot have welcomed the idea of one of its lady missionaries being towed about by young Africans in some 'box on wheels', and it was clear that she was very definitely going to 'trifle with' her health. But it could not allow its famous missionary to break away and once more it was getting a good bargain. The Committee made the gesture of pronouncing that in future she would please suggest and it would do the deciding, but then since it knew there was no hope of this, it laid down that in future she would have no fixed station. She was free to go forward and to start new stations where the Africans wanted them, provided always that she did not commit the church to additional expense. She was indeed now 'dragging a great Church behind her' into Africa.

With this victory behind her she went back from Ikot Obong to Duke Town to try to persuade the Mission Council to take Amasu and Arochuku off her hands. If, with the help of the Aro, she built a house and a church-cum-school in one of the towns would the mission appoint two women to take it over?

The Council agreed to send an ordained missionary, John Rankin, up to Arochuku with her to survey the area. He reported: 'Close to Arochuku . . . are nineteen towns each of which is bigger than Creek Town. The people are a stalwart race . . . the majority are very anxious to help. A section is strongly opposed, even to the point of persecution of those who, under the influence of Miss Slessor and others [her teachers] have already begun to live in "God's fashion" . . . The head chief of all the Aros is one of the most favourable . . . A new church will be built and he offers to build a house for any missionary who will come.'

Rankin volunteered to go to Arochuku himself. The Mission agreed, and a few months later he went up and, with help from Mary, took over both Arochuku and Amasu. For the time being therefore Mary's journeys up the Enyong Creek ended at Asang about five miles below Amasu.

Meanwhile Janet Wright was going on leave before marrying Dr Rattray and going to live at Unwana with him. The mission decided that young Mina Amess could not live among the Okoyong on her own, so until a companion could be found for her, it sent her across the river to live with Mary.

Miss Amess wrote home about how she had pictured the formidable Miss Slessor before she met her: 'She had been so courageous that I imagined that she would be somewhat masculine and of a very commanding appearance, but I was pleasantly disappointed to find that she was a true woman with a heart full of motherly affection. Her welcome was the heartiest which I received. Her originality, brightness, and almost girlish spirit fascinated me . . . One could not be long in her presence without enjoying a right hearty laugh.'

Mina, of course, knew all about Mary's primitive way of life and brought all her own household equipment up from Akap with her. It took sixteen men to carry it all and she was rather worried about how she and her train of bearers would be received. Mary however only laughed, and when the new recruit produced her water-filter, made her usual joke about them never having been created.

Like Partridge, who found Mary 'surprisingly well-informed', Mina was surprised at the veteran's 'grasp of everything going on in the world'. This was because Mary had several political journals sent out to her each month along with the Scottish newspapers and the *Record*. But after her stay with Mary, Mina wrote that there was never any routine with 'Ma'. 'One never knew what she would be doing. One hour she might have a political discussion with a District Commissioner, the next, be supervising the building of a house, and later on judging native palavers. Late one evening I heard a deal of talking and also the sound of working. I went to see what was going on and there was Ma making cement and the bairns spreading it on the floor with their hands by candle-light.'

Mary got on well with her: 'What a relief it is to have someone to lean on and to share the responsibility of the bairns. Miss Amess is sane and capable and helpful and is always on the watch to see what is to be done ... A dear lassie.' Mary was particularly glad to have her because Jean was in hospital in Duke Town with 'a female complaint' and would be away for several weeks.

The old leopardess was beginning to learn to live with her cage, to delegate authority, and quietly to steer others instead of always pushing herself. She was undoubtedly helped towards this new frame of mind by the fact that day by day events were proceeding in the way she was praying that they should. Had she been losing the battle she would have been fighting and raging and worrying away at her problems as she had always done.

She had found a site which would have been ideal for her women's settlement if it had not been too far from Use market. It was on a hill two miles from the river and had a good view and a good water supply.

Often in the past when she had been ill she had wished that there had been a rest camp for the women missionaries where they could recover their health without having to go to crowded Duke Town or Creek Town. So she wrote to the Council and recommended that a rest camp be built on this site. In the meantime she obtained permission to clear part of it and proceeded to build a hut on it.

After the rebuke which it had received from Edinburgh for sending two ladies to live in Mary's house at Akpap, the Council decided that it ought to send a senior woman to inspect the place. Miss McKinney was warned to take her own camp-bed. This was just as well because she found Mary sleeping on the floor of the new hut with a mattress and a sheet of corrugated iron under her: concessions to old age.

Miss McKinney came back with a story which had Duke Town laughing for weeks. She had been surprised to find that Mary had no alarm clock and had asked her how they could be sure of waking at sunrise in time for her to get to the river and catch the launch back to Duke Town. 'Dinna worry!', Mary had said, 'I hae an alarm.' She had then gone out and caught a cockerel which she proceeded to tie by one leg to the corrugated iron with a piece of string. 'When we blow out the lamp', she said, 'he'll bide quiet till dawn . . . he aye does!'

Nothing ever came of her rest camp idea, probably due to lack of money. But now, due to malnutrition Mary began to come out in crops of boils. This was not altogether surprising because, when in any particular place the food did not agree with her – or only dog, cat, or monkey, was available – she was known to exist entirely on shortbread and toffee. She wrote to thank one woman in Scotland who had sent her tins of shortbread and biscuits: 'I had been much upset by the local food and now I have been able to live on nothing but shortbread and buns for a week and that has made me better.'

Some of the boils were on her head and part of her hair fell out. A government doctor told her that she really must now go to Scotland for a complete rest. But this verdict seemed only to cure her for the boils disappeared. She wrote to him, 'It looks as if God has forbidden my going.'

But in January 1907 after more fever she found that once again she could not walk. She admitted in a letter to Partridge that this time she thought she was paralysed for good.

There could be no argument now about going back to Scotland. One of the mission staff, Mr Middleton, was going on leave in May and he volunteered to look after her on the voyage. In the meantime Mary refused to go back to Duke Town and carried on with her court work and her teaching and services, although she had to be carried everywhere. When the time came for her to leave she decided to leave Jean in charge of Ikot Obong and to take only Dan to Scotland with her. Miss Amess had returned to Akpap with a new recruit, Miss Reid.

She wrote to Partridge on 20th May 1907 from on board the SS *Orcades* to say that she was sorry that his duties had prevented him from seeing her off. 'The water has been delightful, so deep and green and clear and the lap-lap of the waves most restful to wearied nerves.'

She had been carried on board but, with Mr Middleton's help, could climb a few stairs. 'I am leaning hard on my limbs and after going up the stair I can still fetch a bit of breath. I hope to be walking quite well in about a week more.' They had to sit beside the door in the dining saloon because she could not walk up it.

At Liverpool she sent her usual telegram to Mrs McCrindle asking her to meet the train at Edinburgh.

Until she heard her voice her friend did not recognise the stooping, grey-haired woman talking to a porter, so shrunken and wrinkled had she become in the eight years since she had gone back to Calabar. She was wearing a hat too, to hide the top of her head which was bald.

Mrs McCrindle took Mary off to her home near Edinburgh from which, after a few weeks' rest, she began the inevitable round of speeches and sermons. Daniel proved to be as big a success as Janie had been twenty-three years before.

At the McCrindles', Mary used to stretch out on the rug in front of the fire and tell them about life in Calabar. They often heard her talking in her room and thought that in her old age she had developed a habit of talking to herself. They discovered however that she was chatting away to God. Mr McCrindle wrote: 'One afternoon she arrived home to us after visiting friends in Dundee. She was somewhat worn out as she had had a slight attack of fever, to which she was constantly subject, and sitting down at the tea table all alone, she lifted her head and uttered these words, "Thank ye, Faither, ye ken I'm tired", as if she had been speaking to one of us.'

She wrote several letters from Scotland to Charles Partridge. In June she told him, 'I can walk now and go up and down stairs like anybody.'

In September she was sorry to hear that he had been ill but was glad that he was going back home to Suffolk to recover. 'It's nice to be called by your Christian name and to hear people say "How like your mother you are." But it is hard on my dear old mother . . . I have been revelling in frocks and furbelows. It is simply lovely to see the shop windows and very nearly envy the beautiful creations the girls wear, and to look at their milk-and-roses complexion and the beauty and roundness of form which they possess . . . But all this is most unbecoming in the senior

member of a Presbyterian Mission. So you must keep my
weakness a secret'.

She was enjoying herself – 'behaving like a young lady.' But
she could not for long keep off the subject of Calabar. 'I am
longing to get a home of some kind started for women in Ibibio
and my friends are willing to come to the rescue . . . I have a
promise of £300, but only for the home. . . . I am hoping that
shoe-making may be given them for an industry as I believe
there will be a great demand for shoes and the plant costs little.'
What a shrewd businesswoman Mary Slessor would have made.

At the end of September her enjoyable time came to an end.
She received a letter from Calabar telling her that there was a
rumour that Jean was misbehaving herself with a chief. Mary,
desperately worried, announced that she must go back to her
bairns immediately.

Friends argued and so did the Foreign Missions' Committee.
But it was no use. The Slessor mind was made up. The best the
Committee could do was to persuade her to stay on until October so that she could speak at three big meetings which they
had arranged. She wrote to a Mrs Melville who had sent her a
large donation for her home: 'They [the Committee] much
against my will and pleading, have ruled that I must stay . . . till
one big meeting be held in Glasgow, one in Edinburgh, and one
in Aberdeen . . . I suppose I must obey.'

She asked Mrs Melville to pray that God's cause would be
worthily represented by 'these stammering lips of mine'.

She actually wrote out two of the sermons which she
preached in Dundee and they are preserved in the Dundee
Museum. One of them reads like an old woman's testimony to a
young woman's simple, indestructible, faith: 'Why then are you
fearful . . . The rage and scorn of men cannot harm you for "He
shall hide thee in His presence from the pride of Man" . . . No
foe either from without or within can prevail against you while
He, the omnipotent, is with you . . . No weapon formed against
you shall prosper . . . "Thou shalt be free from fear and from op-
pression for it shall not come nigh thee" . . . The change, the
decay which is stamped on all around need not disturb you while
the unchanging love of God is pledged to you, while His
everlasting arms encircle you. "Fear not for I am with thee." '

At the end of October 1907, after only five months' rest instead of twelve, and with her health still bad, she sailed back to
Calabar.

During the voyage she wrote to Partridge about her time in Scotland: 'Life is full of conventional duties, which are as hard in their way as the real things in life, but much less satisfactory. Still I have enjoyed it, the white-washings and pullings about to get me into society shape notwithstanding'.

At Ikot Obong she found that the rumours about Jean had been false but was 'too grateful to be angry'.

16. TOWARDS WOMEN'S INDEPENDENCE

In November Mary wrote from her hut at Use to Charles Partridge, who was still on sick leave in Suffolk. She told him that she was surprised that she could walk up hills 'so easily'. She was 'rudely healthy' now. 'It has been worth getting home to get such a welcome. The chiefs were down the morning after we arrived and they cleared all the bush and the road [track] before the sun was high. The place is beginning to look homelike and clean now.'

In a letter to Miss Adam of the Foreign Missions Board she described how she had received a deputation, 'of forty fine looking men from a large market town called Ikpe'. They came to remind her that two years earlier when she had been 'itinerating' she had promised that one day she would go and start a school for them. Now, in a town nearby, they had built a little church in the hope that this would bring her to them.

Ikpe unfortunately was a difficult place to reach. It was about twenty miles beyond Amasu up a tributary of the Enyong Creek. For six months in the year this tributary dried out so that to reach the town Mary would have to walk from Asang to Amasu, then six miles to Arochuku, and then another fourteen miles to Ikpe. The very idea of her making such a journey was ridiculous. But the delegation told her that some of the chiefs of the towns round about were afraid that, because the Christians were not obeying the old customs, they would bring disaster on the area. In consequence the young Christians were being flogged and branded. They had only the sketchiest idea of Christianity and none of them could read but, in spite of the floggings, they were still holding prayer meetings in their little church. Mary was in no doubt that, since she was partly responsible for the situation, she had a clear duty to go and try to stop the floggings.

In later years, after he visited her there, the young Dr John

Hitchcock described the last stage of the journey, that from Arochuku to Ikpe. 'We set out at 6.45 am and walked steadily for three and a half hours along a bad and little frequented track, through miles of native farms rich in palms and cassava.' They then had a rest at a village: 'We walked on from this village again until we struck a river. A canoe took us over . . . now our path was through primeval forest abounding in beautiful flowers and gorgeous butterflies. Now and again there was a surprising crash overhead as a monkey ventured a flying leap. But most of our attention was required to pick our path for it was intensely muddy and the track in many places was faint. It was about noon when we got to the town . . . We took the same way home . . . the lights here pass description . . . Night was falling when we reached Arochuku . . . the passing of the day and night here is almost pompous.'

This was the kind of journey which Mary had been making often over the past thirty years and one which would have delighted the young Miss Slessor. Over the next eight years, however, the journeys which she felt bound to make to Ikpe were an ordeal which the pain-wracked woman dreaded. She had to keep going back there because, although the floggings stopped during her visits and for a few months afterwards, they always began again.

Her station at Ikot Obong and her out-stations round it were now well established, so, since she wanted to start her women's settlement and free herself to stay longer at Ikpe, the mission agreed to appoint Miss Peacock and Miss Reid to Ikot Obong. With Dr Robertson at Itu, John Rankin at Arochuku, and Miss Amess and Miss Welsh at Akpap, her church was beginning to back her up.

Martha Peacock, who was a tall girl and at this time shy and withdrawn, was the second of the Falkirk girls. She had arrived in Calabar a few years earlier but Mary hardly knew her and was worried about how she and her companion would react to living conditions at Ikot Obong. She was afraid that they, like the women who had first taken over Akpap, might find the house too primitive, so she and Jean worked hard at improving it.

On 1st January 1908 Mary wrote to Partridge to thank him for the Christmas puddings which he had arranged to be sent to her although he was still in Suffolk. She told him that she was going to build her settlement in a disused government camp near

Use, 'but not until the house here is ready for the ladies . . . I can climb ladders again now.'

But when, two months later, the 'ladies' arrived, she found them 'very enthusiastic' and decided that she could leave Ikot Obong to them and move on to the camp near Use. Once installed there, she and Jean and 'the bairns' set to work to repair the old buildings.

She had to keep cycling back from Use to Ikot Obong to preside over the Court. Motor cars were beginning to appear on the road now, and when one was heard, court proceedings were suspended while Mary, chiefs, police, accused, witnesses, and spectators, ran out to have a look at it.

Partridge had obviously been telling her in his letters that she must look after herself better, wear a hat, and filter the water, because she replied: 'I never once removed my hat all day from 7 am to 8 pm and − I had fever! It is the first time in my experience that I have been able to keep my hat on so long, and the woeful result is quite expected . . . I am sleeping sometimes under a net, when it is not too hot . . . and several times this term I have taken quinine. The filter I may indulge in soon . . . and I WORE MY HAT, will that satisfy you?' Her hair was growing again. 'The poor white threads that barely covered the scalp during my last two or three years, have multiplied exceedingly during my trip to Bonnie Scotland.'

A few weeks later she wrote to tell him how difficult it still was to get twins and their mothers accepted into the communities. She had persuaded some of the mothers to take offending chiefs and husbands to court to enforce their rights. But most of the women were too afraid of a flogging to do this. When the Government Report on the area for 1907 was published it included a reference to Mary's success in getting a few mothers of twins accepted back into their families. 'The result is a sign of the civilising influence through the Court by that admirable lady, Miss Slessor.'

Donations were now coming in from Scotland for her settlement and some of her out-stations were collecting enough money to begin paying for their own teachers and books. Soon she had enough money to start moving her unwanted women to Use where she helped them to build their own huts. The government sent up fruit trees for her to plant and she bought goats and cattle but lost most of them to the leopards.

The mission too had promised to support the settlement but

Mary with David and their two children

only on condition that Mary stayed on it for a year to see it properly established. This of course she could not do. Places like Ikpe had been waiting for years for her to go to them and time for her was running out. Anyone, she felt, could run the settlement once she had started it, but only she could move into areas where the chiefs were clinging to the old barbarous customs. So because the mission refused to send anyone to take over the settlement, and she was only able to visit it from time to time, it was never properly run until her death forced the mission to take it over.

In July Partridge wrote to say that he was returning to West Africa but had been transferred to Lagos. Mary replied, 'What a sell! – What a dead down dump!' She was disappointed that he was not returning to Calabar and upset because while she had been at Amasu a troublesome chief had persuaded a junior official to send her favourite court messenger, Ekpenyong, to an outlying town to make a proclamation and he had been murdered. 'I am so mad', she wrote, 'I can't feel sure of myself to go into it all.' Probably the chief and the junior official never knew how near they were to being thumped over the head with the Slessor umbrella.

In the same letter she told Partridge, 'I am rejuvenated, I now have false teeth – when I remember to put them in!'

While she was at Use, to save a man from going to prison for debt, she bought his cow. Within weeks, until finally she had to get rid of it, the animal became famous as far away as Duke Town, as 'Ma Slessor's Coo'. Mary wrote to Partridge: 'She took us all in tow the first week, every night and morning, and gave us a run through the bush and everything until of course we had to let go, and then we had wild excursions all over the bush with an occasional race after her again, till again she took the rope and thus we played in the moonlight, till I was at my wits end and everything was broken in pieces . . . One night she took the young men of Use for a run and had them well up the road to Ikot Obong, but at length she did arrive dragging three or four of them . . . Speak of milking the creature? . . . But she lets me scratch her nose now.'

Mary's 'daughter' Annie – who on 4th August 1888 had travelled up that black path to Ekenge astride her shoulders – had married an African trader and was living happily with him at Itu. Now, in October, young Mary married no less a person than David, the driver of the government motor car. Mary saw

to it that he was baptised before the ceremony. A big glass bowl
stood in for a font.

She had sent Dan and Asuquo off to the Hope Waddell Institute and now relied more than ever on Jean. She was usually
too tired at the end of the day to wash or undress or brush her
hair, 'which is as thick as ever now and still has gold glints in the
sun', until she had lain down for what she called her 'first rest'.

In December 1908, probably as a birthday present, the
Macgregors sent her a real bed and a carpet for her hut at Use.
A rapturous Mary wrote to thank them, 'Oh what a difference it
[the carpet] has made to our comfort . . . the mud and the cement
were transformed and the cosiness was beyond belief. It
did not look a bit hot and it was so soothing to the bare feet.'
And the bed – what a change from a hammock! 'I have been
jumping my tired body up and down on it just to get the
beautiful swing, and to feel that I am lying level. I'm tired and
I'm happy and I'm half ashamed at my own luxury . . . Oh what
a lovely sleep I've had!'

James Macgregor was now looking after her money for her at
Duke Town. Donations of fifty pounds and more were now
coming in from individuals and from parish collections in
Scotland specifically for her work, so that, with the money
which she continued to save from her own salary, she had over
two hundred pounds banked with him. But, to Mary, her work
did not include herself. She wanted the money for her settlement
and to pay teachers and maintain the churches-cum-schools and
she grudged every penny which had to be spent on anything else.

Notes which she sent to Macgregor asking him to draw out
some of her money showed how worried she was that it should
be spent 'properly'. She needed a new lamp and a new Bible.
Now that she had a 'guest room' she had better have a basin and
water jug for visitors who could not be expected to wash in a
bucket as she did. 'Is that extravagant?' she would ask, 'Is that
too selfish?'

A woman in Scotland sent her fifty pounds and asked her to
spend some of it on herself. Mary replied, 'Dear Friend, I need
nothing. My every want is met and supplied without my asking.'
Her primitive way of life was now the only life she thought of
living. The people for whom she was working had so little that
she was ashamed to have anything more than was necessary for
her work. She knew that they looked on the food which they
gave her as a gift to *Abassi* through her, for they had always

offered food to their gods and their ancestors at their shrines. But in spite of their gifts, in the remote places in which she now lived for weeks at a time, she was often near to starvation.

Early in 1909 she went down with dysentery and 'the funniest illness I have ever had'. She did not say what this was, but it seems to have involved long spells of giddiness. Dr Robertson took her off to hospital at Itu, and, 'He brought me out of the valley of the shadow, and when I was convalescent, lifted me up in his strong arms and took me to see the church and the garden, and anywhere else I wished, just as he might have done to his own mother.'

When she had recovered, the Macgregors removed her, protesting, to Duke Town for a complete rest. 'I am doing nothing but eating and am growing fat and shedding my buttons all over the place.' But, although she wrote this to Partridge, she was still little more than skin and bone.

In Africa she was as completely indifferent to clothes as she was to accommodation. The Macgregors once found her presiding over her Court, bareheaded, barelegged, barefoot, in a cotton overall. For her rest at Duke Town she had fitted herself out, as usual, from the boxes of second-hand clothes. But shoes were painful to her splayed out feet and she had a habit of slipping them off when she sat down. This, she noticed, upset some people, so for their benefit she ostentatiously kicked her shoes off. And, as part of the clowning which she now used to annoy people who looked down on her or who thought her 'quaint', she began to wear extraordinary mixtures of clothes and of colours.

For the benefit of a lady journalist from the London *Morning Post* Mary excelled herself. The journalist had been most anxious to interview such a famous 'character' but Mary had refused, until Macgregor persuaded her to change her mind. He said that when she finally agreed to be interviewed she had a wicked gleam in her eye and that he had feared the worst. Eventually this report appeared in the newspaper:

I am not given to admiring missionary enterprise. The enthusiasm which seems to many magnificent, seems to me but meddling in other people's business. But this missionary conquered me if she did not convert me. She was a woman close on sixty with a heavily lined face and a skin from which the freshness and bloom had long departed, but there was fire in her old eyes still, tired though they looked, there was a sweetness about her heavily lined mouth. Heaven knows who had dressed her. She wore a skimpy tweed skirt and a cheap nun's veiling blouse, and on her iron-grey hair was perched rakishly a forlorn, broken, picture-hat of faded green chiffon with a knot of bright red ribbon to give the bizarre touch of colour.

The report ended with a quote from the High Commissioner:

She Miss Slessor can go where no white man can go. She can sway the people when we cannot sway them. Because of her they are not as hard on twins and their mothers as they used to be.

After this episode the Macgregors and her other friends tried to see that Mary was properly dressed when invited to meet people or to a function. They did not always succeed.

After 'five idle Sabbaths' at Duke Town, Mary pronounced herself fully recovered and went off back to Use. There she happily resumed her cycle tours and her journeys by canoe up to her out-stations along the Enyong Creek and then across country to Ikpe through Arochuku. She was becoming more and more ashamed at not being able to go and live at Ikpe or to find a teacher who would do so.

She took Martha Peacock up there and they made several tours of the area round about. Martha wrote home about how much she was enjoying the tours and how much she was learning from them. She described how at one place they were met by a crowd of women who were completely naked except for coloured chalk patterns and head-scarves; how Mary turned to her and, remembering the evangelist's rules about women covering their hair, said, 'Do you suppose Paul was here before us?'

To Partridge Mary wrote that Martha was now 'One after my own heart . . . the old stiffness is greatly gone and she is most successful in her work . . . She is as kind to me as if she were my own born sister. Her sane ways of looking at things now that she has the right clue, are a great help to me.'

But Mary's new-found health lasted for only six months and then she went down with her most painful illness yet. Partridge received no reply from several letters and became so worried that he sent her a telegram. Her writing in her reply is barely legible.

Use. 7/7/09

Very dear old friend,

I only got your telegram last week . . . I went very ill with at least a hundred boils over my head . . . I lay down, or stretched across is nearer the thing, Mrs Wilkie's bed and for a whole month was in a prolonged agony of pain. The boils came in shoals all over my face until you would not have recognised me . . . all over my neck and ears and, whenever I got over one operation of having the cores pressed out, another began and I cried like a child . . . when I was not shrieking. No sleeping draught could keep out the pain . . . I am a very shaky bundle of nerves . . . I could not read because my eye-lids were full and letters were left unopened. I have often joked with you, in my mind though, about the pretty hair and the halo. Poor hair! Poor head! It is as bald as a sixpence all over the back and I wear a handkerchief knotted at the four corners as we did in schooldays . . . The few hairs left at the front are like those of a doll's head put on with bad glue.

It was in this letter that she told him about newly arrived Europeans finding loopholes in the African laws on land purchase and grabbing all they could get.

Without the Gospel . . . the very men you are educating with guns and motors and telegraph will one day turn you all out and keep Africa for the Africans.

It was typical that she wrote 'turn you all out' and not 'us'. What can Partridge have made of such a prophecy in 1909?

In reply to this letter he must have tried to persuade her to give up now and go back to Scotland, for she replied, 'I love my Master and I will not go out from Him, and I do believe that I am doing Ikpe and Use good by giving them that which turns away the hunger of the spirit and gives them a tangible Helper and hope of life . . . So there! . . . I am to stick to my post and you would be the first to cry shame if I turned tail for a bit of fever or even a bald head. My hair is growing in nicely and I hope that it will be covering the scalp before you come over and see me.'

She told him that her Christian faith had, all along, given her peace, she had 'proved it often' and it would do the same for him if only he would try it.

There was talk at this time of his being transferred back to Calabar from Lagos. But this never happened and she never did see him again.

In her letters to him she came out of her tough shell and sometimes the loneliness and nervous tension, with which she had lived for so long, shows through. He was the only one whom she told about how upset she had been over the circumstances of her resignation from the vice-presidency of the Court. There had been a misunderstanding over the death of a woman and a new District Commissioner had sent her a very rude letter in which he accused her of attempting 'as usual' to protect the

Africans. She had replied that if this was his opinion of her then she could not continue to serve under him. Later the Area Commissioner had accepted her resignation.

Her colleagues had thought that she was glad to have the work taken off her hands. But a long letter to Partridge showed how she really felt about the matter: 'I am cast aside by strangers and not to be trusted.' But she ended, 'Then the ludicrous side dawned on me and I laughed.'

The people of course continued to consult their *Eka Kpukpro Owo* about everything and the new District Commissioner did not last long.

With Martha Peacock too the old warrior began to let down her guard. The young recruit wrote that, although Mary was as fearless as ever in facing up to people, snakes now frightened her, and if a canoe even lurched, 'Ma would cling on with both hands to my arm.'

From a letter which Mary wrote earlier to a boy called Ratcliffe in Edinburgh, Jean seems to have been the one to deal with snakes, as she was with so many things. 'One night in the dark . . . Janie was jumping about and Annie was throwing things and by the light of the fire it looked awful. Janie laughed back to my scream, "It's a snake! Don't come!", and she was lashing all she was able with a stick. Annie was making noise and not much more. Janie forced it back until she and Maggie and Annie were on the outside and could run, but Janie held on, and I threw her a machete and she hacked the thing to bits.' When it came to standing up to danger Mary and Jean made a good pair.

In December 1909 Mary wrote to Partridge, 'I was sixty years old last week.' She had once more lost count of time – in 1905 she dated several letters 1904 – for there is no doubt that she was born in 1848 and was therefore sixty-one.

At Christmas he sent her his usual plum-pudding (he never once missed when he was in Africa), and a new bicycle too: her old one had rusted up in the rains. On 3rd January 1910 she wrote to him from Duke Town, 'I have been so excited for over a week about my new cycle. I saw it for the first time when I came down here for Presbystery.'

In March she wrote to his parents to apologise for being so long in thanking them for sending out the cycle. Once more her writing is barely legible. 'I can't write a letter as I am nearly blind. I have had that neck and head of boils again.' But a new

District Commissioner. whom she liked, had brought a government doctor to treat her and he had not been stupid enough to insist on pressing out the cores. 'He has worked a miracle of healing . . . and made life quite bearable again. I feel mad at the months of agony which I spent last year . . . Only yesterday have I been able to read and write again . . . though I am groping over the paper by instinct . . . There is no pain in the eyes now and in a couple of days I shall be on my cycle again.'

But of course she was not. She was able to use her cycle so seldom now that she began to think again about her 'box on wheels'. She wrote to friends in Scotland asking them to try to find a large wheelchair for her which would be light enough to be pulled along tracks and lifted into canoes. She hated, she wrote, being carried in a hammock: 'I feel a brute in it. It seems so selfish to be lying there while four boys sweat like beasts of burden. To push a little carriage is like skilled labour and is no degradation.'

Her friends tried once again to get her to go to Scotland for a complete rest. But there had been more deaths and she refused. 'We were never so short-handed before. I can do what others cannot do; what medical opinion would not allow them to try. No one meddles with me and I can slip along and do my work with less expenditure of strength than any . . . I begin every day, every journey in pain and such tiredness that I feel I can't go on, and whenever I begin the strength comes and it increases.' From this she concluded that God wanted her to persevere in her work otherwise he would not be giving her the strength to do it.

Another delegation came to tell her that the young Christians were once more being flogged at Ikpe. Now she decided that visits were not enough. Since no one else would go, the only way for her to get peace for her people was to go and build a house and live there herself.

17. 'THE MOST WONDERFUL HOLIDAY I EVER HAD'

The only land at Ikpe which Mary could lease was near a creek, swampy in wet weather, and in the dry swarming with mosquitoes. Macgregor did not like the sound of it and asked her if he and his wife could go up there with her to look it over.

When they arrived at Use Mary told them that the Lord did not want them to go to Ikpe next day because, although she had tried several people, she had been unable to hire a canoe and crew. They would have to wait a few days.

Then, on the evening before they were to set out, she went down with fever and they thought that the journey would have to be postponed again. However Mary was up just after midnight, supervising the loading of the canoe, although Jean was having to help her to walk. Two hours later she announced that they were ready to go.

Macgregor protested to Jean that Mary was much too ill to travel but Jean laughed and said, 'She is often like this. She just takes laudanum and lies down in the canoe and sleeps. By the end of the journey she is better. She has been doing it for months.'

They set out by moonlight and reached Amasu, where they were to spend the night, eight hours later. Mary, sure enough, had recovered.

At Ikpe they camped in the little church. Macgregor found the people 'degraded' and the town filthy. Most of the women wore only blue beads and patterns of coloured chalks.

The Christians thought that he must be the teacher whom Mary had promised them and were most upset when they found that he was not. They said that she had promised them a teacher years before but now always said, 'Wait! . . . Wait!' Was she never going to get them one?

'You see?', Mary said to Macgregor, 'I'm honour bound to come.' Just what there was about the place which put off

African teachers, then or later, from taking it on was not explained. Perhaps it was the combination of swamps, mosquitoes, and floggings.

The Macgregors thought that the site, what with the night mists on the swamp, the stink, and the mosquitoes, was unbearable. They did their best to persuade Mary that the very idea of her living there was ridiculous. But she said that since she was honour bound it would have to do. She told the people that she would be back in a few weeks with materials to build herself a house so that she could live among them. After the floggings and so many years of waiting, the news that *Eka Kpukpro Owo* herself was coming to live with them would have seemed almost unbelievable. 'I am committed now. No more idleness for me. I am entering in the dark as to why or when but my mind is at perfect peace about it and I am not afraid. God will carry it through.'

She ordered timber and fifty sheets of corrugated iron and took it all up in canoes from Duke Town the following month. Two hundred and fifty of the Ikpe people turned out to help clear the site.

It was all quite like old times. And when a fight between two groups started in the market place and she had to wade in and stop it, she might indeed have been back with her Okoyong.

After she had stopped the fight an old chief came up to thank her. 'He held out both his hands for mine, which I gladly gave to him . . . It is a real life that I am living now, not all preaching and holding meetings but rather a life and atmosphere which people can touch and live in and be made to believe in, when the higher things are brought before them. In many ways it is a most prosaic life, dirt and dust and noise and silliness in every form, but full too of the kindliness and homeliness of children who are not averse to be disciplined and taught, and who understand and love just as we do . . . The excitement and surprises would not however need to be continuous, as they wear and fray the body and rob one of sleep and restfulness of soul.'

While her house was being built at Ikpe she went back regularly to visit her other stations and her settlement at Use. She could not always manage the walking part of the journeys and had to be carried.

Martha wrote home that Mary was often in great pain both during and after these journeys. Once, when the pain had been greater than usual, she asked Mary how she could possibly have travelled at all. 'Ach! I just had to take as big a dose of laudanum as I dared and wrap myself in a blanket and lie in the bottom of the canoe all the time, and I managed fine.'

She came back to Use for Christmas and New Year and wrote to Partridge to thank him for his usual plum-pudding: 'There is a deadness here [at Use and Ikpe] as in the Church at home, an indifference about spiritual things . . . This morning I have just answered a very prudish epistle from a black clerk asking me to, "Tell your church member women to cover their nakedness when they pass here, else I shall make the boys drive them away." . . . I've answered him!'

She was always pleased to get away from the isolation and the appalling conditions at Ikpe to Use and to Martha Peacock. But while she was away her hut lay empty and when she and the bairns returned to Use they had to work for hours to clean it up. In the rainy season of 1911 they arrived back in the dark and she found that her matches were too wet to light so that they could have neither a lamp nor a fire. The bairns were afraid that snakes would have taken up residence – they often did – and Mary had to shuffle round poking into corners with a stick to 'prove' there were none. She had been taking her turn at carrying five chickens in a box on the walk from Okopedi and she was so exhausted that she lay down on her 'beautiful' bed and slept in her soaking clothes.

Events like this – and there were many of them – did nothing to improve her health. But she continued to go her own way until later in the year Dr Robertson went on leave and the young Dr Hitchcock came into her life. They, as he put it, 'collided'.

His first letters to his parents from Itu were full of references to his obstinate patient,

For thirty years she has lived in Calabar. She has ever been the pioneer going ahead into unexplored districts and paving the way, not only for mission work, but for the Government as well. Without exaggeration here is a name to conjure with. Her influence is felt over hundreds of square miles. She had been ill before we came into collision. She wanted to go to some outlandish place [Ikpe] 15 hours by canoe far from any white man. The idea was unthinkable but I only stopped her by threatening to close all work at Itu and to follow her. This was effectual and since then she has been amenable. She has really been very ill – it is her heart – and I am obliged to see her every day. She has only a native house – the floor is of beaten earth and the walls of clay, the windows are bits of absent wall – She compels admiration, she is utterly heroic. She has a brilliant mind,

Mary after her illness

incredibly keen. I am glad to say that she is improving but she is so fright-fully headstrong. She will not rest and resting is the one thing which is essential.

From the first [in Calabar] she was regarded as a forceful personality of splendid gifts . . . She went fearlessly up country . . . For the most part she was entirely alone, and by sheer force of personality she cut her way . . . until 'the good white woman who lives in the bush' became known and venerated; her name literally an open sesame . . . Now the poor creature is worn and weary. Often her wit flashes out and her splendid discernment shows itself. She is exceedingly vivacious, an excellent conversationalist.

Since this was the effect which the 62-year-old Mary had on young John Hitchcock it is hardly surprising that 'Mariolatry' had been much in use by the young recruits at Duke Town when she was at her peak nineteen years earlier. But it was a good thing that Mary did not see his letter. She would have given him 'poor creature'!

Their first 'collision', when he threatened to close the hospital, would have been well worth watching, and during the year in which he looked after her, they fought continually. To Partridge she wrote that, 'He is a rare man . . . a rare Christian . . . a rare doctor . . . a physician for soul and body . . . I am beginning to love him like a son. Of course to the doctor my health is the only thing but I can't get rest for my body while my mind it torn about things . . . I am vexed at vexing him.'

Both Mary and the doctor knew that she had this special influence over the people and they both knew that time was running out for her. But, whereas he wanted to protect her body, she wanted only to force it to go on further still to take that influence out to more and more people in the time remaining.

She told Partridge that the doctor was killing himself with overwork. She worried about him and quoted his own instruction back at him and they battled on while their friends watched with glee. James Macgregor described one of their arguments:

'You are hopelessly undernourished', said the doctor, 'You must eat meat.' 'I am not a meat eater, doctor. Why did you send me that cooked chicken?'

'Because it could not get here by itself. And you will eat it!'

And the old warrior ate it.

After a journey to Ikpe had to be cancelled because Mary had collapsed, the doctor ordered her to bed and told her that she must not make any more journeys until he gave her permission. She wrote a note to Macgregor, 'The doctor has sent me back to bed under a more stringent rule than ever. I dare not rise.'

He ordered her back to Duke Town for a complete rest. She refused to go. He lost this battle and called in Macgregor's help. But this, to begin with, made no difference. 'Na! Na! My plans are all made. I canna draw a salary and not do what I can!' Macgregor said that she had done more than enough already, but she snapped back, 'I've been well paid for what I've done.' In the end she went back to Duke Town but there she only fretted and got worse. Hitchcock had to fetch her back to Use and keep an eye on her himself. She would obey no one else. 'Life is hardly worth living, but I am doing what I can to help him to help me, so that I can be fit again for another spell of work.'

Mary was now bent and wizened and grey, and because she rarely wore her false teeth her chin seemed to jut out even further. When she was getting her own way in her work she was humorous and charming. But when her plans were opposed she got angry and looked very like a bad tempered witch. The Scots have a word in their 'Doric' for old people who are obstinate and cantankerous but very likeable: it is 'thrawn'. And there is no doubt that in her sixties Mary Slessor was thrawn as thrawn can be.

Now, in the middle of her running battle with John Hitchcock, messengers came from Ikpe to ask when she was going back to them. 'Not for another seven weeks', said the doctor firmly. But Mary wrote to Macgregor, 'I may run up sooner than that. I am quite well if only he would believe it.' And, sure enough, when the doctor was away she ran off back to Ikpe.

When he heard that she was coming back to Okpo, which was near Okopedi, for the opening of a new church, the doctor seized the chance to go up and check on her health. The people had built the church themselves and, in a letter home, he described the opening: 'The sun was blazing mercilessly and all the kirk members were there with their neighbours and friends, all seething with excitement. Everybody was as smart as possible but it was amazing to see how quickly boots were removed and collars flung away, the simple loincloth and singlet replacing the suit, the moment the ceremony was over . . . The place was packed and the heat was intense but everybody was supremely happy.'

Miss Slessor was 'much better than I expected'.

In letters to Scotland Mary herself had taken to adding 'this spluttering candle' to her descriptions of her 'poor carcase'. And now she suffered a disaster. At Ikpe she lost her spectacles and could therefore neither read nor write. For days she went forlornly about her duties, occasionally praying aloud, 'Faither, please give me back my spectacles.' Dozens of young men searched for the precious things, the loss of which was making their Ma so miserable, until the great day when a group of them went whooping up to her hut, with one of them cradling the poor things in his huge hands. Much battered, this pair are preserved in Dundee Museum; one leg is still neatly mended with her whipping of cotton and one lens is missing.

She had been itinerating round the Ikpe area, and several other towns now wanted 'God' and 'Book'. So, to let her move on, she had asked the mission to consider sending two 'ladies' to take over Ikpe. She had at last convinced its chiefs that the extra protection of her God would be good for them. That any other European would be willing to live there was most unlikely since only a Mary Slessor could have endured it. But anyway the mission refused to consider such a move until Dr Hitchcock had approved the site. When he made his journey to Ikpe and saw where his patient had been living he was horrified and declared that the town was the filthiest which he had ever seen and that the site was totally unfit for Europeans to live on.

Mary was furious. Her diaries for 1912 and 1914 are the only two which have survived. On January 7th 1912 she wrote, 'I object to the doctor's findings. He has absolutely no experience.' But the entry in the diary ends, 'Could not take school as I have been vomiting . . . tried hot water bag [bottle] and used it all day in church and was helped well.'

The 'candle' was spluttering again:

10th January. Fever. Two women murdered, Heads taken.

15th January. Full up with work till late at night. Dead tired.

21st January. Vaccinated for three hours until lymph finished.

31st January. Fine catechism class. Fever after. Sleepless night. Baby screaming every few minutes.

She had as usual been rescuing unwanted babies around the Ikpe area. She did this wherever she went. In February she took them back to Use with her and was upset when, a few weeks later, three of them died.

Her anger with Dr Hitchcock soon evaporated. She wrote to Partridge that her 'dear doctor' had taken malaria and would soon kill himself if he did not slow down.

In March she went back to Ikpe by way of Arochuku, where she 'arrived at dawn after a moonlight trip'. She could get no sense out of the chiefs because an Egbo celebration was in progress, so the day which she spent in the town was wasted: 'Egbo screaming and drumming all night. All drunk.'

Next month she went back to Use again and found that her hut had been damaged in a storm. She had to work on the roof next day and finished up with cut and bleeding hands. All through the month she had fever. 'Night of delirium. I wash a big washing.' and 'Scarcely able to stand upright in church.' are typical entries in the diary.

On May 7th it was, 'A grand day notwithstanding intense weakness almost to fainting. Heavy pain at night.'

She had several 'lovely visits from Miss Peacock' during the month but by the end of it was back at Ikpe.

Her letters to friends, apart from a few to Partridge, were usually cheerful and concealed the real state of her health and the conditions under which she was living. But the two diaries show the true picture.

She was often forced to sell things in order to buy food. 'Alice did very well as we had not a penny to buy food . . . sent a few things, machine oil and thread to sell [at the market] and got as much as would buy yams and oil.' A few weeks later she sold '3 books for 6d for 5 small yams, oil and shrimps . . . and a few small fish.' The chickens which they had intended to keep them in food had been lost or stolen.

The diaries show too how dependent she was on the gifts of food from the Africans. If her other diaries had survived they would almost certainly have shown that this had been her situation ever since she began itinerating ten years earlier.

By the end of May she was itinerating again: 'A fearful night with mosquitoes and the hard filthy ground on which we lay. . . . Night of misery.' And again: 'Troubled by mosquitoes.' At the beginning of June she was having to be carried again. But just the same, 'Began to make a staircase.'

By the middle of the month she had to give up the travelling and the building work at Ikpe and go back to Use where: 'That dear Dr Hitchcock, as if he had not enough to do with two wards full of patients, was here before 6 am. Examined my poor carcase. He gave orders I am not to go to Ikpe or cycle. I am confined to bed.'

Next day, 'Am up again.' But the doctor caught her and promptly sent her back to bed again and made her stay there ... some of the time.

By July she was complaining: 'feel extremely weak and useless. From lying idle I expect.'

In answer to her request for a large wheelchair, her friends in Scotland now sent her out one with a light basket-work body, two wheels at the back and one at the front, and handles for pulling and pushing. It was just what she wanted. She called it her 'rickshaw' and, with its arrival immediately abandoned any thought of going back to Scotland. 'Instead of going home as I had planned, in order to get strength for a wider range of work, I shall stay on and enjoy the privilege of going over ground impossible for my poor limbs.'

In September 1912 she wrote to friends that she had completed thirty-six years as a missionary. She had got her dates right for once. 'I'm lame feeble and foolish; the wrinkles are wonderful − no concertina is so wonderfully folded and convoluted. I'm a wee, wee, wifie, very little buikit [built] but I grip on well none the less.'

But by the end of the month the diary records that 'Fever is back' and the fight against sickness and pain was on again.

9th October: 'Pain in whole side much worse.'

She could not use her cycle at all now so she had lent it to Miss Welsh, who had taken over one of the out-stations which Mary had established at Ibiaku, between Ikot Obong and Ikot Ekpene, and made it into a main station with several out-stations of its own.

The terse entries in the diary for the end of November and the beginning of December sum up Mary's situation. She was back living at Ikpe again. 'Sore throat. Boy child kept me awake and afoot the whole night.' . . . 'Bad night. Cross child. Sore throat.' . . . 'Baby's head suppurating. He is bound to die in the long run from this. Made three slabs of cement.' . . . 'Boils on my head very sore. Throat and catarrh still bad.' . . . 'The boys brought a bag of rice and a fowl as a present. I think they knew we were scarce of food. It was most kind of them.'

On 26th December she wrote to Partridge to thank him for

the usual Christmas puddings. She had been to Ikot Ekpene in a motor and came back in her rickshaw. He would never recognise the place now. It had several large brick buildings and was full of motors and motor cycles.

Agnes Young, another young girl who had heard Mary speak in Scotland, had joined the mission and had gone up occasionally to help Mary at Use. Now she was going to Scotland to get married. She was a particular favourite of Mary's who wrote from Ikpe to say goodbye to her: 'I am a nasty, mean, grudging, thing. I'm telling it to myself often and often, for I am not glad that you are going. I won't pretend to be . . . Bah! . . . I am not feeling well today . . . And yet in my heart I am truly glad for you and for him who waits for you . . . I am, dear heart, yours affectionately, and lovingly, Mary.'

When her husband died Miss Young, now Mrs Arnot, was to return to Calabar. She was one of the four women who completed the work which Mary had to leave unfinished.

Meanwhile news of Mary's failing health had reached Scotland. Since to return there in winter would probably kill her, one of her friends, Miss Cook, suggested that she should go with Jean to the Canary Islands for a complete rest. Miss Cook and her friends would pay for everything.

Mary was against the idea at first. But the Macgregors and the Wilkies and Martha Peacock worked on her and, when in a box from Scotland she found warm material just right for the Canaries, she decided that God was in favour of the holiday and agreed.

When she emerged from the forests again the European community was shocked once more at the wasted appearance of its fabulous character. Dr Robertson, who was on his way back to Itu, told her that he hoped from now on she would look after herself. 'You should have been dead years ago. Anybody else would have been.'

She and Jean were to stay at the Hotel Santa Catalina at Las Palmas. But of course they had no clothes fit to be seen in such a high-class establishment. This problem was solved by the ladies of Calabar, mission, military, and colonial. They measured, cut, and sewed with enthusiasm and Mary and Jean suddenly found themselves with a complete wardrobe. This bewildered them a little because they had never had such a thing before. Mary thanked the ladies for making the two of them look 'wiselike and decent'.

They had to change ships on the voyage and Mary was carried from one to the other and Miss Cook's cash box was passed from captain to captain.

On board the ships she was carried from her cabin and back again for meals, passengers and crew fussed over her, and one captain was heard to remark that he was prouder of having shaken hands with her than with King George himself.

At the hotel the two missionaries, white and black, were considerably taken aback by all the splendour. 'We were certainly a frightened pair.' But the tourist season had not yet begun and the staff and what visitors there were made as much fuss of her as the people on the ships had done.

'What love is wrapped round me. All are kind, the manager's family, the doctor's family, and the visitors. It's simply wonderful. I can't say more.'

The hotel had a garden full of European flowers and there she was able to sit and enjoy the sea breezes and, after so many years of being hemmed in by trees, watch the clouds sailing across the blue sky and the blue sea rolling in from the horizon. 'I sat and knitted and worked my way through the Bible all day long. And the good house-keeper sent up lunch and tea to save my walking . . . the most wonderful holiday I have ever had.'

On the return voyage she received a bouquet of flowers from the Governor of the Gold Coast himself.

She had recovered considerably in health, but when she sailed into the anchorage at Duke Town, Jean had to lift *Eka Kpukpro Owo* down into the boat.

18. 'END O' THE ROAD'

It was fortunate that she had a respectable dress because the Governor-General of all Nigeria, Sir Frederick Lugard, who was on an official visit to Calabar, 'commanded' her to attend one of his receptions.

Anxious friends pleaded with her to obey; the good name of the mission, indeed of her church, demanded that she should. If she had come straight from the forests she would probably have refused and slipped away back into them. But fortified by her eight weeks of civilisation, she agreed.

When her name was announced, members of the Governor-General's staff craned their necks to see this formidable character and saw instead the little old woman, wizened and shrunken, and limping a little but, thanks to her holiday, able to walk without help.

She was wearing one of her new dresses and a new hat which probably someone had lent her. He was resplendent in plumed hat, white uniform with gold epaulettes, scarlet sash, and gold-hilted sword. As he bent to take her hand and to say that he was proud to do so, his brother Edward found: '. . . a great lump in the throat. The long years of *not* quiet but fierce devotion – for they say she is a tornado – unrecognised, and without hope of, or desire for, recognition'.

Mary had of course been quite certain for a number of years that she had all the recognition which she either wanted or needed. But it came from 'up higher'.

While she was at Duke Town her friends were successful too in persuading her to have a complete medical check-up. Two doctors examined the poor carcase and pronounced that, if she took care of it, it would be good for a number of years yet. They gave her written instructions on what she must do to preserve her health. She read them, pulled a face, and said, 'Life will hardly be worth living now.'

She had every intention at the time of doing what they suggested, but the mission, through yet more deaths and illness, was desperately short of staff again. There was no one to take over from her at Use and of course the site at Ikpe had been condemned and the mission would not have allowed anyone else to live there.

If she had been content to stay at Use she would have been able to carry out her instructions. But that would have meant abandoning all the people in the Ikpe area who had built their little mud churches for her and abandoning her itenerating as well. This *Eka Kpukpro Owo* could not do.

She went back to Use laden with the medicines, tonics, and special tinned foods which the doctors had ordered for her. She even had a water-filter and a new mosquito net. But all this paraphernalia would have been impossible for her bairns to carry. When she went back to Ikpe most of it was left behind, and within a few weeks her list of instructions had somehow disappeared. She 'got a great welcome' from her people.

The British were building a road up from Ikot Ekpene to link up with one coming round from the Niger delta. It had reached a place called Odoro Ikpe five miles from Ikpe itself, and since Brooks, the Area Commissioner, now let her have the use of a motor whenever she wanted one, she was spared the miles of canoe journeys and the muddy tracks from Amasu.

The government officials could not now do enough for her, although one at this time did introduce himself pompously as 'your new Vice-Consul' and get a terse, 'I can't help that, laddie' in reply. She had usually got on well with them especially with the youngsters, many of whom, after being posted to some other lonely place, still wrote to her. 'Dear Lady, I hate the idea of you going so far up into the bush. Don't go. There are plenty of men eager and willing to be of service to you, but away up there [Ikpe] you are far away from help or care.' Another wrote: 'Do be careful. Do take quinine and sleep under a net and drink filtered water – Don't be so ridiculously unselfish. Learn a little selfishness. It will do you all the good in the world.'

In emergencies she was able these days to send a messenger to the nearest telegraph station and have packages sent up from Duke Town. These were too precious to be entrusted to messengers and were passed from one official to the next.

'Very urgent!' one would say, 'She must get it right away.'

'What's in it?'

'Feeding bottles.'. . . . Or it might be, 'Tea.'

Even the Governor of Southern Nigeria, Sir Walter Egerton, seems to have been pressed into service. He arrived at Use bearing gifts of two cakes, a box of crystallised fruits, a box of chocolates, and also two cases of tinned milk which he was probably just delivering.

At Ikpe she was building again and an accident, in which a pellet of mud hit her in the eye, showed how concerned about her health the British had become. She had simply asked Jean to wipe out the mud with a handkerchief and gone on working and it was not until a day later that Brooks heard about it. He immediately sent a message asking Mary to come to the road in her rickshaw where he would meet her with a motor and a doctor. The eye, he wrote, must be properly examined. It was inflamed and painful so Mary did as she was told. This was a good thing because in spite of treatment at Itu she went blind in it for a fortnight and was 'very ashamed of being laid up after so fine a holiday.'

When she recovered she began to push out again into the country beyond Ikpe where the British described the people as 'arrogant and dangerous'. These had not invited her to come to them and told her forcefully that they had no intention of abandoning the old customs. White man's ways were no good against witchcraft.

She had become so used over the past ten years to Africans being anxious for her to come and live with them, that in her old age, to be back where she had been in her early days with the Okoyong, both surprised and worried her. She was back among killings for witchcraft, poison bean trials, and of course the murder of twin babies and the outlawing of their mothers. And there was so little time now. Where were the new recruits? 'We are lower in numbers in Calabar than ever . . . Surely there is something far wrong with our Church, the largest in Scotland . . . Where are the men? . . . We have really no workers to meet all this opened country, and our Church, to be honest, should stand back and give it to someone else . . . But oh! I cannot think of that . . . For how could we meet the Goldies, the Edgerleys, the Waddells, and the Andersons? . . . It is not committees and organisations from without that . . . send the Gospel to the heathen at home and abroad, but the living spirit of God working from within the heart.'

She hoped that when she died another freelance pioneer

would be appointed to replace her to move out among the people and bring Christianity to them, not with elaborate churches but as simply as possible. She wrote that the African did not look on life in the European way and that there was no reason why he should: 'To give him an elaborate building is to give him a foreign thing in which he will worship a foreign God . . . These infant churches need so much to be instructed . . . They are children in everything that matters . . . And when we have led them to Christ we are apt to forget how much more they need to make a strong, upright, ethical, character on which to build a nation. Then we need a literature and this too is work for the Church.'

Some people would have held that to push herself forward where she was not wanted was indeed 'meddling in other peoples business'. But it never for one moment occurred to Mary Slessor that to replace their old cruel customs with Christ's teaching of love even for enemies was in any way questionable. And it was this simple teaching without the trimmings which Europeans had tacked on to it, which she was trying to bring to the people. She knew only too well at first hand the misery which the old customs created.

At this time she scribbled in the margin of one of her Bibles – what with the intinerating and the damp and the constant handling and scribbling they never lasted her long – against Exodus, chapter 20, 'Elaborate ceremony, costly buildings are not allowed'.

These scribbles, when they are legible, give some insight into the thinking of a lonely, sick, old woman. For they, like the diaries, were never intended to be read by anyone else and there was therefore no need to keep cheerful in them.

Against Job, chapter 7: 'Pain! What a pathetic but perfectly truthful picture of human sickness and despair. Every street on earth can tell it. A mighty sob from the heart of man.'

Jeremiah's 'Be not afraid of their faces for I am with thee to deliver thee saith the Lord', she heavily underlined. And, here and there in the margins against his letters, 'Paul, laddie' comes in for applause: 'No worldly truck or muck there! Direct on lad!'

Meanwhile, now that Dr Robertson was back at Itu and Dr Hitchcock had gone off on a survey into the interior behind Unwana, Martha Peacock took up the role of chief protector of Mary's health. She retaliated by calling Martha 'My Bishop'.

The friendship between them had grown even stronger. But it suffered a setback when Mary went to Duke Town to put more plans for pushing forward before the Council and Martha had the temerity to speak against her. As a result the old warrior completely ignored her all the way back to Itu in the launch, and wished her a very huffy 'Goodnight Miss Peacock' on arrival.

Next evening Martha, anxious about how she would be received, cycled over to Use. She found Mary sitting under her verandah reading the Book of Exodus. As she approached, rather apprehensively, Ma closed the book and sighed, 'Poor wee Mosie! He never did see the Promised Land!' Then she grinned and said, 'Come away, lassie! I'm awful glad to see you!'

One of her friends now reported that 'A new softness and graciousness has stolen into Miss Slessor's life.' And at this time Mary even wrote, 'My opinions may not suit everyone and it is possible that other people may be right and I far wrong'.

The first part of the statement she knew only too well to be accurate. The second part however could have shown an entirely new attitude. But since she continued serenely to go in the direction in which she was certain that the Lord was pointing her, in spite of anything anyone said, it is doubtful if her colleagues took it seriously. Those who considered her little mud churches and schools a complete waste of time certainly did not. To them her ways were just as haphazard as the Africans' and they thought that she should do things in the proper British manner or not at all.

Fortunately for the mission Mary, with the support of the British, the Africans, men like Luke, Robertson, Macgregor and Wilkie, and of her young protegées Beatrice Welsh, Martha Peacock, and Mina Amess, could not now be held back. And even her opponents would have had to admit that the way in which she had travelled for ten years, living often on the food which the Africans gave her, in areas where any other lone white was likely to *become* food rather than be given it, was, to say the least, remarkable.

Mary, as usual, gave any credit which was going to God. 'My life is one daily, hourly, record of answered prayer . . . for guidance given marvellously, for errors and dangers averted, for enmity to the Gospel subdued, for food provided at the exact hour needed, for everything that goes to make up my life and my poor service, I can testify with a full and often wonder-stricken awe that I believe God answers prayer. I know God answers prayer . . . Food is scarce just now. We live from hand to mouth. We have not more than will be our breakfast today but I know that we shall be fed for God answers prayer . . . It isn't Mary Slessor doing anything but Something outside of her altogether uses her as her small ability allows'.

At Odoro Ikpe she had her eye on another old government rest camp near the road for herself and for whoever should succeed her, to replace the condemned site at Ikpe. Now that, instead of marching, officials could bowl along in motors, it was no longer used. But before she could start work on it she received a very welcome invitation from Mina Amess in July 1913 to attend the opening of a new church at Akpap. Her old one was now crumbling and too small for the Okoyong congregations.

Mary had not been back to Akpap for eight years. She had thought that for her to do so would have been unfair to Mina. But now, so anxious was she that Mary should be present for this great occasion, Mina asked the Macgregors to go and fetch her in the mission launch.

A huge crowd of Okoyong met the launch at Ikonetu beach. They had not changed. Their welcome was as riotous as it had always been. The strangers who were carrying her ashore were swept aside and her 'own very dear people' carried her in procession up to Mina's house.

The 'seething with excitement' which Hitchcock had seen at Okpo was nothing to this. Scores of Okoyong squatted happily round the fires near the house to wait their turn to go up and talk to their *Ma Akamba*. Mary herself was so excited that on the first evening she refused to take time off from meeting old friends even to eat.

Eme, 'my dear old friend and almost sister', came to see her and they talked about Edem and about the gin bottle. Eme told her that she was sacrificing regularly to *Abassi* and to the other gods.

Many of the people whose lives she had saved came to see her too and everyone was amazed to see what fine young people Maggie, Alice, and Whitie, who were all twins, had grown into. Four hundred Okoyong attended the ceremony and Mary preached to them for half an hour.

Next day she said farewell to her tribe. Once more they came with so many presents that there was not enough room for all the goats and chickens and yams in the launch. Once more they wailed as the launch drew away and she waved to them with the tears streaming down her cheeks. And once more she sat in silence and the bairns left her alone.

What the Okoyong thought of seeing the woman who had punched them in the stomach, beaten them over the head, gone down their paths barefoot as fast as they could, and broken up their fights, changed into a wizened old woman is not on record. But back at Use Mary wrote at once to Janet Wright, now invalided home with her husband Dr Rattray and living in Edinburgh: '. . . Akpap is full of memories of you and you are not forgotten . . . I had only one disappointment, so many seemed interested only in me, with no concern for the things of God.'

Later in the year she had to leave Use again for an event which she had dreaded but ended up by enjoying. Edward Lugard's concern for her lack of recognition had caused Sir Frederick to recommend that she be admitted as an Honorary Associate into the Order of St John of Jerusalem which took with it the award of a silver cross. She had been notified that 'His Most Gracious Majesty King George the Fifth' had approved the award but she had kept it secret. The cross and scroll however had now arrived at Duke Town and the secret was out.

Her friends were worried, as usual, about what she would wear. Her holiday dresses would, they were quite sure, have gone mouldy in the rains, have been eaten by ants, or just been given away. They asked her if they should make a dress for her and were even more worried when she thanked them but said that she had a 'nice' dress'.

However on the great day they were relieved to see that she was wearing one of her Canaries dresses, a trifle crushed but clean, and a clean straw hat. But, alas, as she went up to the platform, from underneath the dress, peeped an old pair of canvas shoes.

She was embarrassed at the speeches in praise of her work and when she stood up to speak was silent for a time. Then she turned to the young people from the Hope Waddell Institute and spoke to them first in Efik before switching to English for the British.

As the longest serving Scottish member of the mission, she said, she received the award on its behalf and not for any special work of hers. 'If I have done anything in my life, it has been easy, because the Master has gone before.'

Duke Town now took the chance to make a real fuss of Mary Slessor. The Army put on a display and gave a reception for her and invited her to a cricket match, though it is doubtful how much she made of this since she had almost certainly never seen the game before. The mission held a big tea-party in her honour and a few days later she was presented with a bouquet of roses by the High Commissioner's wife and escorted back up the river in his launch.

Roses were her favourite flower and when these began to fade she stuck the stems into the soil outside her hut at Use. She was delighted when one of them took root. She barricaded it off from the chickens and the livestock, and when she was away her African women solemnly watered it. What was so good about it they would not have been able to see, but it was clearly one of *Ma Akamba's* ju-ju's and therefore deserving of every care.

Then the rains came and Ikpe was flooded. The hostile chiefs blamed the disaster on the Christians for not following the old customs and Mary was involved once more in endless palavers. They went on so long that she ran out of tea. The government motor could not get through because of the muddy roads and she was forced to use old tea leaves again and again until the brew was beginning to be tasteless and Mary's temper shorter and shorter. Food was of little interest to her these days. But to be without tea was disaster. She and the bairns prayed, no doubt earnestly, statedly, in a businesslike manner, and even desperately, for the tea to get through. But no tea came. Then one day a messenger arrived to say that there was a box on its way to Ma from Amasu. Jean and Alice hurried off to meet it. They carried it up to Mary's hut and then Jean had to look for a hammer and chisel with which to open it and this took time. Meanwhile Mary and the bairns and a few well-wishers squatted round the box and regarded it in silence. If it were not after all the tea, the disappointment would be unbearable. But it was and the hymns were sung with extra fervour that night.

Towards the end of the year Mary had a bad bout of fever in which she dreamt in her delirium that the mission had a motor and was using it for teams of Scottish missionaries to tour round scores of out-stations all over the Aro and Ibibio territory to supervise the work of the Africans who ran them. 'The bairns were afraid, for I was babbling more than usual, but to me it was as real as if it had all happened.'

So Mary made the last of her novel suggestions to the mission. Why not have a motor and use it in this way? It had taken the mission over thirty years to get a steam launch but there was no need to wait so long for a motor. Once again however she was well ahead of her time and this suggestion too was shelved.

She spent Christmas 1913 with Martha at Use. The church was decorated with flowers and palm leaves: 'A bonnie kirk . . . Miss Peacock my dear comrade was there . . . so we had a grand time . . . the biggest Christmas I have ever had in Calabar.'

In January she was off back to Odoro Ikpe, against everybody's advice, to start work on the old rest camp building. For the first few days she and the girls had to camp in the old place with no furniture and no proper facilities. They cooked over a fire in the yard and washed their clothes piece by piece in a bucket.

The house was falling to pieces and she was ill and making heavy weather of repairing it.

> 14th January: End of wall fell down during the night.
> 16th January: Couldn't get to catechism. Can't get rid of fever.
> 17th January: Fever most distressingly bad. A lost day.
> 21st January: Rose at 4 am . . . Could not sleep. Finished the wall before the sun was clear. Some letter writing but back would not sit up.
> 28th January: Dear Miss Peacock offered me a camp-bed or a hammock . . .

Presumably therefore she was still sleeping on the floor at this time.

By February she was pushing on from Odoro Ikpe to the towns of Endot and Ekri Mornu. Sometimes it was dark before she got back and her young Africans took to going out to meet her armed with machetes. This seems to have amused her for she wrote in the diary: 'I have never been so protected before!' And she underlined the entry.

> 10th April: A great reception at Use . . . Puss is quiet now. [Somebody had given her a huge yellow cat of which she was very fond.] . . . Dirt reigns supreme . . . Rat's dirt everywhere . . . clothes eaten by them . . . A box of milk eaten through by white ants . . . Nauseating! . . . Jam leaking but house intact.

She and the bairns had to work for hours to clear the place up. Afterwards she had fever. But her letters were as cheerful as ever. To one woman in Scotland she wrote: 'Don't grow up to be a nervous old maid. Gird yourself up for the battle outside somewhere, and keep your heart young. Give up your whole being to create music everywhere, in the light places, and in the dark places, and your life will make melody . . . I'm a perfect witness to the joy and satisfaction of a single life . . . with a human tag-rag hanging on . . . It is rare! It is exhilarating as an aeroplane or a dirigible or whatever they are, that are always trying to get up and are always coming down!'

To another woman she wrote: 'Mine has been such a joyous service . . . God has been good to me . . . I cannot thank Him enough for the honour He conferred on me when He sent me to the Dark Continent.'

In May some of her youngsters came to see when she was going back to them: 'Thirty lads from Odoro Ikpe marched into church . . . mostly clothed.'

So in July she went back and itinerated again in the Ikpe area by rickshaw. She was making progress now with towns which had turned her down earlier. But, as usual, the acceptance of twins and their mothers was holding up negotiations and palaver followed palaver on this subject. Then early one morning one town sent a message to say that they were ready now to settle for 'God' and 'Book' and would *Ma Akamba* please come for a final palaver. She was still in her nightdress. But, as she wrote to a friend, 'It could have been Court dress for all they knew.' So she hurried off and finished up the day surveying a site for a school still wearing it.

Martha Peacock came to see what Mary was up to and at one place had to share a mattress on the floor with her. Next day she complained to Mary that rats had been running over them in the night. 'Na! . . . Na! lassie', said Mary, 'It couldnae be rats.' But the next night when Martha, lying awake, accidentally nudged her shoulder, the old warrior's elbow came whizzing up and she grunted, 'Awa! . . . ye brute!' Next morning, when she saw Martha's black eye, she was most apologetic and admitted 'Well! . . . Aye! . . . mebbe there are one or two rats.'

Her diary records her unequal battle with the old rest camp building. A sheet of iron slipped off the roof, just missed her head, made her hair fly, and cut the back of her chair in half.

August 12th was 'A miserable drag-out of a day . . . All day long putting in one door.'

Shortly afterwards she heard a rumour that war had broken out in Europe. The motor had not been up to them for weeks, probably because of the rains, and she had no definite news. But when the mail and the newspapers did get through by canoe and she read of the early defeats of the British and the French, she was so upset that she could not get out of her chair and Jean had to carry her to bed.

As more and more news of the heavy casualties in France came through, nearly every day in September has an entry of 'Fever'. Just the same on the 9th she wrote, 'I find the sawing hard work.' And on the 10th, 'Trying vainly as yet to put frame into window.'

But by September 24th she was so ill that she could not get out of bed: 'Boys came for me, lifted me in camp-bed and took me to Ikpe – so tenderly. Four fowls smothered to death on road. Boy took my cat and lost it in the bush.' She was most upset about 'Poor Puss'.

Next day the boys put her in a canoe, still on the camp-bed, covered her with a tarpaulin, and paddled her down with the bairns to Okopedi beach. They landed by moonlight and Jean sent to Itu for Dr Robertson. Mary lay unconscious on the bed by the side of the road with the crew from Ikpe squatting round her while Jean bathed her forehead with water from the river. Jean said afterwards that Mary had been 'babbling' in her delirium about two friends who were naval officers and had been drowned.

Dr Robertson arrived and asked the crew to carry her the four miles to her hut at Use. They took her through the dense bush and the mud and the moonlight, stopping occasionally for Jean to quieten her when her 'babbling' grew worse.

Next day, to everyone's amazement, the old lady was herself again. The doctor wanted to have her carried to Ikot Ibong from where a motor could take her on to hospital at Itu, but she refused to hear of it. No, her bairns would look after her just as they had done hundreds of times and she would be fine.

The diary starts again. Miss Welsh had been to visit her in pouring rain. Silly girl would catch her death of cold. 'Dear Miss Peacock' came to see her often and held church services for her. She herself was having to be carried into church and had to sit all the time.

She was thinking that perhaps she better go to Scotland to recuperate when it was summer there again and 'When I have finished the house at Odoro Ikpe.'

She was worrying about Ikpe itself. 'It is seven years since I took them on and they have never got a teacher yet . . . It is bitterly hard'.

Time was now nearly at an end for her. The pages of the Book of Revelation are smothered with her scribbles. She marked the words 'And I looked and behold a door opened in heaven'. And to Paul's words to the Corinthians: 'Death is swallowed up in Victory' she added 'Hallelujah! . . . What a climax!'

Early in December Martha found her burning her personal papers. When Dan came home on holiday for Christmas he wept at how wasted she looked.

She underlined the entry for December 15th. 'Have received a lovely pair of spectacles from Mr Hart as Christmas present.' Her old ones were now almost useless and she was delighted with the new ones and kept taking them out of their case and trying them on. But there are no more entries in the diary.

No doubt however she used her present to write her last letter to Charles Partridge:

Use. 24th December 1914

My Dear Old Friend,
   The plum puddings have just come and as this is Christmas Eve I have ordered one to be opened and the whole lot of us are to have it tonight, which has caused great excitement and all are jumping about like crazy things . . . If I can hold out until March I shall probably take a trip to Scotland or at least to the Canaries . . .

She wrote too to a friend in Scotland saying that she might be coming home. She seems to have been writing it at sunrise for she went on to say that whereas in Scotland they were now in the dark days of winter and of war: 'With us it is all brightness and beauty with the long summer months opening out before us . . . If you saw the lovely pearly skies in the dawn; the earth all refreshed and cooled, and saw all the mystery of a new day opening out, you would enjoy it as I am doing.'

For New Year 1915 Martha made Mary a huge plum pudding. She sent it with a message that she and a new recruit, Miss Couper, would be coming to tea. She later wrote home: 'The plum pudding, with a rose out of the garden, stuck in the top, was on the table, Miss Slessor was as happy as a girl and said she had to exercise self control to keep from tasting the pudding before we arrived. We had a merry meal'.

But the following day Mary collapsed again and Jean sent for Martha and for Dr Robertson who came with medicine and ice. Mary could not rest and kept asking to be moved to a chair and then back to the bed again. The bones of her shrunken body had now so little flesh to comfort them that even lying in bed was painful.

By the night of the 12th of January it began to look as if not even Mary Slessor would recover and Martha, Jean, Alice, and Whitie, took it in turns to watch beside her.

Martha wrote an account for the *Record*: 'It was not a grand room . . . the walls were of reddish-brown mud very roughly built, the floor was of cement with a rug here and there and the roof was corrugated iron'.

She noticed that Mary's breathing was becoming more and more difficult and sent the girls to ask two men to go to Itu for Dr Robertson. It was a very dark night and they had forgotten to wind the clock. They were pleased when they heard a cock crow. But when Martha pulled aside the curtain they saw that it was not yet dawn.

It was hot and airless in the hut and Mary tossed and turned and sweated and babbled. But she was conscious when Martha bent again to bathe her lips, and whispered, 'thanks lassie, but it's nae use.' Then, in Efik, as was proper, '*O Abassi, sana mi yok.*' 'O God release me.'

She was breathing harshly now, struggling for air. To the girls, who had watched so often before for her recovery, it would have seemed as if her breathing was the only sound in all the world; as if on its continuance their own lives depended. As it faltered and they realised that their Ma was dying the three younger girls ran out of the hut leaving only Jean and Martha. When the door opened they saw that it was dawn at last.

Along the river the mists would be curling. The night hunters, animal and bird, would be turning for shelter as the glare of another day glowed on the rim of the forest. In the lull between the sleeping of the night hunters and the wakening of the day the hut's harsh breathing ceased.

Use. Dawn. January 13th 1915. Boys, those messengers and postmen of the bush, ran to pass the awful news. The wailing of the women grew to a great chorus of misery as the children of

The hut at Use in which Mary died

the dead *Eka Kpukpro Owo* came crowding to the hut. Soon, over their shrill voices, came the deep voice of the drum. It thundered close to. But in the still of the Enyong Creek and of Mary's far-away places it whispered through the trees like the blossom petals or the big slow flakes of January snow which feather the silver branches of the birch trees and silver the frost-bleached grasses in that other country which she could call her own.

> How I long for a look at a winter landscape – only a peep you know – to feel the cold winds and see the frost on the cart ruts of the road, to hear the ring of horseshoes on the frozen clay . . . (Letter, Christmas 1904).

The scroll and silver cross had been sent to a friend for safe-keeping. In a drawer in her mother's old sideboard Martha found the other possessions of *Eka Kpukpro Owo*. There were mementos of her family: her mother's ring, an old scent bottle, a pebble brooch, a memorial hair-bracelet, and two old lockets. There were her spectacles, her pocket compass, her pen, two Bibles, an Efik hymn book, and the two books which Charles Morrison had given her twenty-five years before.

The mission sent a coffin from Itu and a launch from Duke Town and the 'poor carcase' of the no longer expendable Miss Slessor made a last night journey down the river. The launch arrived at the government beach at Duke Town just before midnight. The coffin remained on board until morning, while the canoes came in, their torches flaring, Efik and Okoyong, Itu and Enyong, Aro and Ibibio.

Funerals were still all too frequent and the drill was well known. Next day, for Mary Slessor, all flags flew at half-mast. The Commissioner asked all the government officials to attend and was there himself. The route to the cemetery from the beach was lined with troops and police and the boys and girls from the Hope Waddell Institute and Duke Town School. As the procession passed they joined it.

Word had gone round among the Africans that it was to be a very solemn and dignified occasion. And they paid *Eka Kpukpro Owo* one last tremendous tribute which she herself would never have asked nor expected from them. There was no wailing, no tearing of clothes, and no beating of breasts. To those who knew their Africans this was the most impressive thing that happened in Duke Town that day.

They buried Mary Mitchell Slessor next to William and Louisa Anderson, in the place where once they used to throw the corpses of the slaves.

EPILOGUE

As soon as he heard of Mary's death Sir Frederick Lugard telegraphed to the Mission Secretary: 'It is with deepest regret that I learn of the death of Miss Slessor. Her death is a great loss to Nigeria.'

There was an official announcement in the *Government Gazette*:

> It is with the deepest regret that His Excellency the Governor-General has to announce the death at Itu, on 13th January, of Miss Mary Mitchell Slessor, Honorary Associate of the Hospital of the Order of St John of Jerusalem in England.
>
> For thirty-nine years, with brief and infrequent visits to England, Miss Slessor has laboured among the people of the Eastern Provinces in the South of Nigeria.
>
> By her enthusiasm, self-sacrifice, and greatness of character she has earned the devotion of thousands of the natives among whom she worked and the love and esteem of all Europeans, irrespective of class or creed, with whom she came in contact.
>
> She has died, as she herself wished, on the scene of her labours, but her memory will live long in the hearts of her friends, Native and European, in Nigeria.

T D Maxwell, Justice of the Supreme Court of Calabar, her 'dear laddie' of Okoyong days, wrote: 'Her outlook on this life – and on the next – was never narrow. Her religion was above religion – certainly above religious differences. I have often heard her speak of the faiths and rituals of others but never without the deepest interest and sympathy. She was young to the end; young in her enthusiasm, her sympathy, her boundless energy, her never-failing sense of humour, her gift of repartee, her ability always to strike the apt, even the corrosive epithet. A visit to her was, to use one of her own phrases, "like a breath o' caller air to a weary body".'

Another official wrote, 'Her life was carried out with immeasureable courage and capacity. Her strength of character

Daniel Slessor with his two daughters, laying a wreath on Mary's grave

was extraordinary and her life was one of absolute unselfishness
. . . for years I personally would have trusted her judgement on
native matters in preference to all others.'

The *Record* published the official tribute to her from The
Women's Foreign Missions' Committee. It described her insight
into character, and her letters, 'full of terse statement, pictur-
esque flashes, humour, and tenderness . . . But above all Miss
Slessor was a saint. Her devotion and self-sacrifice was absolute
. . . Careless of convention and making nothing of comfort, she
fared forth into lonely regions . . . and endured all privations.
And she did it in no spirit of artificial asceticism or self-
immolation but out of the depths of an energetic and loving
heart.'

But when he read this, a mission carpenter who had worked
with Mary in the forests – Charles Ovens had been invalided
home ten years before – nodded and said, 'Aye! . . . But she was
nae jist a' that holy!' And when later the people of Scotland sent
out a huge granite plinth to mark her grave, he said, 'It'll take
mair than that to hold doon oor Mary!'

James Macgregor said much the same thing: 'Mary Slessor
was a whirlwind and an earthquake, and a fire, and a still small
voice, all in one.'

Mina Amess summed up on Mary, 'She was very child-like
with her bairns and really loved them . . . She really had two
personalities.'

After Mary's death Jean and Whitie stayed on at Use with
Annie and her husband. Alice and Maggie went to live with
Martha Peacock. Dan stayed on at the Hope Waddell Institute
and Asuquo went off to sea.

Jean died in the big influenza epidemic in 1918. Dan worked
for the Nigerian Forestry Commission and then became a
journalist. Annie and Mary lived on with their husbands near
Use. Alice seems to have become a nurse, but what eventually
happened to her, to Whitie, and to Maggie is not known.

While Mary Slessor had been opening up the Aro and Ibibio
territory to the mission James Luke had, with the help of new
recruits, been pushing on up the Cross River again. In spite of
more deaths and more illness they had opened stations with
several new tribes.

Dr John Hitchcock, when he left Itu, was asked to make a
survey into the Ibo territory up the Asu River which flows into
the Cross from the west above Unwana. He settled at a place

called Uburu where he estimated that there were 150,000 people within a day's walk. In 1915 he set up a hospital there. It was immediately as overcrowded as the Mary Slessor Hospital at Itu had been. He was hopelessly over-worked and collapsed and died there in January 1919. So Mary had been as right about his health as he had been about hers. He was buried near her own grave at Duke Town.

Her four protegées, Martha Peacock, Beatrice Welsh, Mina Amess, and Agnes Arnot, consolidated her work and proved that her ideas about Africans running their own out-stations, under the supervision, to begin with, of travelling white missionaries, were not only workable but the correct policy to meet the existing circumstances.

By the 1920s, using bicycles on the new roads, Beatrice Welsh was supervising ninety out-stations from Ibiaku, and Martha Peacock over fifty, first from Ikot Obong and later from Asang.

Mina Amess set up several out-stations from Akpap and worked there with the Okoyong until she retired thirty years later.

Agnes Arnot was appointed the first Mary Slessor Memorial Missionary specifically to carry on her work using a fund set up by Mary's friends in Scotland and Calabar. She moved the women's settlement to Arochuku and enlarged it, and ran Ikpe and several out-stations round it from the old camp building at Odoro Ikpe which had given Mary so much trouble, until an ordained missionary took over the area a few years later.

And when in 1954 the Presbyterian Church of Eastern Nigeria was established, run by Nigerians, and the remaining Scots and Jamaicans joined it, the great dream of the early pioneers, now 'working up higher' finally, after one hundred and six years, came true.

In the nineteenth century, because he had been so isolated for hundreds of years from new ideas and came so late into the modern world, the black man was looked down upon by most whites as a 'savage'. But in the twentieth, the bloodiest century ever, we can see more clearly just how thin is the veneer of civilisation over the coarse human greed and aggression of all nations: see more clearly too perhaps the importance of the basic teaching of Jesus of Nazareth in the affairs of man. It remains as revolutionary in our day as it was in his. We cannot escape the truth that in our century the atrocities of the 'developing' black man pale into insignificance against the atrocities of the 'civilised' whites. The builders of bridges are as desperately in short supply as ever they were, and as desperately needed, not least in Africa where tribalism threatens to wreck all that has been won. The importance of people like Mary Slessor lies not so much in what they achieve as in what they are. The stories of their love remain as part of the lesson which the human race is lunatic enough never to learn.

When the dust has finally settled on the struggle of the Africans for recognition as human beings of equal intelligence and dignity with other races, and on the struggle of the African nations for independence, historians will perhaps argue that, in the end, the black man with his modern systems of education, medicine, law, roads, railways, airports, and industries, has done as well out of the white man as the white man did out of him. Perhaps then too it will be recognised that, of all the foreigners who came to Africa in the nineteenth century, only the missionaries came to give something for nothing. They gave a system of education and a new attitude towards human relationships. They have been accused of being 'the running dogs of British imperialism' but, ironically, they were the first to teach the Africans that all men, as men, are equal.

Meanwhile people will probably continue to talk glibly about 'all the harm' which the missionaries did in West Africa: an assumption readily made by those who know nothing of the facts and by those who wish to conceal them. Accusations have even been made against the Calabar Mission in its early days quoting parliamentary papers of the time in support. Anybody who bothers to check those papers will find however that they refute the accusations.

Certainly the Calabar missionaries made mistakes. In the chaotic conditions which faced them it would be amazing if they had not. But, because of the experience which they had gained in Jamaica, men like Hope Waddell, Goldie, and Anderson, had ideas about mission work which were ahead of their time. So too did men like James Luke, Peter Rattray, and John Hitchcock, and women like Mary's four protegées. But the one who stands out as being ahead of them all is Mary Slessor because she identified herself with the people years before this was seen to be an essential in mission work.

Mary would hardly recognise modern Calabar with its new docks, city, and airport, but her far-away places have changed little. She would not have been surprised to read in the *Nigerian Chronicle* in June 1976 of the struggle to prevent side-roads round Ikot Ekpene and Ikot Obong from returning to bush. But she would probably have been amused to read that taxi drivers charge a higher mileage rate from Ikot Ekpene to Itu than to other places because of the poor state of the road, which she used to trudge along so often. She would certainly have been delighted to read that same month, considering all the suffering which the first mud school caused her, that to upgrade the school at Ikpe to comprehensive status the Nigerian Government had decided to spend N80,000 on it.

Sixty years ago, when the Scots missionaries wanted to use African musical instruments in their schools, their church elders would not allow it. 'These be pagan things', they said. But as African pride in Africa has grown, the people have learned to tack on their own trimmings to Christianity and to worship God in their own way. This too would have delighted the plain but sparkling redhead who grew into a scrawny but sparkling old woman. So too would the fact that in the film of the great Nigerian Independence procession in 1960 the first of the contingents of young girls is carrying the banner 'ITU'. It is doubtful, though, if any of those girls knew the name of the woman who first established their school and who first made it possible for women to live in independence in Calabar.

In Scotland now Mary is largely forgotten too by her countrymen. They were reminded of her however when, during a visit to Nigeria, Her Majesty Queen Elizabeth – perhaps because of a Scottish childhood – at her own special wish, placed a wreath on Mary Slessor's grave. A fitting tribute to one who must rank as one of the greatest Scotswomen who ever lived.

But Mary's hospital is still at Itu and when, as a young man, R M McDonald finished a lantern lecture there with a picture of Mary, an old chief asked if he could keep the table cloth which had served as a screen, and into which her face seemed to have faded. 'She was my friend', he said, 'and I like that face too much.'

Another memory of McDonald's would have especially pleased her. He says that when one spoke to Martha Peacock or Mina Amess about Mary Slessor, 'Their faces would light up and they would begin to chuckle at the mention of her name.'

'For Christ did not send me to baptise, but to preach the good news, and not to preach that in the terms of philosophy in which the crucifixion of Christ cannot be expressed.'

(Paul, laddie, to the Corinthians)

SOURCES

PROLOGUE

Kingsley, Mary. *Travels in West Africa*, pp 74, 474. 3rd edn. London, 1897
Perham, Margery. *Colonial Sequences (1949-69)*, p 173. London, 1970
           Frederick Lugard: The Years of Authority, pp 396-7. London 1960

CHAPTER TWO

Lenman, Lyth, Goldie. *Dundee* (Abertay Publication no 14), pp 9, 29, 59-68, 90. Dundee, 1969
Livingstone, W P. *Hitchcock of Uburu*, p 15. Edinburgh, 1920
Thomson, W. *Women of the Church*, p 316. Edinburgh, 1975

CHAPTER THREE

The Missionary Record, Aug 1869, Oct and Nov 1872, Feb 1877. Church of Scotland Library, Edinburgh
Waddel, Agnes. *Memorials of Mrs Sutherland*, pp 60-70, 116-8. Paisley, 1883
Waddell, Hope. *29 Years Missionary Work in West Indies and Central Africa*, p 335. London, 1863

CHAPTER FOUR

Crowder, M. *The Story of Nigeria*, pp 141-2. London, 1962
Dike, Onwuka. *Trade and Politics in the Niger Delta*, pp 33-7, 73, 101-121. Oxford, 1956
Forde, D. *Efik Traders of Old Calabar*, p. 50. Oxford, 1956
Goldie, H and Dean. *Calabar and Its Mission*, pp 20, 58-60. Edinburgh, 1890
Latham, A J H. *Old Calabar*, pp 1-25, 133-145. Oxford, 1973
McFarlan, D. *Calabar*, p 74. London, 1946
The Missionary Record, May 1853
Talbot, P A. *Peoples of Southern Nigeria*, vol I, P 193. London, 1969
Waddell, Hope. *op cit*, pp 206-292, 335-7, 663

CHAPTER FIVE

Goldie, H and Dean. *op cit*, pp 17, 23-34, 52, 362-3
Goldie, Hugh. *Memorials of King Eyo VII*, pp 19-23. Pamphlet, Church of Scotland Library, Edinburgh

McFarlan, D. *op cit*, pp 65-6
The Missionary Record, Feb 1877, June and Sept 1878
Sealy King. *Okoyong Clan*, p 10, Ibadan University Library, Nigeria
Slessor, Daniel. Letter to Mr Hart. Dundee Museum
Slessor, Mary. Letter to 'Maggie'. Dundee Museum
Talbot, P A. *Life in Southern Nigeria*, pp 190 and 257. London, 1967
        Peoples of Southern Nigeria, vol I, p 193
Thorp, Ellen. *A Ladder of Bones*, p 144. London, 1956
Waddell, Hope. *op cit*, pp 325-331

CHAPTER SIX

Goldie, Hugh. *op cit*, pp 42-52
Livingstone, A. *Mary Slessor Calendar*, p 42. Edinburgh, 1918
Livingstone, W P. *White Queen of Okoyong*, p 40. London, 1916
Minutes of United Presbyterian Foreign Missions' Board, 1880 no 1886, 1882 Appendix p 18, 1883 no 3643. Church of Scotland Library, Edinburgh
Talbot, P A. *Life in Southern Nigeria*, pp 6, 20, 53, 140, 179
        Peoples of Southern Nigeria, vol I, pp 192-9, 213
Waddel, Agnes. *op cit*, p 165

CHAPTER SEVEN

Ellis, J J. *Two Missionary Heroines*, p 81. London, 1926
Geary, W N M. *Nigeria Under British Rule*, p 97. London, 1965
McFarlan, D. *op cit*, pp 74-7
Minutes of United Presbyterian Foreign Missions' Board, 1885 no 4481, 1886 no 5315, 1886 no 5612
The Missionary Record, March 1889
Sealy King. *op cit*, p 11

CHAPTERS EIGHT AND NINE

The Missionary Record, March 1889
Slessor, Daniel. Letter to Mr Hart. Dundee Museum
Slessor, Mary. Bible, Psalm 4. Dundee Museum

CHAPTER TEN

Forde, D. *op cit*, pp 18-19
Hutchinson, T J. *Impressions of West Africa*, p 123. London, 1970
Luke, James. *Pioneering in Mary Slessor Country*, P 130. London, 1929
The Missionary Record, Dec 1889

CHAPTER ELEVEN

Geary, W N M. *op cit*, p 100
Luke, James. *op cit*, pp 104-5
McFarlan, D. *op cit*, pp 83-8
Marwick (née Hutton). Diaries. MSS GEN 768, Edinburgh University Library
Minutes of United Presbyterian Foreign Missions' Board, April 1880 Appendix, July 1890 no 7991
The Missionary Record, Jan 1892

CHAPTER TWELVE

Ellis, J J. *op cit*, p 77
Kingsley, Mary. *op cit*, pp 74, 473-6
Marwick, W. *William and Louisa Anderson*, pp 653-4. Edinburgh, 1897
The Missionary Record, May 1897
Slessor, Mary. Letter to Mr Hart. Dundee Museum
Thorp, Ellen. *op cit*, p 239
Wallace, K. *This is Your Home*, pp 54, 64. London, 1956

CHAPTER THIRTEEN

Goldie, Hugh. *op cit*, p 391 (Dean's additional material)
Luke, James. *op cit*, pp 155-7
McFarlan, D. *op cit*, p 109
Minutes of Women's Foreign Missions' Committee, Sept 1904 no 35.
Church of Scotland Library, Edinburgh
Slessor, Daniel. Letter to Mr Hart. Dundee Museum
Thorp, Ellen. *op cit*, p 119

CHAPTER FOURTEEN

Geary, W N M. *op cit*, pp 119, 126-7
Talbot, P A. *Peoples of Southern Nigeria*, vol I, P 215
Women's Missionary Magazine, 1904, p 295. Church of Scotland Library,
Edinburgh

CHAPTER FIFTEEN

Livingstone, W P. *White Queen of Okoyong*, pp 16-17
Slessor, Daniel. Letter to Mr Hart. Dundee Museum
Slessor, Mary. Letters to Charles Partridge. Dundee Central Library
Women's Missionary Magazine, May 1915, p 59

CHAPTER SIXTEEN

Livingstone, W P. *Hitchcock of Uburu*, pp 16-19
              White Queen of Okoyong, p 176

CHAPTER SEVENTEEN

Slessor, Mary. Letter to Agnes Young. MSS GEN 766/6, Edinburgh University Library

CHAPTER EIGHTEEN

The Missionary Record, March 1905 and March 1915
Perham, Margery. *Frederick Lugard: The Years of Authority*, p 397

EPILOGUE

Livingstone, W P. *Hitchcock of Uburu,* pp 84-5
McFarlan, D. *op cit*, pp 121-131
The Missionary Record, March 1915

INDEX